# The Immigrant Threat

## The Integration of Old and New Migrants in Western Europe since 1850

LEO LUCASSEN

UNIVERSITY OF ILLINOIS PRESS
Urbana and Chicago

1  2  3  4  5  C  P  5  4  3  2  1

Library of Congress Cataloging-in-Publication Data
Lucassen, Leo, 1959–
The immigrant threat : the integration of old and new migrants
in western Europe since 1850 / Leo Lucassen.
p.    cm. — (Studies of world migrations)
Includes bibliographical references and index.
ISBN-13: 978-0-252-03046-8 (ISBN-13/cloth : alk. paper)
ISBN-10: 0-252-03046-x (ISBN-10/cloth : alk. paper)
ISBN-13: 978-0-252-07294-9 (ISBN-13/paper : alk. paper)
ISBN-10: 0-252-07294-4 (ISBN-10/paper : alk. paper)
1. Europe, Western—Ethnic relations—History—19th century.
2. Europe, Western—Ethnic relations—History—20th century.
3. Immigrants—Europe, Western—History—19th century.
4. Immigrants—Europe, Western—History—20th century.
5. Europe, Western—Emigration and immigration—History
—19th century.
6. Europe, Western—Emigration and immigration—History
—20th century.
I. Title. II. Series.
D1056.L836    2005
305.8'0094'09034—dc22        2005007138

# Contents

## Part 1: Old Migrants

## Part 2: New Migrants

# Tables and Figures

## Tables

## Figures

# Acknowledgments

I wrote this book during my 2002–3 stay at the Netherlands Institute of Advanced Study (NIAS) in Wassenaar. I profited enormously from the comments and suggestions of other fellows who were also working in the field of migration studies, especially Klaus Bade, Pieter Emmer, Anita Böcker, and Dietrich Thränhardt. Furthermore, those who read parts of the book's manuscript—David Feldman, Nancy Foner, Mies van Niekerk, Wim Willems, Jan Lucassen, Hans Vermeulen, Maurice Crul, and the various anonymous—preserved me from many errors while at the same time gave me a lot to think about. Instrumental in helping me to keep the book focused was Leslie Page Moch, who—together with Donna Gabaccia—convinced me that their new series at the University of Illinois Press was the right place to publish the book. Leslie Page Moch, moreover, read the manuscript very carefully, and her suggestions were invaluable. I also thank my colleagues at Amsterdam University's history department, Clé Lesger, Marjolein 't Hart, Boudien de Vries, and Leo Noordegraaf, who graciously accepted my absence from teaching during this period. My time at NIAS was made so easy by the wonderful staff, especially the staff of the library, who, led by Harriet de Man, only very seldom could not comply with my insatiable hunger for ever more books and articles. Equally important was the help of Petry Kievit-Tyson and Kathy van Vliet-Leigh, who tried to turn my pidgin English into readable text. Kate Williams finished the correction of the second part of the manuscript, after I left NIAS in the summer of 2003. Additionally, I would like to mention Dirk Hoerder, Jochen Oltmer, Annemarie Cottaar, and Corrie van Eijl, with whom I have had interesting discussions about the historical approach to migration and integration. Finally, there are the people with whom I share my life: my wife Wil and my daughters, Emma and Marie. They are rarely interested in my work-related obsessions and remind me constantly that there is more to life than reading and typing.

# Abbreviations

| | |
|---|---|
| AMGT | Avrupada Milli Görüs Teskilati (European branch of the Milli Görüs in Cologne) |
| CDU | Christlich Demokratische Union |
| CSU | Christlich Soziale Union |
| CUKC | Citizenship of the United Kingdom and the Colonies |
| DITIB | Diyanet Isleri Turk Islam Birligi (German Diyanet) |
| ENA | Étoile nord-africaine |
| FIS | Front Islamique du Salut |
| FLN | Front de la Libération Nationale |
| FN | Front National |
| GCSE | General Certificate of Secondary Education |
| HLM | Habitation à Loyer Modérée |
| IRB | Irish Republican Brotherhood |
| INED | L'Institut National d Études Démographiques |
| MHP | Milliyetçi Hareket Partisi |
| MICUM | Mission Interalliée de Contrôle des Usines et des Mines |
| MNA | Mouvement National Algérien |
| NATO | North Atlantic Treaty Organization |
| NSR | Polish National Workers Party |
| OAS | Organisation Armée Secrète |
| ONI | l'Office Nationale d'Immigration |

PKK           Partiya Karkerên Kurdistan (Kurdistan Workers Party)

SDF           Söcmen Derneuleuri Federasyonu (Federation of
              Immigrant Associations from Turkey)

SGI           Société Général de l'Immigration

SONACOTRA     Société Nationale de Construction de Logements pour
              les Travailleurs Algériens

SPD           Sozialistische Partei Deutschland

WI            West Indian

WTC           World Trade Center

ZZP           Zjednoczenie Zawodowe Polkskie

# The Immigrant Threat

# Introduction

## American Situations

Since the arrival of non-Western immigrants in the late 1940s, public discussion in western Europe has been dominated by the fear that the immigrants will turn into unassimilable segments of the population. Initially, scholars and politicians pointed their fingers at the United States, where African Americans especially, but also more recently immigrants from Africa, Latin America, and Asia, were concentrated in inner-city ghettos characterized by intergenerational poverty, criminality and widespread rioting. From the 1950s through the beginning of the 1980s in particular, the prospect of being confronted with "American situations," as they were called, worried many native western Europeans and inspired various anti-immigrant movements, such as the National Front in Great Britain and the Front National in France.

In the later decades of the twentieth century, fear of social disorder and underclass formation was eclipsed by a more fundamental cultural and philosophical discomfort with the conflicting values of non-Western migrants. Populist leaders, ranging from Jean Marie Le Pen in France to Jörg Haider in Austria, Flip Dewinter in Belgium, and Pim Fortuyn in the Netherlands, may differ in many respects, but they all agree that immigration must be stopped and that non-Western newcomers, especially when they are Muslim, threaten the core values of Western liberal democracies. Moreover, they argue that through their sheer numbers, these immigrants destabilize Western societies and in the near future will become so numerous that the demographic outlook of countries such as France, Great Britain, Germany, and the Netherlands will change dramatically.

National statistics, or rather extrapolations based on them, often provide powerful ammunition in this public debate. Thus, for France it has been argued that Islam will soon become the nation's dominant religious faith, assuming that all Muslim immigrants and their offspring—some three million around the year 2000—are indeed devout believers.[1] Other statistics employ a broader definition of immigrant *strictu senso* to include that of immigrants' descendants. A good example is the use of the term *allochtones* in the Netherlands, which defines immigrants as everybody born abroad as well as people who have at least one parent not born in the Netherlands.[2] On the basis of this definition, which easily leads to static and hereditary interpretations, it is forecast that in the near future a large segment of the population in the Netherlands will consist of *allochtones,* thus turning the indigenous population into a minority. In countries like France, where the Republican *ius soli* tradition precludes such statistics, the perception that the numbers of "Arabs" and other Muslims are on the rise is widespread; but whether people are French citizens or not is irrelevant. Children born in France with French citizenship but with parents born in North Africa may not show up in statistics as such, but they are nevertheless very much considered part of the problematic immigrant population. And the same is true for the offspring of West Indian immigrants, who were British citizens from the start.

The fear of the new immigrants has many different roots, ranging from racist and eugenicist traditions on the extreme Right to principal defenders of the Republican tradition of the Enlightenment and the French Revolution on the Left. Thus, opposition to the rise of Islam, and thereby to the continuing immigration from Muslim countries, can be heard in both neo-Nazi and leftist-inspired intellectual circles. A good example of the latter is the leading French intellectual Alain Finkielkraut, who as far back as the 1980s voiced his concerns about cultural relativism and more recently has criticized the radicalization of Muslims in western Europe, as well as the celebration of cultural differences.[3]

## "Negroes" and "Arabs"

Although there has been migration from Asia and Africa to Europe from the early modern period onward, it was not until after the Second World War that considerable numbers of immigrants settled more or less permanently in western Europe,[4] starting with colonial migrants who, for either political (decolonization) or economic reasons, found their way to the "mother" country. The earliest examples are the West Indians in Great Britain and the Dutch East Indians who left Indonesia between 1946 and 1968. Both were seen as problematic because of their skin color and the social and cultural characteristics associated with it. This is especially true of the West Indians, who caused great unrest and became the brunt of permanent hostility. People from all layers of British society were afraid that these newcomers would never really fit in but would remain isolated aliens for generations in the cities where they were concentrated. From the 1980s onward the principal target of anti-immigrant discourse gradually shifted toward newcomers from Muslim countries. Beginning in the 1970s, natives of Pakistan and Bangladesh in Great Britain had already run a much higher risk of being harassed, attacked, and beaten up than second-generation Caribbean youths, and in the course of the 1980s they would finally move center stage. The emergence of religion and culture as principal markers over color and race was stimulated by the Islamic revolution under Ayatollah Khomeini in Iran in 1979 and culminated in the Rushdie affair in 1989 and the First Gulf War against Iraq a few years later. From that time on, culture, not race, has become the buzzword, often framed in global terms, as Samuel P. Huntington points out in his influential book on the clash of civilizations.[5]

This shift in attention, which occurred throughout western Europe, coincided with a substantial inflow into western Europe of migrants from Muslim countries such as Turkey, Morocco, Algeria, and Tunisia, most of whom were family members who joined the initially much smaller group of predominantly male guest workers from these regions. Thus the Turkish population in the Netherlands has increased from some thirty thousand around 1970 to more than three hundred thousand at the beginning of the twenty-first century. This confluence of changes in the international political climate and the actual settlement of newcomers from Muslim countries, who became highly visible through the establishment of mosques and Islamic dress codes (such as headscarves for women), led to the widespread view that Islamic migrants are problematic. Many people, including scholars, politicians, and considerable segments of the population, believe that the values of these migrants are fundamentally opposed to the "Judeo-Christian" tradition or the heritage of the Enlightenment, rooted in the equality of men and women and the separation of church and state. (This notion, by the way, displays a curious amnesia about the deeply rooted anti-Semitism in western Europe—and not only in Germany!—at least until the Second World War). The terrorist attacks on the Pentagon in Washington and the

World Trade Center in New York in September 2001, as well as the ensuing "war on terrorism," have provided even more fuel to the conviction that the culture of Islam and that of the West are irreconcilable.

This Manichean dichotomy has had a profound influence on the way Muslim migrants and their descendants are looked upon in western Europe, and it explains the emotionally loaded discussions about Muslims' alleged failure to integrate, which have dominated the public debate in western Europe since the 1990s. Islam is seen as an obstacle to integration from both a political and a cultural point of view. Migrants coming from Muslim countries are not only assumed to be more open to the political and terrorist-backed form of Islam, but they are also viewed as people coming from tribal societies whose values are diametrically opposed to the individualistic, secular western European society.[6]

The idea that the new, non-Western immigrants are different from immigrants in western Europe in the past (the Irish in England or the Poles in Germany)—who, after all, originated from within—is not limited to the political Right or to opponents of immigration at large. At the other end of the spectrum are supporters of a society structured around the principle of multiculturalism who, inspired by policies in Canada and Australia, are convinced that the cultural background of the new migrants differs fundamentally from those in the past. Well-known advocates of normative multiculturalism, such as Will Kymlicka and Charles Taylor, have started a worldwide discussion about the political and philosophical justification of multiculturalism.[7] In their view, Western societies have to acknowledge the right of immigrants (and non-immigrants, for that matter) to be different, not only in the private but also in the public domain. Moreover, they argue that the migrants, rather than threaten, enrich western European societies, and that by acknowledging their cultures, Western societies would become more tolerant, more open-minded, and less nationalistic.

Although scholars working in the multiculturalist tradition vehemently resent the anti-immigration discourse, their work can inadvertently strengthen populist ideas that the new immigrants will not fully integrate and will always remain outsiders, at least to some extent. Multiculturalists may argue that transnational identities and ethnic-group consciousness are, in principle, good things because they empower immigrants, but such factors nevertheless make assimilation less likely and undercut the exclusionary power of the nation-state; for those who oppose the new immigration, it confirms their worst fears.

## Lessons from the United States

The principal aim of this book is not to analyze the battle between multi-culturalists and those who see non-Western (Islamic) cultures as a threat to Western civilization. Instead, it focuses on the question of whether, from a historical perspective, it is reasonable to believe that the integration process of these new immigrants will indeed be fundamentally different in the long run (over several generations) from that of similar immigrant groups in the past. Or, to put it in the form of a question, to what extent are past immigrant experiences relevant for understanding the present as well as the near future?

Recent scholarly debate in the United States has stressed the relevance of such a historical comparison. Its central question is: To what extent is the post-1965 immigration and integration process similar to that experienced by the immigrants who set foot on American soil between 1880 and 1920? This debate has mobilized social scientists and historians, yielding a wealth of arguments from both sides. On the one hand we find that it is mostly historians who stress similarities and who predict some sort of assimilation of the current migrants in the foreseeable future. Political scientists, anthropologists, and sociologists, on the other hand, are convinced that structural changes in both the nature of the immigration and the receiving society have made obsolete the old assimilation model, developed by the Chicago School of Sociology in the 1920s and 1930s.[8] In her book *From Ellis Island to JFK*, Nancy Foner produced an exploration and summary of the debate; more recently, Richard Alba and Victor Nee provide an outstanding analysis in *Remaking the American Mainstream*.[9]

Because such a discussion has not yet taken hold in Europe, it is interesting to take a brief look at the core arguments in the American debate. Proponents of the "uniqueness school," who dominate the debate, argue that not only has the composition of immigrant groups changed dramatically (from Europeans to Asians, Africans, and Hispanics), but also that the structure of the present-day receiving society differs significantly from that which existed around 1900. Their conviction is buttressed by at least four major arguments. The first is that migrants, coming from all over the world, are much more visible by their skin color and other phenotypical characteristics. Given the significance of racial categorization in the United States, which places significant value on color and tends to categorize people as either white or non-white, it is expected that this makes assimilation far more difficult than it was for southern European migrants, who were not so very different from the contemporary native population at the end of the nineteenth century. Moreover, the argument continues, a considerable number of these new migrants share values which conflict with those of the Western world.

The second argument points to the unprecedented effect of the transportation and communication revolutions. Inexpensive and fast travel, satellite television, telephone, fax, and e-mail have dramatically enhanced the possibilities of remaining in contact with the home country or one's own ethnic group, greatly facilitating the emergence of *transnational* communities: people from the same region who stay in contact wherever they settle.[10] This enables them to keep some distance from the country in which they settle and retain a transnational or *diasporic* identity that supersedes or at least competes with identification with the new country and thus blocks full-scale assimilation.[11]

Third, many argue that the economic structure of the United States has changed fundamentally since the 1960s, a shift which is summed up by the use of the term "hourglass economy." Through the restructuring of the global economy from the 1960s onward, many stable and well-paid jobs in industry and manufacturing (textile, cars, shoes, etc.) have disappeared or been transferred to low-wage countries. This has reduced the size of this segment of the labor market considerably—and with it the chances of upward social mobility. With the disappearance of many blue-collar jobs and the shrinking of the lower-middle class, the possibility of advancement within one's own company has diminished greatly. Instead, formal education and college degrees have emerged as the gateway to social mobility. At the same time, low-wage jobs in the service sector are blossoming. Whereas many unskilled migrants in the past could slowly rise to a position in the middle class, this road has largely been closed to present-day low-skilled immigrants from developing countries who instead experience a form of downward mobility.

Finally, the idea has been put forward that old migrants in the United States encountered a more open society that was willing to turn immigrants into citizens and thus win their votes. The frequent elections and fierce battles between various factions made the stream of immigrants an attractive reservoir of potential new votes, often mobilized through ethnic networks and communities.[12] These four factors—skin color, access to technology, an hourglass economic model, and a less open society—are presently deemed to be so fundamental that the classic assimilation process is not likely to repeat itself. Instead, many migrants will either experience a form of segmented assimilation into the African American lower classes or hold on much longer to their ethnic communities.[13] As such, this interpretation of the current settlement process is a continuation of earlier criticism on the assimilation model voiced in the 1970s by scholars like Glazer, Moynihan, and many others who preferred the culinary imagery of the "salad bowl" over that of the "melting pot."[14]

This view, which treats the experience of the new migrants as basically different and unique, is criticized by what we could label the "continuity school," represented predominantly by historians but which also finds support among social scientists.[15] They argue that the interpretation of the past is too rose colored, whereas the present is painted too much in shades of gray.[16] Joel Perlmann and Roger Waldinger, for example, show that the adaptation of Italians, Poles, Russian Jews, and others in the first half of the twentieth century went less smoothly than is often assumed. The majority of both the first and the second generation experienced no, or only limited, social mobility, were confronted with considerable racial discrimination, and only gradually became "white, "meaning they were accepted as equals by the native population. Moreover, they argue, present-day migrants (with the exception of Mexicans) are generally better schooled than the average American, and many of them enter the labor market in the upper segment rather than at the bottom. Recent research shows that even Mexican immigrants, whose children are generally thought to experience a "second-generation decline," are doing better than expected. As well, the segmented assimilation hypothesis is not confirmed, with women doing even better then men.[17]

Others have criticized the transnationalist factor by demonstrating that this phenomenon is not new at all. The "old" immigrants who came to the United States around 1900 also kept in touch with their home communities through letters, associations, native-language newspapers and frequent return migrations. These critics reject the "technological determinism" and do not share the conviction of scholars who object that the scale and intensity of such connections have made the effect of the modern contacts much more pervasive and fundamental.[18] The same critics are therefore skeptical about the idea that the second and third generations in immigrant families will continue to be interested in their roots and willing to prefer the transnational community to the dominant culture of the receiving society.

Finally, historians and others stress that cultural and "racial" differences are social constructions. In the past, Irish, Jewish, and Italian immigrants were (for various reasons) labeled "black" or "alien," and their race and culture were deemed incompatible with the "American stock" and values.[19] They may have been "white on arrival, " as Thomas Guglielmo so aptly expressed it in his book by the same title, and therefore legal citizens, but they were nevertheless seen as racially inferior.[20] With the historical advantage of hindsight, however, it is clear that these ideas have faded and that those former "black" migrants, or "in-between-peoples" have become "white." It is not inconceivable that this process will repeat itself in the future with Hispanics, Asians, and even immigrants of African descent. Although those who stress continuities and similarities acknowledge that the post-1965 immigration is to some extent different (involving people with less physical resemblance to Europeans, ongoing immigration, changes in the economy, stronger transnational ties), they maintain that it is still too early to draw up the balance sheet.

## Back to the Old World

Taking the American debate to the Old World comes at a timely moment, because assimilation theory, so despised in the last decades, has been making a modest comeback in the social sciences, both in the United States and Europe.[21] The recent reassessment of this theory regards assimilation in the long term as a complex sociological process and not as a political and ideological program.[22] The reformulation of the theoretical position of the Chicago School does not ignore new developments and discontinuities; rather, it downplays these differences (especially in the long run) and emphasizes the autonomy of the integration process, which is to a certain extent independent from the context in which it takes place.

Comparing old and new migrants in western Europe, however, is not without its pitfalls, mainly because such an exercise may be hampered by disciplinary biases. In a recent interdisciplinary discussion between European migration scholars on the newness of transnationalism,[23] one of the interesting points that arose was that historians and social scientists often reach different conclusions, because to a large extent their disciplines determine their interests and ensuing research designs. In the words of Nancy Green:

> We should explore, I would argue, the ways in which each discipline has its own perceptions of time and newness. Historians can study moments of newness in the past (the marvel of Marconi, the speed of steam over sail, etc.); however, we often tend to look for signs of continuity (while, of course identifying moments of rupture). Historians then, are perhaps more inclined toward a mode of *déjà vu* in understanding today's migration and (un)settlement

patterns than sociologists who see contemporary detail with disciplinary eyes that emphasize newness. Indeed, as anthropologists, who used to study "tradition"—elsewhere—have begun to study modernity within tradition and vice versa—at home, they, like other social scientists have placed their emphasis on the contemporary world, postulating a difference of the present from the past, which is distinct from the historian's lens.[24]

Even when we keep this insightful warning at the back of our minds, transplanting the American discussion to the Old World can be problematic. Before explaining how such a comparison could be structured, we first have to deal with a number of obvious differences in the structure of the receiving societies of the United States and western Europe.[25] In Europe there was no internal slavery tradition akin to that which underlies and explains America's pervasive racism and obsession with color. Second, western European countries, with the exception of France,[26] have never really considered themselves as immigration countries, so that the reception of immigrants and the ensuing integration policy is rather different from that of the United States. In addition, one major difference between the United States and Europe is the welfare state, which creates a different opportunity structure for migrants and has effects on the way migrants are perceived. It is helpful to look a little more closely at these three divergences.

## Race and Whiteness

The works of David Roediger and Noel Ignatief[27] have made us more aware of the elasticity of concepts such as "race" and "blackness," as they are subject to changes in the social construction of difference. Roediger and many others have pointed out that various immigrant cohorts were originally labeled in terms of race, but that this racialization has changed and even vanished over time. Extensive studies have been made of the "whitening" of groups such as Jewish Europeans and Italians, who lost their stigma as racially distinct groups in the course of the 1950s.[28] This whitening process of European immigrants is partly explained by the mass migration of African Americans, descendants of former slaves, to the northern United States after the First World War.[29] This offered Jews and Italians the chance to distance themselves from these internal migrants, whose status was much lower and more enduring than theirs, and enabled them to gradually vanish in the expanding white population.

Although this argument is convincing in itself, from a European perspective it seems highly probable that the racialization of Jews and Italians would have vanished anyway, without this "black factor." Three arguments may suffice to substantiate this expectation. First, in many cases first-generation immigrants have been, and still are, viewed in a negative way, albeit to varying degrees; but all the same, these stereotypes and discriminatory practices faded after a few generations. With regard to Europe, we might mention the examples of Jews, Gypsies, Poles, and the Irish, and in more recent times migrants from third-world countries, who in varying degrees were considered to be different in religious, social, cultural, linguistic, and even racial respects well into the twentieth century.[30] Overall, one can say that they lost their racial stigma in the course of the integration process, without the "help" of any subsequent black immigration.

A second factor that has been put forward to explain the successful whitening of formerly "swarthy" European immigrants in the United States is the absence of official discrimination, codified by law. Allowing only certain numbers of Jewish students to enter universities, for example, may have been widespread until the Second World War,[31] but "equality before the law" was a crucial difference between Jews on the one hand, and black Americans and Asians (who had to fight legal discrimination until the late 1960s) on the other. To quote Nancy Foner: "That the law declared [Jews] white—and fit for naturalizable citizenship—was a powerful symbolic argument in their favor."[32] The importance of legal equality can also be illustrated by examples from Europe. Looking at the last four centuries, it is clear that the integration process of at least three generations of only two groups has been seriously blocked or slowed: that of Jews and Gypsies.[33] These are precisely the groups that have been legally discriminated against for a long time[34]—Jews until the French Revolution (and in many countries even later) as well as under Nazi rule, and Gypsies in most countries until the 1970s. How important this legal "apartheid" was to the understanding of minority formation in various nations, and the persistence of ethnicity over several generations, is finally indicated by the slow but undeniable assimilation process of the Jewish inhabitants of France, Belgium, the Netherlands, Great Britain, and Germany, notwithstanding ongoing social discrimination.[35]

It is important to understand that "blackness," because it is directly attached to the discourse on race and slavery, has a highly specific meaning in the American context. In Europe, especially on the Continent, the connotation of "blackness" as it applied to all kind of immigrants dates only from the 1980s onward and is linked to a specific, highly politicized interpretation of post–World War II colonial immigration. It is interesting, though, that this "imperial legacy" produced a much less fixed racial categorization than one might expect.[36] Clearly, in the era of decolonization, which led to the subsequent flow of half-caste or colored migrants from the colonies—the Dutch East Indians in the Netherlands, West Indians in Great Britain, and Algerians in France—racism already played a role, but it never acquired the semi-primordial status that exists in the United States.[37] Even in Britain, where the definition of "race" bears the greatest resemblance to the term as it is used in North America, policymakers did not generally label black migrants as undesirable in the 1950s, as Randall Hansen in a recent analysis of postwar immigration policy shows. The Colonial Office, especially, stressed the importance of *civis Britannicus sum*, which safeguarded the rights of all subjects of the British Empire, wherever they lived in the Old Commonwealth, and gave them the right to enter the home country. Even if Hansen's provocative attack on a whole body of literature that stresses the racist character of the postwar immigration policy is too one-sided,[38] it is clear that the issue of race was much more complicated than is generally assumed and is not as fixed in a black-white dichotomy as experienced in the United States.

Hansen's conclusions link up with recent research in the Netherlands by Wim Willems. In his book on the massive immigration of East Indians from Indonesia (1946–68)—constituting some three percent of the total Dutch population at the time—Willems convincingly argues that although many policymakers had outspoken racist ideas about at least some of these colonial migrants (especially those with the darkest skin color), the government decided to follow an inclusive policy for the whole group, stressing their Dutch citizenship. Moreover, a large-scale integration and relief program was set up to prevent the emergence of a distinct category of former colonial migrants. Although this brand of forced programmatic assimilation ignored the wishes of the newcomers to hold on to their home culture, one of the results was that the deviant skin color never became an issue so that the group as a whole was "whitened" within one generation.[39]

The position of immigrants from the other Dutch colony, Suriname, illustrates how social and cultural differences—real as well as perceived—offer a better explanation for the attitude of the native population toward newcomers than skin color. The fact that a significant number of descendants of former slaves in Suriname (who immigrated to the Netherlands beginning in the early twentieth century) are black in a phenotypical sense has not, nevertheless, led to a rigid race barrier for these Creoles. It is, rather, the lack of an *internal* Dutch slavery tradition that has allowed these migrants, as well as the descendants of indentured workers from India who left Suriname for the Netherlands en masse beginning in the late 1960s, to avoid falling into a well-defined racial category. In fact, these people often experienced a modest level of upward social mobility; some rose very high on the social ladder.

The explanation for this development, especially when we consider that the mass migration of the Surinamese coincided with the economic recession of the 1970s and 1980s, seems threefold. First, migrants from Suriname were Dutch citizens, and before the independence of Suriname in 1975, they could enter the Netherlands freely. Second, the cultural affinity of most of the Surinamese with Dutch society prevailed in the long run and eased their integration.[40] Finally, they have benefited from the influx of other newcomers who arrived at the same time (or only somewhat later) and who differed much more from the native population in cultural and linguistic respects. The socioeconomic position of the two largest groups, the Turks and Moroccans, was (and still is) considerably lower, due especially to their low human capital and vulnerable labor market position. Moreover, owing to their adherence to the Islamic faith, Turks and Moroccans are considered to be much more alien. It is striking that these factors make them more "black" in public opinion than the Surinamese. Even the discourse of policymakers is dominated by this use of the term "black": the expression "black schools," for example, is generally used to designate schools where a large proportion of the pupils are first- and second-generation Moroccans and Turks. As official target groups for policymakers, "minorities" are defined on the basis of socioeconomic handicaps; migrants from Suriname are less "black" than the Turks or Moroccans because, on average, they perform better at school and in the labor market. Thus, in this context, "black" clearly transcends its original racial meaning and has turned into a proxy for class.

A similar argument has been made in the case of France, where the "beurs" (second-generation Algerian migrants) are deemed much more alien than the much darker-skinned Francophone immigrants from central and western Africa. The American sociologist Michèle Lamont, who compared working-class attitudes toward blacks in the United States and France, attributes the lower salience of racism in France partly to the Republican ideal: "Indeed, if republicanism strengthens the boundary between a French 'us' and a foreign 'them,' it also has had a powerful effect in downplaying the salience of skin color in the French public sphere: it presumes a voluntaristic or contractual approach to political participation that posits that anyone can join in the polity as long as he or she comes to share a political culture based on the universal (and superior) values of reason and progress."[41]

The Dutch and French cases both shed an interesting light on the situation in the United States. Thus, it seems not far-fetched that the phenotypically black Surinamese have benefited from the immigration of other groups and in a sense have become more white (meaning less problematic) in a manner somewhat similar to the process that Jews and Italians experienced in the United States. These contrasting cases strengthen the idea that race is a social construction of a more fundamental kind than physical characteristics. As race is disconnected from its phenotypical connotation in certain contexts, then even the "real" blacks can (in principle) escape from it.

## "We Are Not an Immigration Country"

The primary reason the American debate on old and new migrants has not effectively influenced the migration field in Europe[42] is that immigration is not part and parcel of Europe's collective memory. European countries are full of *lieux de mémoires,* to use Pierre Nora's well-known concept,[43] but none of these "sites of memories" are linked to Europe's immigration past. Ellis Islands are nowhere to be found, and only recently have museum initiatives been undertaken to recognize Europe's immigration history.[44] Instead, there are museums partly dedicated to emigration, like the Norwegian Emigration Museum in Hamar and the historical museum in Bremerhaven, where so many Europeans embarked for America.[45] This lack of interest in the history of newcomers in various European states cannot simply be explained by the fact that emigration was much more important than immigration. For some countries this is true, at least up until the 1970s. Italy is the example of an emigration country *par excellence,* which began to receive immigrants only after 1970. For most western European countries, however, emigration was insignificant (France, Belgium, the Netherlands before 1950) or died away after World War I (Germany, Great Britain, Ireland, Scandinavia).[46]

Indeed, many western European states were confronted with considerable numbers of immigrants and became *de facto* immigration countries from the middle of the nineteenth century on.[47] The best-known case is France, where millions of migrants settled beginning in 1870. This process was even encouraged by the French state through its lenient naturalization legislation and, after 1918, active recruitment. Whereas France's attitude was stimulated by the fear of depopulation caused by its remarkably slow population growth, other countries also experienced considerable levels of immigration. For some, the newcomers came from within the borders of the state, like the Irish in Great Britain and the Polish-speaking population from Germany's eastern provinces who settled in the Ruhr area. Other migrants were foreigners and were treated as such, as in the case of the Italians in Switzerland and Germany, and the Germans in the Netherlands. After 1945 most western European states remained immigration countries, either through the arrival of large groups of colonial migrants (the Netherlands, France, Great Britain, Portugal) or through the importation of labor immigrants, such as displaced persons in the 1950s and the so-called "guest workers" in the 1960s and 1970s.

The French historian Gérard Noiriel has rightly argued that this impressive immigration past has barely influenced the collective memory, nor has it created an awareness that western Europe has long been and still is a typical immigration region.[48] People's knowledge about immigration in the past is mostly restricted to their experience with recent waves of migrants. And even when earlier migrations have stood the test of time, many interpret these phenomena as exceptions to the static, sedentary condition.[49] Gérard Noiriel, Klaus Bade, and others have argued that this concept of "permanent exception" has blocked a broad acceptance of migration as an integral part of European societies, and they blame the dominant ideology of the nation-state[50]—the concept of homogeneous nations with stable populations. This idea took root in the nineteenth century and has deeply influenced the self-conception of western European states and their inhabitants, as well as historians, who became prisoners of an image they have themselves helped to create.[51] As a result, many scholars do not realize that most western European countries experienced huge immigration in the period 1880–1930, or, in the words of the German migration historian Dirk Hoerder: "Official recognition of a many-cultured past has been achieved in but few European states. In general, neither the public nor politicians are searching for a past different from the currently imagined national ones. Historians as gatekeepers, with few exceptions, share these nationalist and nation-centered approaches."[52] This denial of a vibrant immigration past and the idea that migration is not a normal phenomenon has made European states much more wary of immigration and explains their refusal to accept the reality that they are *de facto* immigration countries. As a consequence, immigration is looked upon as a threat, whereas the perceived cultural differences of newcomers are regarded as a problem that has to be solved by specific integration policies that result in assimilation. This "democratic impatience" also explains the focus on immigration problems and the idea that integration has failed.[53] Immigrants in Europe are thus under much more official and public pressure to assimilate than those in the United States.

## Immigrants and the Welfare State

With the emergence of the western European welfare states in the course of the twentieth century, the image that migrants are a potential threat to the welfare state as "free riders" who only receive and do not contribute has firmly taken root. This way of thinking is not entirely absent in the United States, as the discussion on admitting children of illegal migrants in California reveals.[54] Some American scholars argue that even the very sober welfare schemes in the United States attract immigrants because these programs still pay significantly more than those in the countries of origin.[55]

In western Europe, concern about the burden immigrants placed on "poor relief" and other types of welfare clearly predate the twentieth century. Internal migrants, especially, were often refused or sent back by local authorities, as the example of the Irish in the next chapter shows.[56] Most foreign migrants were left in peace until the First World War, although in states like Germany, which had developed insurance programs as early as the last part of the nineteenth century, or like France, which had a strong labor movement and early male suffrage, some legal measures were taken to control and monitor the entrance of foreign workers to the labor market.[57] When states became increasingly responsible for unemployment and other benefits, and universal suffrage gave a voice to the native population, calls for restrictive measures against foreigners became louder, especially in the 1920s and 1930s.

After World War II, western European states, in collaboration with labor movements, tried to solve the free-rider problem while simultaneously eradicating the unfair competition of the immigrant workforce by opting for temporary migration schemes and equal rights for all workers, irrespective of nationality: the "guest workers" program has become the prototype of such efforts. But this worked out differently than the states intended: policymakers had not expected that the temporary migrants, especially when they remained longer than initially foreseen, would accumulate "embedded rights," as James Hollifield has so nicely formulated it[58]—rights which eventually entitled them to settle permanently. Because many guest workers did not return home but stayed on to become residents, it proved very difficult to send them back; what is more, they acquired the legal right to send for their dependents, which led to mass immigration in the 1970s and 1980s.

## Linking the Past to the Present

It is fair to say that, so far, the American debate on old and new migrants has had virtually no resonance in the European context. Although historical migration research on Europe has made considerable progress in the last decades,[59] it has been very difficult to influence the interpretation of national or European histories. This may explain why the gulf between historians and social scientists is much deeper and communication even more sparse than it is in America. As a result, the scholarly research on integration processes then and now is divided into two mutually isolated domains that seldom interact, so that a common forum for discussion and mutual incorporation of research results and perspectives is virtually nonexistent.

To date, social scientists have barely noticed the historical studies on immigration in western European countries, and only rarely have historians themselves explicitly pointed to the relevance of social scientists' analyses for current debates on immigration and integration.[60] This lack of interdisciplinary communication is not only the result of historians' very late discovery of Europe's immigrant past; it is also a product of the often implicit assumption that intra-European migrants (not to mention the huge movements of internal migrants) were in cultural and physical respects far more similar to the population of the host societies. Even if this holds true, however, comparisons are equally interesting. Moreover, there are numerous indications that in the early twentieth century, immigrants from other European countries, especially the Italians, Irish, and Poles, were perceived as culturally and "racially" different. Just as in the United States, they were often seen as "swarthy," primitive, and unassimilable, a categorization that only gradually dissolved over time. Some of the present-day migrants, especially those from central Africa and Asia, may be more conspicuous because of their skin color and other phenotypical characteristics, but it remains to be seen whether these are relevant in all situations and contexts, and how these perceptions will evolve in the long term.

Any interdisciplinary debate is hindered by the fascination with current immigration: a good example of this is the currently fashionable interest in transnationalism. Many scholars argue that, due to technological advances, it only recently became possible for migrants to enjoy regular and sustained social contacts across national borders. Cheap telephone rates, frequent holidays in the countries of origin, especially among former guest workers from Turkey and Morocco, satellite television, access to e-mail and the Internet, as well as the active involvement of sending states and Islamic mosques with the immigrant communities in western Europe, have given rise to the impression that integration will take place much more slowly than in the past, and that the character of integration has changed quite drastically. Moreover, it is now easier for immigrants to maintain their culture because the receiving states, influenced by multiculturalism, allow more room for group expression.

For most social scientists, the past is mainly a strange and highly irrelevant country that has little in common with the present. Historical studies showing that transnationalism is nothing new (as historians in the United States argued much earlier on) are therefore left unread and remain largely isolated. This is true, for example, in research on Germany and Italy, which illustrates how these countries, from the 1870s on, created policies to support nationalist organizations abroad with the explicit aim of keeping *Deutschtum* and *Italianità* alive by stimulating schools, newspapers, and all kinds of associations that furthered patriotic feelings among fellow Germans and Italians.[61]

It would be unfair, though, to blame only social scientists for being blind to the ever-increasing body of historical migration research. Historians also fail to frame their conclusions and findings within an interdisciplinary paradigm. Comparisons seem useless because the differences with the past are considered to be self-evident. Only occasionally is historical knowledge explicitly embedded in the social-scientific discussion about migration and integration.[62] Often, studies remain descriptive and—even when a more analytical approach is taken—other historians remain the primary audience.

A number of scholars, however, have moved beyond case studies and tried to make comparisons between migrations then (mostly 1870–1940) and now (1950–present). One of the earliest attempts is the seminal book *Le creuset français,* by Gérard Noiriel, which stresses the importance of immigration to France in the past and shows the similarities in settlement processes and reception.[63] A more in-depth case study, which also compares immigration through time, is Marie-Claude Blanc-Chaléard's study on Italians in Paris.[64] In Germany, historians such as Klaus Bade and Ulrich Herbert have incessantly beaten the drum of continuity where the migration experience is concerned and with respect to policies toward labor migrants. They have even gone so far as to compare labor migrants with forced labor, which has produced a number of valuable new insights.[65] Jan Lucassen and Rinus Penninx have analyzed migration and integration in the Netherlands in the long period from 1550 to the present, in which they claim that assimilation is the most likely outcome, both in the past and in the present.[66] Moreover, Klaus

Bade and Leslie Page Moch have recently published excellent overviews of migration history in Europe.[67] Finally, there is Nancy Green's very interesting double comparison (in time and in space) of immigrant workers in the garment sector in Paris and New York, using more or less the same period as in the American "old and new" debate.[68]

The studies mentioned above have been trailblazing, and I am very grateful for the insights they offer. Notwithstanding the quality of current research, most studies are restricted to one country and do not make comparisons with other western European countries. Those who do cover Europe are more interested in movement (migration) than in what happens once migrants have settled, especially over generations. As well, these studies do not select similar groups for their comparisons, which often makes it difficult to assess the factors leading to specific outcomes of the integration process.

## Definition of Integration

Many scholars have justly criticized the often normative, one-sided, and linear connotations of many words or phrases that set out to describe the settlement process of immigrants, such as assimilation and integration. However justified this criticism may be, renouncing concepts like integration and assimilation altogether makes scholarly discussions and progress even more difficult than they already are. Changing words is no solution; whether you call it inclusion, adaptation, insertion, or incorporation, in the end we all will have to answer the question: "Assimilation or integration into what?"

Keeping in mind the warranted criticism of its original definitions and applications, I prefer "integration" and start from a very broad definition of the word: the general sociological mechanism that describes the way in which all people, migrants as well as non-migrants, find their place in society. This basic element of the functionalist sociological school explains how processes of socialization turn people into workers, consumers, voters, soldiers, and gendered beings, by looking at the school, the workplace, the neighborhood, the local state, the church, unions, the army, the family, etc. This broad definition of "integration" does not assume that it produces a uniform, unitary, and harmonious society or national culture, but rather allows for important differences according to class, gender, ethnicity, and sexual orientations—to mention a number of important distinctions—and in this sense every society or nation-state *is* automatically multicultural.

The particular nature of the integration of migrants, both internal and external, is that they are already socialized in another society. By migrating, they face different social structures and value systems at a more advanced age. To what extent the various domains of a new society are new depends on the background of the migrants (their own human capital, value systems, etc.) and can theoretically range from virtually no differences to a great many. Whether they like it or not, immigrants, just like non-migrants, always integrate to some extent.[69] The crucial questions, however, remain: in what domains, to what extent, and at what speed? It is important to note that using a functionalist model does not preclude asymmetric power relationships. Integration is never a neutral process; it is embedded in power relations. Its course depends on the specific configuration of various actors, including migrants themselves.

Finally, it is important to make clear that although this definition is inspired by the assimilation model of the Chicago School of Sociology, scholarship has progressed since the early works of Robert Ezra Park, Anthony Burgess, and others, and the initial definition has been modified on at least five points:

1. Integration, just like assimilation, is viewed as a non-linear, long-term, and thus intergenerational process. Following Milton Gordon's classic dichotomy, this implies that integration is defined as a *process* and not as a *program*.[70] By focusing on the social process of mutual adaptation, the "moral imperative" trap can be largely avoided.

2. Integration takes place in many different domains, and within these domains the speed of the process may differ.[71] This "differentialist model" distinguishes between levels of analysis and various domains, such as the economic, the social, the cultural, and the political.

3. For analytical purposes, I distinguish between *structural* integration, which can be measured more or less objectively by mapping social mobility, school results, housing patterns, etc., and *identificational* integration, which is subjective and refers to the extent to which migrants and their offspring keep on regarding themselves as *primarily* different *and* to the extent that they are viewed as primarily different by the rest of society.[72]

4. Integration is not a one-way process. Not only do the migrants change, depending on their precise interaction with the receiving society, but the receiving society changes, too, although this may often take place slowly and be barely noticeable to contemporaneous observers.

5. Integration is always structured by both class and gender, factors which should therefore be structural elements of analysis.

## Central Questions

Following this modified concept of integration, the central questions that result are:

- To what extent does structural integration in various domains (social, political, cultural, economic) over at least two generations differ in Europe *in the present* from what we have seen its past?
- As far as we can discern such generational differences, how important are they, and how can they be explained?
- To what extent do the different structures of receiving societies in western Europe produce different integration paths than are present in the United States?

Bearing in mind the different disciplinary perspectives of historians who stress continuity and social scientists who are primarily interested in newness, it is of the utmost importance that the long-term integration processes in the past and in the present are analyzed by looking at roughly the same factors. Keeping a number of characteristics of the immigrant groups constant, such as size (large) and social status (predominantly low), I have chosen to compare a limited number of immigrant groups in the recent and more remote past:

- Stereotyping and stigmatization (the social construction of the threat)
- Social and political mobilization among migrants (including transnationalism)
- Rates of intermarriage[73]
- Social mobility, occupational specialization, and school attainment
- Criminality
- Residential patterns

Although it was not always easy or possible to find the right data, especially when studying the past, I will sketch the rough outlines of how migrants and their descendants fared in these different domains. By using this comparative method, I want to bring historical and social scientific approaches into the same paradigm, one in which history is more than a "fun science" that produces amusing and moving (but largely irrelevant) stories. Instead, I consider history to be a social science specialized in long-term developments. Knowing that a number of contextual factors, such as the role of the state and the structure of the economy, have changed fundamentally between then and now, the key question is whether this has really influenced the course of the integration process. This question can only be answered by a careful comparison in which it is essential to keep in mind that the developments in the present are still in full swing and far from complete. This implies that, in a certain sense, this book has arrived too early and can only provide provisional and conditional answers. Only when the life course of the third generation draws to a close—and for the recent immigrants in Europe that will take at least another half century—will final answers be possible. By that time, unfortunately, social-science scholars will probably no longer be interested, as they will be too busy analyzing the new immigrants of the future.

## Sources, Comparability, and Structure

Comparative analysis is only possible thanks to the numerous studies on the migration and integration processes that have been published by historians and social scientists, especially in the last two decades of the twentieth century. The work at hand restricts itself mainly to secondary literature. Only for the case studies of recent migrations have I occasionally been able to use primary printed sources, mainly government statistics.

The present work does *not* deal with the entire migration experience, focusing instead on what one could call "large and problematic" groups— immigrants who are perceived as a threat in one way or another and who came in considerable numbers: hundreds of thousands rather than tens of thousands. This choice rules out many migrants and therefore gives only a partial picture of Europe's migration experience. The advantage of this limitation, however, is that it enables us to understand much more precisely the extent to which the present-day fears, which are centered around "large and problematic groups," are justified in the long run, and what we can learn from the past in this respect.

The three chapters that follow encompass "big and problematic groups" in western Europe: the Irish in England, the Poles in Germany, and the Italians in France. There have been more groups that were perceived as problematic or threatening in the period before the Second World War (like Gypsies, eastern European Jews, Chinese, and the Moroccans in France), but their numbers were relatively small. By focusing on the "big three," it soon became clear that, interestingly enough, these countries and their respective immigrant groups not only shared certain characteristics, like size and low-skill job levels, but also constituted three different *types* of threats: religious, national, and social.

Irish workers who migrated on a huge scale to England by the mid-nineteenth century were *generally* detested because they were poor and nationalistic, but *predominantly* so because they were Catholics. Catholicism was perceived by the largely Anglican native population as representing an entirely different culture and worldview, and it was feared because of the faith's global and expansive aspirations, symbolized by the Pope in Rome. Moreover, as Linda Colley has demonstrated so well, Catholicism was the main ideology against which English nationalism was constructed.[74] In the eighteenth century the hereditary enemy, France, was equally hated for being alien as for being Catholic. This anti-Catholic tradition, which reaches back to the sixteenth century, explains why the anti-Irish atmosphere focused so much on religious aspects.

In the case of the Poles, who arrived in the West after 1870, it was not so much their Catholicism—despite the anti-Catholic *Kulturkampf* waged by Bismarck in the same period—nor their proletarian status as unskilled workers. It was, rather, their nationalism that posed a major threat, especially to the Prussian state, which feared that Polish nationalism could eventually lead to a separation of the Polish-speaking part of Germany and the reconstitution of the Polish state.

With the Italians in France, whose migration coincided with that of the Poles in Germany, religion played virtually no role, and nationalism was only important during the first decades of their migration. The chief complaint about the Italians was their role in the labor market. Most of them were unskilled men who worked in teams on construction sites, mines, and quarries; many French workers accused them of lowering wage rates and breaking strikes. This engendered a widespread and violent discourse in which Italians were seen as invaders who put the position of French workers at risk, leading to a number of violent clashes and even to the hunting down of Italians in the last decades of the nineteenth century.

The second part of the book defines the major threats posed by large immigrant groups in the present. Many people, both in the United States and in Europe, assume that the unprecedented large-scale immigration of "colored" migrants, mainly of African and Asian descent, has turned the tables. Unlike migrants suffering discrimination in the past, "coloreds" remain visible through generations which—so the argument continues—will make integration much more difficult, especially because color often coincides with a low social status. To test these assumptions I will analyze the reception and integration process of a major colonial migrant group in a context where color was perceived as extremely problematic, which led me to the West Indians, or Caribbean, migrants in postwar Great Britain.

The second major threat is *religion,* only this time the threat is not Catholicism but Islam. It goes without saying that the Muslim threat is on many people's minds, especially since the terrorist attacks on the World Trade Center in New York and at the Pentagon in Washington in September 2001. But before those events, Islamic migrants from North Africa, the Middle East, and Asia were already seen as an obstacle to integration because it was assumed that the core values of Islam clash fundamentally with those of the Western world. And one need not agree with Samuel Huntington[75] to argue that the Islamic faith may slow down integration, especially where Islam's conflicting ideas about women's emancipation and the separation between church and state are perceived as important stumbling blocks. As a case study, we will consider the Turks in Germany, who, since the 1980s, have created a large infrastructure of religious institutions, which are, in part, actively supported and governed by the Turkish state.

A third threat—fear of social problems like criminality, poverty, and ghettos— is associated with the second-generation migrants. Whether one looks at the young Algerian French in the *banlieues* of Paris, West Indian youth in London's suburbs, Moroccans in Amsterdam, or Turks in Berlin's Kreuzberg, one is confronted with young, second-generation migrants, some of whom (often boys) cause trouble by petty but nonetheless annoying criminal behavior, who fail at school, and face a gloomy future of more or less permanent unemployment, or at least bleak perspectives in the labor market.[76] Moreover, among the second generation with an Islamic background, the soil seems fertile for the mobilization of extremist pan-Islamic or pan-Arabic sentiments and organizations, especially in the polarized, tense atmosphere after the attacks on the World Trade Center buildings. To move beyond impressionistic tales, in the third chapter of the second part of this book I will focus on the first and second generation Algerians in France.

Not all possible intergroup comparisons will be drawn. I will concentrate first on comparisons between the Irish, the Polish, and the Italian immigrants in the past; second on the West Indians, Turks, and Algerians since World War II; and finally on a comparison between the developments in the two periods. The last chapter will draw up the balance sheet and map out the similarities and differences as far as they relate to different paths of integration in the past and in the present. Along these lines I will offer explanations for possible divergences within the European context and finish by contracting the outcomes of this European study with the American discussion, taking the debate back to where it began.

# PART 1

# Old Migrants

# 1

# The Religious Threat:
# Irish Migrants in Britain
# (1840–1922)

The nineteenth century witnessed great movements of people from one continent to another. Considerable numbers of Europeans translocated either temporarily or permanently to the New World, and the United States in particular.[1] Many migrations, however, by both men and women, also took place within the Continent, and even within states.[2] These can be described as local movements between cities, and between the countryside and cities.[3] In general, internal migrants did not cause much resentment, as high mobility was a feature of everyday life in many parts of Europe. Although many people, for whom migration was part of their lifecycle or work cycle (domestics, sailors, journeymen, and seasonal harvesters, for example), had to adjust—at least temporarily—to a new geographical and social environment, most local migrants were not collectively treated as alien or considered a threat by the indigenous population. In some cases, they established migrant organizations at their respective destinations, like the Frisians in Amsterdam, the Welsh in Liverpool, or the Bretons in Paris, but these organizations functioned primarily as a cushioning network and a base from which to explore the new (urban) environment, and as such created no problems in themselves.[4]

The situation was different, however, for immigrants who crossed salient political, religious, cultural, or linguistic borders. These groups were often confronted with negative stereotypes, discrimination, and, sometimes, outright violence. The three most outstanding examples in nineteenth-century western Europe are Italian workers in (the eastern parts of) France and Switzerland, the (German) Poles in the Ruhr area, and the Irish in Great Britain.

All three cases concerned large numbers of unskilled and semiskilled workers who were easily recognizable by their language and—at least in the case of the Irish and the Poles—deviant (Catholic) religion. Although both the Irish and the Poles moved freely within the same political space (the United Kingdom and the German empire), their migration was perceived as problematic for social, religious, and political reasons. Moreover, in both cases the aversion of the local and national receiving societies to these migrants was fed by long-standing negative stereotypes, which occasionally took a racist turn.

The highlights of these migrations and the ensuing problems of integration are well known to most migration historians,[5] but their relevance for the discussion on integration processes of present-day immigrants has not been fully explored, and no structural comparisons between these three groups have been made. Such omission is due not only to the lack of communication between historians and social scientists, but also to the often fragmented and isolated study of different immigrant experiences, as well as the low status of migration as a relevant theme in the general historical field.[6] Even within the field of immigration history, specialization into numerous subfields has not particularly stimulated overarching comparisons. We know, for example, a great deal about the Irish migrants in England, Wales, and Scotland, but results of that research have not generally reached migration scholars who work on other topics. Both the Polish and the Irish migrants play an important role in the national histories of Poland and Ireland, as well as in the history of the labor movements of Germany[7] and Great Britain,[8] but they are nevertheless predominantly studied as a special case. There is a widespread impression that these groups have been confronted with discrimination that initially slowed down their integration, but that after one or two generations, their assimilation was progressing well.

This impression is not entirely accurate, however, as it provides too rosy a picture and ignores the fundamental and enduring contrast between the migrants and the receiving western European societies. Moreover, many elements that are considered crucial stumbling blocks on the road to integration of present-day migrants (especially those from Muslim countries), such as a threatening religion, homeland politics, transnational ties, (low) social status, and criminality are not as new as we might think.

At first glance, the Irish migrants in England, Wales, and Scotland do not seem to be particularly relevant to a discussion of the present-day immigrants in Europe. Legally, the Irish were internal migrants, as the Act of Union in 1801 made Ireland an integral part of the United Kingdom. Irish migrants were thus free to enter Britain; moreover, most Irish migrants spoke English, albeit with a strong recognizable accent. But this was not the essence of the immigrant experience for hundreds of thousands of Irish men and women. They may have been subjects of the British crown, but their mass migration to Britain from the 1840s onward was perceived as an alien invasion and a serious social and a political threat. The most serious problem was that the large majority was Catholic, and at the time, most Anglicans and Protestants perceived Catholicism to be a dangerous religion. As well, most of these Irish migrants were poor, un- or semiskilled, and soon filled the slums of the major English and Scottish cities. Finally, political awareness was stimulated by Irish nationalist propaganda, through which secret societies in England tried to mobilize Irish migrants into supporting an independent Ireland. To illustrate the deep gap between the Irish migrants and the receiving British society, it is useful to consider the social, political, religious, and cultural aspects of their integration process.

## The Irish Emigration to Britain and the Legal Position of Immigrants

There is a long history of people born in Ireland living and working in Britain. Most of these Irish went to England as seasonal laborers to work on farms in England, Wales, and Scotland at harvesttime and returned to their own small farms once the harvest was over. This is a phenomenon that we also encounter in the rest of western and southern Europe from the sixteenth century on.[9] Apart from these seasonal workers, Irish men and women also settled permanently in England, although not in great numbers. Liverpool, for example, became one of the largest areas of settlement after 1840, but the city had only 2 percent Irish-born citizens in 1790; by 1831 this number had increased to 11 percent, and the Great Famine in the 1840s brought with it a mass exodus that doubled the percentage of immigrants in the following two decades.[10]

The Liverpool experience was merely part of a much greater and dramatic demographic and social picture. No fewer than three million people left Ireland between 1841 and 1861, resulting in a net 30 percent decrease in the Irish population. In subsequent decades the population would shrink even further, reaching a constant level of slightly over four million around 1900—about half the number of inhabitants than there were in 1841.[11] Two-thirds of these Irish went to the United States, but Britain also received a considerable share, absorbing almost a half million in a twenty-year period.

The immediate reason for the exodus may have been the repeated failures of the potato crop, but this was not a structural cause. Since the 1980s, it has become clear that the mass emigration cannot be considered as a "Malthusian check" (people leaving because the available land does not produce enough food for the population). Emigration was well on its way long before the Great Famine, and what is more, the emigrants came from the more advanced counties, not from the poorest and most backward regions of Ireland.[12] Thus, almost one million Irish settled in the United States in the first four decades of the nineteenth century, twice as many as in the preceding centuries. Their main reason for leaving the "emerald isle" was not the lack of food, for there are even indications that the diet of the Irish workers was better than that of their English brethren: they simply could not pay for it.[13] A more convincing argument points to structural economic shifts, especially the collapse of the textile industry and the de-industrialization of the Irish countryside due to technical changes in the English textile industry. As a result, many Irish weavers moved to the British textile cities, such as Dundee and Aberdeen in Scotland, and to Manchester in Lancashire.[14] A second reason for the exodus was the commercialization of the dominant Irish agricultural sector, which resulted in the reduction of small farms and an increase in landless laborers.[15] Since these socioeconomic changes were accompanied by a rapid population growth, it was clear that permanent emigration would become inevitable.

The Irish men and women who immigrated to Britain can be divided into roughly three groups. Those from the north (Ulster) went predominantly to the urban centers in Scotland; those from the middle (counties Leinster and partly Connaught) to Lancashire; and those from southern Munster to Wales and London.[16] Most Irish were very unevenly distributed throughout England, Scotland, and Wales, as they settled predominantly in four big cities (see table 1). In absolute numbers, most of the Irish immigrants ended up in London; Liverpool and the Scottish cities Glasgow and Dundee ranked much higher when the Irish are represented as a share of the population (see table 2).[17]

Immigration to Britain decreased sharply after 1860 but did not cease altogether. Expanding towns such as Birmingham, Leeds, and Preston continued to attract Irish migrants. After 1880, however, the total annual numbers of Irish immigrants to Britain dwindled from fifteen thousand in 1879 to one thousand in 1908.[18] This number increased again in the interwar years, especially in the 1930s, when Irish immigration totaled thirty-two thousand (1936).[19]

Table 1. The Irish-born Population in the Four Main British Cities of Settlement

|  | 1841 | 1851 | 1861 | 1871 |
|---|---|---|---|---|
| London | 75,000 | 109,000 | 107,000 | 91,000 |
| Liverpool | 46,639 | 83,813 | 83,949 | 76,761 |
| Manchester | 33,490 | 52,504 | 52,076 | 34,066 |
| Glasgow | 44,345 | 59,801 | — | 68,330 |
| Percent of total | 48 | 42 | 37 | 34 |

Source: MacRaild, *Culture, Conflict and Migration*, 6.

Table 2. Percentage of the Irish-born Population in British Towns, 1841–1901

|  | 1841 | 1851 | 1861 | 1871 | 1881 | 1891 | 1901 | N (x 1000) (1851) |
|---|---|---|---|---|---|---|---|---|
| Liverpool | 17.3 | 22.3 | 19.0 | 16.0 |  | 12.6 | 6.7 | 376 |
| Dundee |  | 19.0 |  |  |  |  |  |  |
| Glasgow | 16.0 | 18.0 |  | 14.0 |  | 11.0 |  | 329 |
| Manchester | 11.0 | 13.1 | 11.0 | 9.0 |  | 5.0 | 3.7 | 401 |
| Stockport |  | 10.6 |  |  |  |  | 2.4 | 54 |
| Bradford |  | 8.9 |  |  |  |  | 1.5 | 104 |
| Newcastle |  | 8.1 |  |  |  |  | 2.1 | 88 |
| Preston |  | 7.4 |  |  |  |  | 2.2 | 70 |
| Bolton |  | 7.3 |  |  |  |  | 2.0 | 61 |
| Wolverhampton |  | 7.0 |  |  |  |  | 0.8 | 50 |
| Durham |  | 7.0 |  |  |  |  |  | 56 |
| Edinburgh |  | 6.5 |  |  |  |  |  | 191 |
| Sunderland |  | 5.6 |  |  |  |  | 1.4 | 64 |
| Leeds |  | 4.9 |  |  |  |  | 1.5 | 172 |
| Merthyr Tydfil |  | 4.8 |  |  |  |  | 3.7 | 63 |
| London | 3.9 | 4.6 | 3.8 | 2.8 |  | 1.6 |  | 2,400 |
| Birmingham |  | 4.0 |  |  |  |  | 0.8 | 233 |
| Bristol |  | 3.5 |  |  |  |  |  | 137 |
| Kingston/Hull |  | 3.5 |  |  |  |  | 0.8 | 85 |
| Sheffield |  | 3.3 |  |  |  |  | 1.0 | 135 |
| Nottingham |  | 2.7 |  |  |  |  | 0.6 | 57 |
| Leicester |  | 1.4 |  |  |  |  | 0.5 | 61 |
| Lancashire |  | 8.6 |  |  |  |  |  | 2,232 |
| England & Wales | 1.8 | 2.9 | 3.0 | 2.5 | 2.2 | 1.6 | 1.3 | 17,931 |
| Scotland | 4.8 | 7.2 | 6.6 | 6.2 | 5.9 | 4.8 | 4.6 | 2,875 |

Sources: Dennis, *English Industrial Cities*, 37; Pooley, "The Irish in Liverpool," 72; Neal, "The Foundations," 73; O'Tuathaigh, "The Irish in Nineteenth-Century Britain," 15; Neal, *Sectarian Violence*, 8–11; Jackson, *The Irish in Britain*, 11; Lowe, *The Irish in Mid-Victorian Lancashire*, 47.

With the incorporation of Ireland into the United Kingdom in 1801, the inhabitants of Ireland enjoyed the same rights as British citizens and were therefore free to migrate to England, Wales, and Scotland.[20] Because the Irish were not aliens in a technical sense, this free migration could only be curtailed through the poor-relief system, enshrined in the Acts of Settlement. This system, which resembles others in continental Europe,[21] made it possible to return internal migrants who appealed for poor relief to the place where they were actually entitled to the relief—generally their birthplace. At the height of the Irish exodus (1849–54), some sixty-three thousand migrants were sent home from Liverpool alone,[22] although this number represents only about 5 percent of the 1.4 million immigrants arriving in this port city during the same period. Most of the Irish arriving in Liverpool soon left for the United States and so were not affected by these measures.

In spite of these regulations, there was widespread belief among the native population that the Irish were parasites, although only a very small percentage of them turned to local poor-relief officers,[23] not in the least because they were afraid that this could lead to deportation.[24] The public perceived the immigration of tens of thousands of Irish men and women as highly threatening. As is true of present-day western Europeans with regard to immigration, many Britons at that time were afraid that the migrants would only cost them money for relief and medical aid and add nothing to society. This partly explains the resentment against the Irish and the demands for a far harsher application of the settlement laws, including the prosecution of those who returned to Britain after they had been rejected.[25] In 1861 and 1865 the Law of Settlement was adapted to fit the real problems of large rural-to-urban migrations and the accompanying very high level of mobility in general, so that migrants who had lived in a place for more than a year could not be sent back.[26]

## Settling Down

What happened after these Irish people settled in British towns and cities? To what extent, and for how long, did they remain a visible ethnic minority that managed to integrate only very slowly? The answers to these questions seem quite simple: the Irish were discriminated against, stigmatized, and, as a result, kept to themselves. After a few decades, however, the ethnic walls began to crumble, and by the end of the nineteenth century the Irish had more or less been absorbed into the mainstream English working class. The most well-known proponent of this view of the situation is the famous historian E. P. Thompson, who, in his seminal book *The Making of the English Working Class*, argued that "the Irish were never pressed back into ghettoes. It would have been difficult to have made a people who spoke the same language and were British citizens under the Act of Union into a subject minority."[27] In the course of the 1980s this interpretation came under attack by social historians who explicitly rejected what they called the "ethnic fade" approach. They argued that the Irish have themselves kept alive their ethnic identity much longer, even into the twentieth century—more than a half century after the mass migration. Moreover, this persistent ethnicity would have mirrored their inferior socioeconomic position. To ascertain to what extent this claim is supported by historical facts, we turn to the most relevant domains of integration: residential patterns, labor market position, negative stereotypes, political activities, criminality, and mixed marriages.

## "Little Irelands"

In a recent historiographical overview, Roger Swift, one of the leading scholars on Irish migration to Britain, has appropriately remarked that the settlement process of the Irish does not offer a homogeneous picture and varies according to time and place. The diverging local opportunity structures, especially, make it difficult to generalize. The reception of the Irish, and also the residential patterns and possibilities for social mobility, varied greatly.[28] This does not imply, however, that there are no clear lines to be discerned. As we have seen, the great majority of the Irish settled in big cities and saturated the poorest areas, usually the slums where they could afford accommodation. This was a fate they shared with many other migrants at the time, but from a wealth of local studies it is clear that the Irish clustered together far more than other groups, including the Welsh migrants. In Liverpool, for example, the Irish were concentrated in the inner city, close to the docks where many of them found work. Around 1850, Irish-born migrants made up 30–50 percent of the population in the most populous wards (Vauxhall, Exchange, and Scotland).

Students of Irish migration in Britain have long discussed whether the Irish formed ghettos; they finally concluded that ghettos—in the sense of residential areas more or less inhabited completely by Irish—did not exist.[29] There were many "little Irelands," but as the Liverpool example shows, the maximum concentration at ward level never exceeded 50 percent, so Irish-born residents were more widely spread over the city than is often assumed. More interesting than this rather technical discussion is what these concentrations tell us and whether they can be considered as an expression of a tight ethnic community. Residential segregation in itself does not reveal much. Moreover, the fact that most of the Irish lived in inner-city working-class areas can largely be explained by their limited choice. Those on low incomes, including the English, were dependent on cheap housing.[30]

It need come as no surprise that historians concluded that more or less ethnically homogeneous ghettos did not exist. The same is true in present-day European cities. The concentration of a particular ethnic group in a specific ward seldom exceeds 20 or 30 percent. To understand the real situation, however, getting down to the street level is more telling. In the Liverpool example given above, it is clear that high concentrations did occur frequently. Chisendale Street, for example, counted 1539 inhabitants in 1851, of whom 1269 (82.5 percent) were born in Ireland.[31] In Manchester, census-takers in 1851 not only differentiated between Irish- and English-born residents but also counted the second generation (born in Britain, but with two Irish-born parents); in a central part of the town almost 50 percent were Irish. Of this category almost three-quarters lived on streets that had a majority of Irish residents, clustered in the southern part of town. Domiciles associated with small courtyards and alleys showed high Irish concentrations of up to 95 percent.[32] Detailed research shows that within these Irish pockets, the composition of the population was strongly structured along local and regional lines as a result of specific patterns of chain migration. In Birmingham, for example, people from Roscommon accounted for 24 percent of the Irish population, those from Connaught as much as 50 percent. In this stronghold of Gaelic, which was also spoken in Birmingham, the migrants were concentrated in central parts of the city. In Green's Village, a section of Birmingham, more than half of the inhabitants were born in Ireland, with 9 out of 10 from Connaught.[33] In York, where the Irish-born made up only 6 percent in 1851, 71 percent came from the county Mayo and another 18 percent from the adjoining county of Sligo.[34] These strong chain-migration links, which were also quite common among contemporaneous immigrants in American cities and still structure residential patterns of migrants throughout the world today, suggest that Irish migrants and their offspring (who are not counted as Irish in the British census) were very likely not only just living in concentrated groups, but they were also were embedded in strong ethnic networks.

These networks were formed at the informal level, among neighbors.

Women, who spent more time in the neighborhoods than their men, played an especially important role in maintaining and building ethnic ties. Furthermore, in cities with a considerable number of Irish migrants, a network of Irish pubs and shops strengthened the ethnic infrastructure. These institutions, together with Catholic churches and schools, formed the backbone of Irish social space, which was even more important than the geographical component. As Lynn Lees has observed regarding the Irish in London, what Hubert Gans called an "urban village" was in fact more a cultural than a physical community: "In mid-nineteenth-century London, the pattern of ethnic residential settlement reflected a symbiotic but hierarchical relationship between English and Irish. . . . They lived close to the English, but they remained apart. . . . The result was a chain of Irish buildings and enclaves located within English working-class territory."[35] This does not imply that the Irish ethnic social space was something natural. As John Belchem rightly observed, ethnicity was far from primordial but had to be constructed, implanted, and upheld against competing identities and affiliations.[36]

Furthermore, we should realize that the Irish were far from being a homogeneous group.[37] The Protestant minority among them clearly remained outside the ethnic enclave, as did a minority of more skilled and educated migrants. For the unskilled and Catholic majority, however, the ethnic urban village was an important infrastructure for most of their lives. As with most migrants, their ethnic identity was activated by the migration process and led to what Ewa Morawska has labeled "ethnicization."[38] In the foreign and hostile British environment, an Irish identity was molded, and it consisted of at least three elements: a working-class identity, Catholicism, and Irish nationalism.

## Jobs and Social Mobility

The rapid extension of English industry could not have taken place if England had not possessed in the numerous and impoverished population of Ireland a reserve command. These people having grown up almost without civilization, accustomed from youth to every sort of privation, rough, intemperate, and improvident. . . . The worst dwellings are good enough for them; their clothing causes them little trouble, so long as it holds together by a single thread; shoes they know not; their food consists of potatoes and potatoes only; whatever they earn beyond these needs they spend upon drink. What does such a race want with high wages? . . . Whenever a district is distinguished for especial filth and especial ruinousness, the explorer may safely count upon meeting chiefly those Celtic faces which one recognizes at the first glance as different from the Saxon physiognomy of the native, and the singing, aspirate brogue which the true Irishman never loses.[39]

This portrait by the famous Friedrich Engels from his book *Die Lage der arbeitenden Klasse in England,* published in 1844, had a profound influence on Karl Marx's thinking about class struggle.[40] Engels's widely read and cited chapter on Irish immigration has been used by many to illustrate the low position and status of the Irish migrants in the British labor market, especially during the first decades of their settlement. Moreover, Engels's assertion that the Irish *Lumpenproletariat* lowered the wages and thus posed a threat to the British working class was mixed with a pessimistic expectation for the future. While many contemporaries might have disagreed with Engels's political views, they overwhelmingly shared his gloomy forecast concerning the assimilability of the Irish. In an address on "Social Economy" some twenty years later, James Emerson Tennent wrote:

> The Scotch or Welsh peasant, who finds his way to the manufacturing towns of England, from a labourer becomes in his turn an employer, a tradesman, a shopkeeper, a capitalist, a merchant, a magistrate, or a mayor: but strange to say, as a rule, in that humblest of all capacities in which the Irish immigrant lands on the quay at Liverpool or Glasgow, for the most part, he is contented to continue for the remainder of his life. He lands as a labourer, without a shilling, rarely aspires to any higher position, seldom returns to revisit the place of his birth, but at the close of a life of toil and privation . . . he leaves the world as penniless and helpless as he entered it.[41]

Does this picture of the Irish as down-and-outs reflect the reality around 1870, and to what extent do the Irish resemble migrants in the late twentieth century with a similarly inferior position in the labor market?

Although many historians on Irish migrants rightly warn against creating a picture that is too bleak and one-sided, stressing instead local and regional differences, the overall picture is quite grim. Lynn Lees' study on London shows that the Irish were heavily concentrated in the lowest social and economic groups and were clearly underrepresented in almost every specialized industrial occupation. Many worked as street vendors or unskilled dock laborers and were generally found in a range of casual jobs. Only 20 percent occupied skilled jobs, although many of these skilled workers were, in fact, condemned to the sweated trades as tailors, shoemakers, and the like. Compared with the English-born workers, the concentration of Irish in unskilled jobs in 1851 London was four times as high.[42] A similar conclusion was reached for Liverpool, which, like London, was also dominated by the service and transportation sectors that employed large numbers of immigrants.[43]

In cities with different opportunity structures, such as the industrial Lancashire and Scottish textile towns, the Irish fared little better. In Lancashire (especially Manchester) the Irish were unevenly concentrated at the bottom of the occupational ladder and wage scale. That so many Irish men and women ended up in the textile industry is no coincidence. Many of them had learned to spin and weave in their home counties, thus supplementing their income from agriculture. Ulster was known for its linen industry, whereas the production of cotton and wool, on a domestic basis, was widespread in other parts of Ireland.[44] These labor patterns were structured by gender and age: women and children were concentrated in spinning, whereas men worked as (handloom) weavers.[45] In Dundee, fathers took their children (especially girls) into the mill to assist them, just as had been the case in the cottage industry in Ireland.[46] Apart from work in the textile industry, Irish men also worked as unskilled "laborers" in mining, building (brick makers, masons), and road and railway construction. Irish women were well represented as domestic servants and street traders.[47]

From these data it is tempting to assume the existence of a dual labor market in which the Irish immigrants were more or less condemned to the second segment, characterized by low pay and very little opportunity for upward social mobility. A study on immigration in Wales argues that this was the case for the Irish who settled there, many of whom worked in the coal mines. The selective recruitment of unskilled persons by the employers, exclusion by native workers, and the negative stereotyping of the Irish as pariahs explains their inferior position in the labor market.[48]

The negative stance toward Irish workers was stimulated by the conviction, as expressed by Engels, that many of them would undercut wages and break strikes. These accusations, which have infused anti-immigrant feeling in many parts of the world (including Europe) in the last two centuries,[49] were only partly justified, but they easily caused violent conflicts between Irish and native workers. Frequently, Irish quarters were the butt of aggression, as in 1869 when more than a thousand men took to the streets against the Irish in Pont Lottyn (Wales), attacking and badly damaging houses of Irish migrants, killing one person.[50] Irish migrants in the counties Cumberland and Westmorland (present day Cumbria), an area north of Lancashire dominated by heavy industry, experienced less violence, but they occupied similar labor-market positions. Considerable numbers of Irish settled there to work as iron-ore miners, metal workers, and in a variety of unskilled jobs, but the Irish-born population in Cumberland never exceeded 6 percent. In the major towns, the Irish represented between 6 and 10 percent of the residents, and only in the small towns of Cleator Moor (10,420 inhabitants in 1881) did the Irish-born population reach high levels (between 25 and 35 percent in the period 1851–81). Thus, the Irish were predominantly found in un- and semiskilled positions, and only a small minority (13 percent in 1861) worked as artisans, skilled workers, and small traders.[51]

Low wages, poor living conditions, violence, and exclusion were certainly important aspects of daily life in the areas of Irish settlement in the second half of the nineteenth century, but these factors did not necessarily result in a rigid ethnic labor-market segmentation. Most people at the time were unskilled and semiskilled workers, and this certainly applied not only to the Irish. Even in cities like Liverpool and Manchester, where the share of Irish migrants was very high, many natives worked side by side with them in low-wage and low-status jobs. A good example can be seen in the occupational distribution of household heads in 1851 in the areas associated with the streets Bevington and Downe, located in the poorest section of Liverpool. Of all the male Irish household heads, 74 percent were unskilled, but so were 60 percent of the non-Irish, whereas 22 percent of the Irish were skilled, against 38 percent of the non-Irish. Twenty years later the skill difference between Irish and non-Irish had vanished altogether,[52] and recent research has dismissed the idea that the Irish who settled in industrial cities lowered the wage level and were indispensable for certain segments of industry and construction. It can be claimed that, as an overwhelmingly unskilled and illiterate labor force, the Irish had little impact upon the position of skilled English workers.[53]

It is important to note that there was a substantial minority of Irish migrants in skilled positions throughout Britain.[54] Most of the data on the labor market in the examples given so far are derived from towns and cities with a rather one-sided economic opportunity structure, or cities like London and Liverpool, with their great demand for unskilled labor in the transportation sector. In smaller cities, the position of Irish migrants was less bleak.[55] In Cornwall, for example, where in 1881 the Irish made up only 0.5 percent of the population, their labor market position was far more diversified. They worked both in agriculture and in industry and were to be found at all levels on the occupational ladder.[56]

Another argument that opposes the idea of an ethnically segmented labor market is the fragmentary information we have on the social mobility of the Irish in the second half of the nineteenth century. Although most specialists agree that upward mobility was very modest, substantial numbers of migrants and their children managed to obtain skilled positions. A good example is found in the heavy-industry towns in Cumbria, where between 1871 and 1891 the Irish remained predominantly in un- and semiskilled positions, but where their share in skilled trades slowly increased. Between Cumbrian towns, differences could be significant, as table 3 shows.

Whereas Cleator Moor was a rather primitive iron town, Barrow was a growing shipbuilding center with an increasing demand for skilled metal workers and a diversifying economy; as a result, the percentage of skilled workers among Irish males doubled in the space of twenty years. Many of these men worked not only as shipbuilders but also increasingly as artisans and small shopkeepers. Another example comes from the Scottish port of Greenock, where most Irish migrants heading for Glasgow and Dundee first set foot on Scottish land, and which grew from fifteen thousand in 1792 to sixty-three thousand a century later. By 1841, Irish migrants made up almost 12 percent of the population, reaching an all-time high of 16 percent forty years later. Many were unskilled sugar refinery workers, dock laborers, or hawkers. A large proportion of the male heads of household, however, were able to secure skilled positions. A third of them were shoemakers, while others were skilled construction workers, tradesmen, artisans, and shop-keepers.[57]

The overall picture given by Friedrich Engels, and also the pessimistic expectations by his contemporary James Emerson Tennent regarding the social mobility of the Irish migrants, may have been corrected by historical research in the last forty years, yet the indisputable fact remains that the Irish as a whole caught up with the rest of the population only very slowly. Social and economic assimilation in Britain took a long time, and even the second generation made only very modest progress.[58] In the words of Tom Galla-gher, "Second- and third-generation Irish, who were counted as English or

*Table 3.* Occupational Groups of Adult Irish-born Males in Cleator Moor and Barrow-in-Furness, 1871 and 1891

|  | Cleator Moor | | Barrow-in-Furness | |
|---|---|---|---|---|
|  | 1871 | 1891 | 1871 | 1891 |
| Higher status | 1.4 | 2.0 | 1.4 | 4.2 |
| Skilled | 5.8 | 9.8 | 13.4 | 29.0 |
| Semiskilled | 62.9 | 62.0 | 3.6 | 14.8 |
| Unskilled | 29.2 | 19.8 | 79.9 | 50.2 |

Source: MacRaild, *Culture, Conflict and Migration,* 79.

Scottish in the census returns, often retained the attitudes and traditions of their Irish parents or grandparents. They were also likely to retain the same job or remain in the same lowly social position."[59] Although the same conclusion can probably also be drawn for a considerable part of the English, Welsh, and Scottish populations, their socioeconomic diversity had been much greater from the start.

The genesis of this "remarkably conservative pattern of occupational and social structure"[60] among the Irish immigrants, which resembles the developments among guest workers in western Europe in the latter part of the twentieth century, can only be fully understood by addressing the British outlook on Ireland and the Irish, and the social and political interaction between Irish migrants and a rather hostile host population.

## Racial and Religious Stereotypes

Negative stereotypes about the Irish date back to the Middle Ages but became widespread in the course of the sixteenth and seventeenth centuries, when the English tried to colonize the island.[61] From 1600 onward, Englishmen and Scots were enticed to Ireland by the promise of free land on which to set up plantations. The Irish population was considered backward both socially and religiously (being Catholics), which is reflected in the stereotype of the racially inferior, violent, contemptible, and stupid Irishman. Catholicism was in general not seen as the root cause, but rather a symptom of the "natural" trait of the Irish (Celtic) character, which made it impossible for them to embrace Protestantism.[62] This highly negative image of the Irish partly served to sharpen English nationalism that, in the eighteenth century, was increasingly articulated in anti-Catholic terms.[63] Following historian Linda Colley, one might argue that, whereas in the eighteenth century British nationalism was stimulated by the anti-Catholic French propaganda, in the nineteenth century the role was taken over by anti-Irish propaganda. Given the deep-rooted distrust and hatred against Catholics in general, especially among the less-educated English Protestants, it comes as no surprise that the influx of predominantly Irish Catholic migrants from the 1830s onward created a hostile climate in those regions where these newcomers settled. Along with the image of poor, backward, and Catholic immigrants, social, cultural, and religious elements created a powerful anti-Irish atmosphere, which exceeded the well-known stereotypes that migrants (both internal and international, inside and outside Europe) often encountered.

The anti-Irish stereotype had a clearly racist overtone. According to Mary Hickman, from the 1840s onward the existing cultural stigma was further contaminated by nineteenth-century scientific racist discourse. As a result, the Irish were increasingly seen as an inferior, Celtic race, and for some this was an incentive to indulge in unsavory insults, as in the well-known "missing link" article in *Punch* (1862):

> A gulf certainly does appear to yawn between the Gorilla and the Negro. The woods and wilds of Africa do not exhibit an example of any intermediate animal. But in this, as in many other cases, philosophers go vainly searching abroad for it at home. A creature manifestly between the Gorilla and the Negro is to be met within some of the lowest districts of London and Liverpool by adventurous explorers. It comes from Ireland, whence it has continued to migrate; it belongs in fact to a tribe of Irish savages: the lowest spies of the Irish Yahoo. When conversing with its kind it talks a sort of gibberish. It is, moreover, a climbing animal, and may sometimes be seen ascending a ladder laden with a load of bricks.[64]

It is tempting to interpret these kinds of examples, which are numerous in the nineteenth-century English media, as proof of the inherent racist character of the anti-Irish stance, even when we acknowledge the fact that such views were inextricably bound up with other religious and social stereotypes. It remains to be seen, however, how pervasive this racist discourse was and how seriously readers took it. Portrayals of the Irish as "ape-faced and small-headed," as a Glasgow newspaper wrote,[65] clearly had racist and biologistic connotations, but they were also ambiguous, ephemeral, and did not result in a widely accepted racial categorization, certainly not in the long run.[66]

The most enduring, salient, and explosive ingredient of the anti-Irish mixture was religion. Anti-Catholicism was deeply rooted in a century-old and deeply ingrained level of hostility among the Anglican population, which regarded Roman Catholicism as a foreign church.[67] In her seminal work on British nationalism, Linda Colley thoroughly explored how important anti-Catholicism was. Although the anti-Catholic mood waned somewhat in the first half of the nineteenth century, it remained very much alive among the working classes, as illustrated by the heated debates around the Catholic Emancipation Act in 1829, which gave British Catholics equal political rights and nullified anti-Catholic acts adopted from 1650 on.

The opposition to this act was not linked primarily with Irish immigrants, just as the protests were not limited to the key areas of Irish immigration.[68]

The passionate reactions to the restoration of the Episcopal Catholic hierarchy in 1851 (and the creation of twelve bishoprics), however, led to turmoil in most Protestant areas of western Europe and aroused even more fear because it coincided with the mass emigration from Ireland. The Orange Order, founded at the end of the eighteenth century by Protestants in Northern Ireland, played an important role during this time. Seventy-seven of the 230 British Orange lodges could be found in Lancashire alone.[69] One of the organization's primary tactics was, under the guise of patriotism, to provoke Catholic reactions by spreading anti-Catholic propaganda and holding marches in Irish Catholic cities and neighborhoods.[70] With the powerful slogan "No popery!" it was easy to mobilize large crowds, and in many English and Welsh cities, anti-Catholicism coincided with anti-Irish (anti-immigrant) feelings. In the years 1851 and 1852 reactions to the "Papal aggression" led to widespread, collective violence against Irish immigrants. The most notorious riots occurred in Stockport, immediately south of Manchester, which at the time counted fifty-four thousand inhabitants, of whom almost six thousand were Irish-born. In June 1852, twelve days before the yearly procession of the Catholic Sunday schools, the town council forbade Catholics to process through public streets with symbols of their religion. Although the Irish Catholics left their symbols and flags at home, fights broke out during the procession the next day, leaving twenty-four Irish houses pillaged and the furniture destroyed, fifty-one Irish wounded, and two chapels ransacked. According to Pauline Millward, the Stockport riots were clearly staged by the local Protestant elite, who urged on the English working-class population and did little to prevent trouble. The fact that 111 of the 113 people arrested were Irish speaks for itself.[71]

After 1852 the violence connected with the "Papal aggression" soon waned, although it would bounce back in the 1860s, when rabid Protestant, anti-papal lecturers toured the country, causing considerable unrest and provoking new anti-Irish riots. The most well known of these lecturers was William Murphy, who wanted to free Great Britain from the "yoke of the Roman Catholic priesthood and its abettors."[72] He targeted Irish settlements, especially in the north. His standard operating procedure was to advertise his lecture well beforehand, hire a large hall, and hope for trouble. As was the case with many fanatical anti-Catholic preachers, Murphy was born a Roman Catholic in Ireland (Limerick) in 1834 but later converted to Protestantism. At age eighteen he became a scripture reader for the Irish Society, an evangelical Protestant organization. In 1862 he migrated to London, where his talent for oratory was soon recognized by the Protestant Electoral Union, launching his career as an anti-papal lecturer.[73] He became known nation-wide for his five lectures in Wolverhampton in 1867, where twelve thousand Irish-born lived, and in Birmingham a few months later. In both cases his lectures led to large-scale riots. In his addresses he tried to demonstrate the theological untenability of the Catholic faith, especially with regard to the transubstantiation and the sacraments. Furthermore, he made allegations of Catholic atrocities in the past and emphasized the intrigues of the Jesuits. He warned against the Catholic aspiration to dominate the world and against the priests in particular, whom he accused of interfering with the family by insinuating themselves with the Protestant *pater familias* and thus influenc-ing his wife and children. These religious attacks were delivered in a furious style and were stocked with offensive language, labeled by Walter Arnstein as "the pornography of the Puritan."[74] In most places Murphy visited, the interest of the mostly working-class English Protestants was enormous, and he had no trouble at all filling the halls where his speeches took place. The Irish population was also attracted to Murphy, albeit for different reasons. They would try to disrupt his lectures by shouting and throwing stones, both inside and outside the lecture halls. In many cases the police had consider-able trouble controlling the riots that ensued. In 1871 Murphy was to speak in Whitehaven (Cumberland), but soon after beginning his first lecture, he was seized by Irish miners, who beat him into unconsciousness. Although he was saved by the police and taken home, he never fully recovered and died within a year.

Apart from a few incidents involving Murphy, the public religious stig-matization against Catholicism died out, and collective violence against the Irish became more sporadic. The anti-Catholic campaign had stimulated the already existing Irish ethnic feeling. From the 1840s onward the small English Catholic Church had established many new parishes and churches wherever the Irish settled. Extensive parish-based welfare support was created in cities like Liverpool and Dundee, support that included schools, church halls, and all kinds of clubs. Church attendance may not have been very high, especially among men, but many scholars of Irish migration have shown convincingly that Catholicism was nevertheless an entire way of life and formed a crucial aspect of their ethnic identity.[75] The introduction of the Irish migrants to the English Catholic Church was not smooth. Many Irish were accustomed to a much more magical form of Catholicism that possessed pre-Christian undertones. The belief in elves, ghosts, witchcraft, and magical healing were widespread, especially in the western parts of Ireland. Moreover, in Lancashire less than 30 percent of the population were acquainted with the discipline of modern Tridentine conformism.[76] Many migrants therefore felt ill at ease in the English Catholic Church. Only after a campaign to help newcomers become more familiar with orthodox Catholicism did church attendance rise and the two forms eventually converge.[77]

## Irish Nationalism

In reaction to the colonization of Ireland by the Protestant English state and its representatives (as well as English landowners), a deep resentment against the English had developed and led to a number of bloody incidents. The insurrection of 1641, for example, in which a number of Protestant settlers were killed, is one of the most well known. It would be anachronistic, however, to label it as an expression of Irish nationalism. In fact, it fit very well with the struggle throughout Europe between the power of the royal state and regional power holders.[78] It was not until the end of the eighteenth century that modern notions of nationalism emerged when, after another insurrection in 1798, Great Britain decided to incorporate Ireland into the United Kingdom.

Lynn Lees has stressed that Catholic Ireland was a conflict-ridden society. In contrast to what nationalists would like us to believe, people were divided along many lines, of which religion, kinship groups, and class (laborers versus landholders) were the most important.[79] Furthermore, local and regional identities remained prominent and, as we have seen, were strengthened by highly selective chain-migration patterns into English towns. At the same time, settlement in Britain created a pan-Irish national identity. Migrants throughout the world have similar experiences. For instance, migration makes people far more aware of their common national characteristics, which, in turn, allows them to perceive themselves as members of an imagined community.[80] In this way, a sort of "retribalization" came about.[81] This new self-perception is matched by how the local population views the immigrants. In the case of the Irish, the national awareness was even stronger because of the anti-Irish mood among the permanent population and because of the Irish's own resentment against England. Many Irish remained heavily focused on Ireland and dreamed of returning to their green island once again. Temporary return migrations were not at all uncommon, in fact, keeping the bond with the home country alive, especially during the first decades. The follow-up immigration of relatives and other chain migrants, who often lodged in with established Irish families, also had an effect, as noted by Lees: "Not only did the Irish provide for their kin, but the ethnic community provided homes for newcomers, for the single, and for those without the means to set up their own households. Those without families regularly boarded within other Irish households, either as lodgers or as visitors, instead of setting up on their own."[82]

The Irish in Britain, as both migrants and Catholics, were a double minority, and they soon expressed themselves in these ethno-religious terms. The most visible collective utterances were the yearly processions on St. Patrick's Day (March 17), which occasionally led to frictions and even riots with organized Protestants, such as the local lodges of the Orange Order. In the 1850s these processions were not a mass phenomenon, because many migrants chose not to irritate the native population by marching.[83] From the 1860s on, however, St. Patrick's Day processions became the rallying point of Irish ethnicity and also became much more of a political manifestation.[84]

Organized Irish nationalism already existed in the first half of the nineteenth century, incorporated in the radical English Chartist movement, which initially was sympathetic toward the Irish cause, and partly organized through secret "ribbonite" societies.[85] After 1850 the nationalist movement in Britain was influenced from Ireland, as in the case of the Irish confederates, also called "young Irelanders," who strove for an independent Ireland and who did not renounce violence to reach this goal. In Lancashire, the heartland of their activities, these confederates were closely watched by the police and in 1858 changed their name to the Irish Republican Brotherhood (IRB), better known as the Fenians. It was their explicit aim to involve all migrants in what we would now call "the diaspora," both in Britain, North America, and other overseas destinations. Notwithstanding the opposition of the Catholic Church, which resented the group's violent nationalism, the Fenians seem to have had wide support among the Irish migrants, many of whom saw themselves as involuntary exiles and victims of exploitative English politics. According to W. J. Lowe, "The IRB was able to capitalise on the desire of the Lancashire Irish to contribute to the national movement and be active on Ireland's behalf because a strong social organization that facilitated communication among the Irish and reinforced a sense of community identity was in place."[86]

Equally important was National Brotherhood of St. Patrick, also founded in Ireland (1861) and soon thereafter exported to the Lancashire target area, as well as to Glasgow and London.[87] Like the Fenians, with whom they partly overlapped, the Brotherhood exploited the exile theme and became very popular among Irish migrants. One of their aims was to revitalize and politicize the St. Patrick's Day processions, and they succeeded. Furthermore, they set up reading rooms in the important Irish centers where nationalists could gather, congregate, and read nationalist newspapers such as the *Irishman,* the *United Irishman and Galway American,* and the *Irish Liberator.* Compared to the Fenians, the Brotherhood had a broader conception of Irish nationalism and also stimulated cultural, linguistic, and historical interests. Nevertheless, they also were condemned by the Catholic Church as a secret society, a fact that deterred moderate nationalists from joining. After 1870 the political struggle increasingly focused on home rule for Ireland; as a result, Fenians and others had to focus increasingly on English politics. Many Irish were eligible to vote— it was, after all, the English parliament who could decide on the status of Ireland.[88] The attempts to mobilize the Irish (some of whom were second-generation by that time) to vote for liberal candidates can in a sense be considered a form of Irish integration into British society, although most contemporaries probably would not have seen it this way.

It is important, however, to realize that, notwithstanding the wide popular support for nationalist causes, there was constant infighting among different organizations and factions concerning the ideal and right course.[89] In the words of Paul O'Leary: "Yet, in spite of the persuasive rhetoric, it is questionable whether the immigrants ever operated politically in such a disciplined and coordinated a manner as Irish politicians wished or their opponents feared. Ethnic politics reflected the divisions and uncertainties which existed in other aspects of immigrant life and as such illuminate the way in which awareness of a particular definition of Irish identity was both cultivated and questioned."[90] This interpretation is supported by the fact that even at the pinnacle of its existence, the Irish nationalist movement was not able to mobilize the Irish effectively. Many did sympathize with the Irish cause, but this remained restricted to symbolic identification. The internal cohesion of the group was simply too weak. But perhaps the most important reason the nationalists failed to mobilize the masses was, as Alan O'Day recently observed, the lack of compelling and exclusively ethnic issues and committed leadership.[91]

## Ethnic Identity and Intermarriage

A Protestant bystander in Manchester, watching the procession on St. Patrick's Day in 1910, commented "You'd think we were in bloody Ireland wouldn't you, why the 'ell don't they play something English?"[92] Almost three-quarters of a century after the mass immigration, the Irish presence in English towns apparently had not resulted in large-scale assimilation. This insight has brought many students of Irish immigration to reject the "ethnic fade" interpretation.[93] One of the field's most prominent spokesmen, Steven Fielding, argued that the Irish ethnic identity remained strong in the second and even third generation and for at least half a century has—among other things—obstructed a large-scale integration of the Irish in the English, Welsh, and Scottish labor movement.[94] He thus follows Lees, who stresses the importance of a relatively closed Irish subculture in London.[95] The numerous Irish pubs and shops, for example, played an important role in maintaining a vibrant ethnic community life functioning as labor exchanges and stimulating the recruitment of labor through Irish channels, known as "Hibernian closed shops."[96] The many Irish-friendly societies contributed as well, acting as collectors or centers for mutual insurance funds against sickness and death (for burial costs).[97]

Important questions arise: How widespread was this persistence of ethnicity? How did it manifest itself in the social life of Irish migrants and their descendants? We have already seen that Irish social mobility was rather slow, and there are indications that for at least part of the Irish working class, their un- and semiskilled position was transferred through generations well into the twentieth century,[98] a phenomenon that bears similarities to what is now labeled as "segmented assimilation."[99] In present-day discussions about general immigrant integration, criminality also is seen to play a prominent role. The overrepresentation of immigrants (and especially their male children) in criminal activities is seen as a disquieting signal, or even as proof of the utter failure of integration. In the Irish case similar opinions were voiced, as is illustrated by the chaplain at the Preston House of Correction in 1848: "When these wretched people . . . settle in a town their children contribute largely to the hopeless class of young offenders. Had they remained in Ireland . . . ignorance, indolence, and begging might have constituted the worst features of their character. But in a town such habits soon grow into more deplorable vices."[100] We know now that Irish men were clearly overrepresented in the criminal records during the first period of settlement. Apart from their membership in big-city street gangs,[101] many Irish were arrested for drunkenness, violence (not in the least against police officers), gambling, and theft throughout the 1860s and 1870s.[102]

Because of the selectivity of these observations, a better measure of the integration process is marriage behavior. Several authors have tried to measure the extent to which mixed marriages existed among the Irish-born migrants, and they have come to the general conclusion that, before the mass exodus of the 1840s, the percentage was much higher, around 50 percent, whereas later, most marriages of Irish born in Britain (about 80 percent) were endogamous. It is conceivable, too, that some of the marriage partners reflected in these numbers were second-generation Irish born in England.[103] In Liverpool, this inclination to stick to one's own people was significantly stronger than among British immigrants from Wales and Scotland.[104] Many Irish men, moreover, preferred to marry a girl from their home village and return to England as a married couple.[105] This theme was idealized in the following song: "Oh the English girls are beautiful, their love I don't decline; but the eating and the drinking is beautiful and fine; but in the corner of the heart where nobody can see; her two eyes of Irish blue always looking out on me; but never mind, Molly, I am still your faithful boy; for Ireland is my country, and your name shall be Molloy."[106]

That such endogamy was relatively high need not come as a surprise. The social distance between Irish migrants and the surrounding population was not only wide for social, political, and ethnic reasons, but because religious affiliation made it even more difficult to cross the line. Even if someone would venture to choose a marriage partner outside the ethnic enclave but still with a preference for Catholics, then the chance was great that he or she would end up with an Irish partner anyway. More systematic research, differentiating between localities as well as generations will have be carried out in order to bring more light to this matter, but for the moment we will have to content ourselves with this somewhat impressionistic sketch.

## Conclusion

At the beginning of the twenty-first century it is difficult to grasp the deeply felt revulsion of Protestants towards Catholics, at least outside Northern Ireland. It seems not far-fetched, though, to posit that the gap between these two groups was even deeper than that which exists between Christian (and agnostic western Europeans) and Muslims at the present time. At least the relative freedom of Protestants to attack Irish migrants verbally and physically was far greater than we experience today. Moreover, the anti-Irish stereotype was further strengthened by the emerging radical nationalism. All elements taken together—low social status, the discourse on primitive races, "deviant" religion, and extreme nationalism—make the Irish case quite similar to that of more recent groups like the Turks and North Africans in western Europe.

Unfortunately, it is difficult to judge how this antagonism toward the Irish worked itself out in the long run. Due to the lack of census data on the second (let alone the third) generation, we are best informed about the migrants themselves. It is clear that their position was far from enviable and that most of them made no socioeconomic progress at all. How the integration of their children and grandchildren took shape, however, is largely clouded. Although the second generation must have felt the Irish stigma, it is less clear in what domains and to what extent they experienced it. Some of them, especially those who managed to climb the social ladder, will have faded into the wider English society. Until the beginning of the twentieth century, class especially played a crucial role in this process, and only in the twentieth century did gender become important as well. From the 1920s on, Irish women who migrated to Great Britain seem to have had slightly better chances at upward social mobility, especially when they worked in isolated jobs as servants and later as nurses, for example,[107] where they were less associated with the negative image of the Irish immigrant, which was predominantly defined in masculine terms. Although the second and third generations were often still recognizable by their surnames, they could afford to move out of the classic Irish quarters and would have identified less with Irish nationalism or ethnicity. Another segment of the second generation (and quite possibly the majority) probably found themselves in the same position as their parents: living with co-ethnics in Irish-dominated quarters, and stuck in the segment of unskilled and semiskilled labor.

# 2

## A Threat to the Nation: Poles in Germany (1870–1940)

By the time the Irish migration to Great Britain was slowing down, the newly founded German empire began to experience a large-scale influx of Polish-speaking migrants from the eastern regions and beyond. The way German society reacted to these Poles, as they were called, and the ensuing thorny integration process bears many resemblances to the way British society reacted to the Irish. Each country had to deal with a large group of people with a distinct ethnic profile who migrated in large numbers over a short period from mainly rural regions, usually to industrialized areas. Immigrants in both countries were often in the lowest social positions; the overwhelming majority of the Poles, like the Irish, were unskilled, landless laborers attracted by the higher wages in the fast-developing industrial areas. Furthermore, the settlement of the Poles was concentrated in particular regions and towns, especially in the capital city (in Berlin, like the Irish in London) and the Ruhr area (which can be considered as the German equivalent of Lancashire), where most of them worked as miners and lived in isolated urban districts. And both groups, although officially citizens of the receiving countries (the immigrants' "home" territories were either entirely, in the case of Ireland, or partially, in the case of Poland, incorporated in the states where they settled),[1] differed in a number of respects from the local inhabitants. Apart from the protestant *Masurians* from East Prussia,[2] most Poles,[3] like the Irish, were Catholics in a (largely) Protestant state. Even more important, however, was that the Poles were regarded as a threat to the new German empire because of their nationalist aspirations, aimed at the establishment of an independent state.

The position of the Polish-speaking minority in the fragile national unity, which came about in 1870, was further complicated by the migration of Poles from the east to the west.[4] This difference in emphasis also explains, to a certain extent, the divergent attitudes in the society where they settled. Whereas in Britain the most violent anti-Irish reactions sprang from the population, in Germany the state reacted most strongly in its attempts to assimilate the Poles as quickly as possible.

## The Polish Migration to the Ruhr Area

The migration of the Poles to the Ruhr area is a classic tale of push and pull, with recruitment and chain migration functioning as channels and bridges linking both the expulsion and attraction factors. The eastern areas of Germany, especially East Prussia and Posen (Poznan), were dominated by large estates owned mainly by German-speaking landholders (*Junkers*), but also by Polish nobility (*Schlachta*) who employed great numbers of landless, Polish-speaking laborers. The power of the *Junkers,* supported by the Prussian state, was extensive and encompassed the economic, cultural, and political domain. Due to the increase of large estates and the dissemination of capitalist modes of production (which replaced the feudal *Gutsherrschaft*), more and more peasants lost their small parcels of land.[5] This proletarianization of Polish peasants coincided with the recruitment of hundreds of thousands of seasonal laborers from the Polish-speaking regions of Russia and Austria, who partly replaced the native workers.

The leaders of the new German state, of whom Bismarck was by far the most prominent, wanted to prevent the settlement of these foreign seasonal workers, afraid as they were of the "Polonization"[6] of the eastern part of the German Reich.[7] They therefore created a rotation system, making it obligatory by law for these foreign Poles (almost three hundred thousand in 1913) to leave the country at the end of each year, allowing them to re-enter after seven weeks. Moreover, they were allowed to work only in the agricultural sector and in the eastern provinces.[8] The legal position of the German Poles—who were, after all, Prussian citizens—gave them much more freedom, but their prospects were equally bleak. Poorly paid, and discriminated against socially and culturally, they had few chances to improve their situation.

As industrialization took hold in the western part of Germany in the 1860s, east-west migration gradually accelerated. The first area to become popular was Berlin, followed soon thereafter by the central part of Germany (Saxony,

Thuringia). The Ruhr area and the Rhineland became more important later; indeed, from the 1890s on, they were the most popular areas for attracting large numbers of migrants, predominantly from the eastern regions of Prussia.[9] The first pioneers had already arrived in the Ruhr area around 1870. Some of them may have hit on the idea when they passed through the Ruhr area as recruits during the short Franco-Prussian war of 1870,[10] but most of the migration to Germany's center of heavy industrialization was triggered by targeted recruitment by the mine owners of Westphalia.[11] The impetus for the Westphalian employers' strategy was the lack of manpower in this rural region, which had been transformed in a very short period into a full-scale industrial center. In the 1850s and 1860s, internal migrants from Hessen and Saxony had already found their way to the mills and mines, as had workers from the Netherlands, Austria, Hungary, and Italy. As industry kept expanding, employers were constantly in need of workers, and in 1871, mine owners in Bottrop sent Polish-speaking recruiting agents to the eastern, Polish-speaking regions of Germany. Their first target was Upper Silesia, as it had a tradition of mining and therefore could provide skilled mineworkers. One of these agents was Karol Sliwka, who was already working in a coal mine in Bottrop in the 1860s. Sliwka and other Polish agents would go to the east in January and entice potential candidates, for example, by handing out cigars and schnapps, and offering them much higher wages than workers could earn in Silesia. The arrival of the recruiting agents was sometimes preceded by letters from mine owners to publicans in Silesia and other Polish areas. One such letter, from 1906, read as follows: "Very confidential! We ask café owners to encourage as many workers as possible to come here [the Ruhr Area, LL], preferably those under the age of 26 and unmarried. For every person who comes we pay you three Marks."[12]

Soon, hundreds of workers, most of them from the Rybnik area, were attracted to Bottrop, paving the way for the large-scale influx of migrants.[13] Whereas these Silesian workers were skilled miners, the mass of the Poles who came to the Ruhr area from East Prussia, West Prussia, and Posen had no industrial experience whatsoever. Most of them were landless agricultural workers or had worked their own small farms. The internal migration to the west was part of a much larger movement from (eastern) Europe to overseas destinations, especially the United States. In the case of the German Poles, however, internal migration dominated, except during the 1880s (see table 4).

It is interesting to note, in this respect, that migrants who went to the Ruhr area did not so much come from the large semi-feudal estates, but predominantly from areas characterized by small land-ownership.[14] (Sea-

Table 4. Migration from the Eastern, Polish-speaking
Parts of the German Empire to the West, 1871–1910

| Period | Internal emigration | Overseas emigration |
| --- | --- | --- |
| 1871–1880 | 54,558 | 18,160 |
| 1881–1890 | 113,558 | 122,160 |
| 1891–1900 | 147,582 | 64,595 |
| 1901–1910 | 148,715 | 31,400 |

Source: Hagen, *Germans, Poles and Jews*, 326.

sonal) labor migration, where the aim was to save money and then return home, was a well-known pattern in western Europe from 1600 onward and was used as a way to increase prosperity and buy more property without actually emigrating.[15]

Although the number of migrants in the Ruhr area was still relatively small in the first decades, after 1890 immigration boomed, increasing from some 110,000 to almost half a million in 1910.[16] Initially, this migration wave consisted mainly of (single young) men who hoped to return home after a few years with the money they had saved, and during the first years many did go back, if only for a short while. However, the lure of high wages and the lack of prospects in the region of origin meant that more migrants opted for permanent settlement in the west. As migrants resigned themselves to the fact that they would not return, at least not in the short term, they started to bring over their spouses or their betrothed. After 1890, in particular, during the period of mass migration, the proportion of women increased dramatically, although their numbers never equaled those for the men.[17] The west was not only attractive to the Poles because of the higher wages (up to 50 percent higher), but also because employers treated workers with more respect (compared to the semifeudal relationship with the *Junkers*), workers had more free time (Sundays off, for example), and they enjoyed better housing.[18]

The anti-Polish policy (Germanization) of the Prussian state also stimulated more permanent emigration from the east. Two acts in particular played an important role. The first was the settlement act of 1886, which made it possible for the Prussian state to buy land owned by Poles. This act was amended in 1904, making it compulsory for people to ask government permission if they wanted to buy land to set up a farm—in effect excluding the Poles, as they did not fit the colonization policy. Another act empowered the state to expropriate land owned by Poles.[19] These acts made it much harder for migrants in the Ruhr area to invest in land or property in their home region.

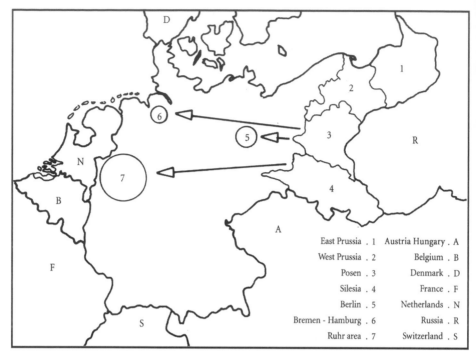

| | | | |
|---|---|---|---|
| East Prussia | . 1 | Austria Hungary | . A |
| West Prussia | . 2 | Belgium | . B |
| Posen | . 3 | Denmark | . D |
| Silesia | . 4 | France | . F |
| Berlin | . 5 | Netherlands | . N |
| Bremen - Hamburg | . 6 | Russia | . R |
| Ruhr area | . 7 | Switzerland | . S |

Figure 1. The Principal Areas of Polish Emigration within the German Empire

Targeted recruitment resulted in a Silesian community in Bottrop made up of Poles (especially from the Rybnik district),[20] an example of chain migration patterns that evolved in many Ruhr towns. However, in most cases, chain migration was a more spontaneous process that led to concentrations of, for example, East Prussian Masurians in Buer and Gelsenkirchen, and Poles in Recklinghausen, Herne, and Oberhausen.[21] Although the Ruhr area was by far the most important settlement area, there were also smaller groups who went to the north, especially to Bremen and Wilhelmsburg (see figure 1). Their migration and settlement process differed in a number of respects from the patterns seen in the Ruhr district. First, the existence of a local labor market in the north (known for its textile, excavation, and metal industries) meant there were jobs, mainly un- and semiskilled, for both men and women. Furthermore, patterns of chain migration were less distinct and settlement was less concentrated than in the Ruhr area. Finally, in part of the north (especially in Bremen), anti-Polish policy seems to have been less pronounced.[22]

Not all the Poles remained in Germany. Coal miners in general were highly mobile, and during the heyday of the mining industry they could choose among employers in Germany and in the adjoining mining areas in the south of the Netherlands, the eastern region of Belgium, and the north of France. French mining companies were particularly eager to attract the Ruhr Poles to work in their mines. Even before the First World War, some twelve thousand Ruhr Poles had moved to France. This movement was the precursor to the much larger community that developed after the war, when the recruitment by French agents (the *Mission Interalliée de Contrôle des Usines et de Mines* [MICUM]) among the Poles in the Ruhr district intensified. In December 1921, the French even set up a recruitment bureau in Duisburg, under protection of the French troops stationed in the Rhineland. Many Poles had good reason to leave Germany, not least because they feared that choosing to become a citizen of the new Polish state, realized in 1919, might mean that they would have to leave Germany. Moreover, Poland and France signed a labor migration agreement in 1920, which regulated the position of the Poles in France.[23] Another factor that may have played a role was the widespread (unsubstantiated) suspicion that the Poles were traitors and collaborated with the French occupiers during the occupation of the Ruhr district in 1923. Although it is impossible to weigh the different possible motives for leaving, economic arguments, such as job stability, wages, and secondary working conditions (social security) were probably most important. Estimates show that some fifty thousand to eighty thousand Polish miners and their families left for France in the 1920s, some of whom may have returned eventually.[24] For some towns, the migration to France had a great impact, as is illustrated by the situation in Herne, where twelve thousand Poles lived in 1910 (22 percent of the total population) and by 1925 only about five hundred (1 percent) remained.[25] It seems that migrants from East Prussia, many of whom were protestant Masurians, were much less inclined to leave the Ruhr district.[26]

## Settling Down

Although hundreds of thousands of German Poles migrated to the relatively small Ruhr area, they never exceeded 6 percent of the total population. The higher concentration of Poles was seen in the mining towns (see table 5).

In the eyes of a contemporary German at the beginning of the twentieth century, Gelsenkirchen, Recklinghausen, Wanne, Herne, and Bochum would have looked like Polish cities.[27] A good illustration is the anecdote of a Polish emigrant who took the train to Wanne, west of Dortmund, in 1921. When he

*Table 5.* Cities in the Ruhr Area with Considerable Numbers of Poles, 1890–1910

| Administrative region | District | % Poles 1890 | % Poles 1910 |
| --- | --- | --- | --- |
| Münster | Recklinghausen Stadt | 5.0 | 23 (26) |
| Arnsberg | Herne Stadt | 15.0 | 22 (26) |
| Arnsberg | Gelsenkirchen Land | 7.0 | 18 (31) |
| Düsseldorf | Hamborn Stadt | 0.5 | 17 (18) |
| Münster | Recklinghausen Land | 6.0 | 16 (24) |
| Arnsberg | Dortmund Land | 2.0 | 12 (19) |
| Münster | Buer Stadt | 5.0 | 12 (39) |
| Düsseldorf | Oberhausen Stadt | 6.0 | 10 (14) |

Note: The percentages between parentheses include the Masurians.
Source: Murzynowska, *Die Polnischen Erwerbsauswanderer,* 44–45.

arrived, he did not get off the train: he thought he was still in Poland because he saw so many Polish language signs and images of the Polish eagle.[28]

As was the case for the Irish in Britain, Poles were not distributed evenly over these towns but were concentrated in specific quarters. The residential intensity of the Poles directly resulted from the employers' policy of providing special housing, so-called "colonies," for their workers. In this way, coal-mine owners hoped to encourage company loyalty and counter the problem that mineworkers were liable to resign as soon as they could get more pay somewhere else (including the mines in the Dutch and Belgian border areas). Moreover, according to some authors, the mines deliberately segregated workers along ethnic lines to prevent class solidarity.[29] Regardless of motives, it is clear that many of the colonies were occupied mainly by Polish migrants, who often originated from the same area. It seems that, in general, the Poles were quite pleased with their relatively spacious houses and gardens, which were reminiscent of the rural environment they came from. Many used their gardens intensively and kept some livestock, especially pigs. By 1900, at the peak of Polish immigration, the number of pigs in the town of Gelsenkirchen had increased more than sixfold.[30]

Mines that had recruited large numbers of Poles were called the *Polish-mines* ("Polenzeche"), and the proportion of Poles living in the colonies often exceeded 50 percent. Increased mobility, especially after World War I, meant that Polish migrants moved to other parts of the town in the course of the twentieth century. However, the stigma attached to colonies in general and Polish colonies in particular lingered on for a long time. In a 1958 sociographical study on a Ruhr town, the authors found that the remaining local Polish colony was still looked down upon by the rest of the population.[31]

## Social Mobility and School Achievement

It is clear that the mining industry dictated the composition of the Polish population (including the Masurians), at least in the Ruhr area. A study on the occupational distribution in Bottrop shows that around 1900, 80–90 percent of the Polish German men were occupied in the coal mining industry.[32] This was a much higher proportion than was seen among working men of German descent or migrants from other countries. While the Polish men found employment in the coal mines, the women usually stayed at home. There were some women who found work in the textile industries of Bremen and Wilhelmsburg in the north, and younger women often worked as domestics. After World War I, many of the second generation themselves became migrants, and several thousands of women from the Ruhr area found jobs as domestics in the Netherlands.[33]

The Polish men were vital to the mining industry. In the 1890s, a quarter of all miners were Poles and this increased to almost 40 percent by 1908.[34] As a result of recruitment policies, Polish men were concentrated in certain mines. In 1899, 41 percent of all the Polish men employed in the Dortmund mining district worked in only 19 out of the 294 mines.[35] These Polish mines, which were much larger than the average mine, were concentrated in Gelsenkirchen (5), in Essen (5), and in Herne (4), towns all very close to one another. The Pluto mine in Herne had the highest proportion of Polish workers (75 percent).[36] The number of Polish mines had grown to 33 (out of 291) by the outbreak of the First World War.[37]

An assessment of social mobility depends on one's point of view. For many Poles the transition from the position of farmhand working on the eastern estates to that of a mineworker with better pay and better housing must have seemed a step forward for most migrants. Moreover, mineworkers started as haulers (the men who had to fill and push the coal wagons) and could be promoted to hewer (mining at the coal face), which was better paid. In this respect, the Poles fared much better than the Italians, who were often stuck in the lowest jobs.[38] However, the Poles especially were recruited with the aim of training them as hewers, so this position was predetermined rather than attained through upward social mobility.[39] Unfortunately, as more Poles came to work in the mines, the occupation of hewer began to lose status. Finally, it is important to note that the fathers of many of the Polish workers were also miners, although the estimates on the extent of this differ widely.[40]

Research on intergenerational mobility is scarce and mainly restricted to two contemporaneous sources. The first of these is a large-scale study carried out in 1937 in Duisburg. Almost fifty thousand children filled out a questionnaire with items about their school level, the occupation of male relatives, and the origin of their parents, grandparents, and great-grandparents. On the basis of a representative sample, occupational mobility was linked to origin.[41] Whereas almost all children were born in Duisburg, their parents and grandparents often were not. The author Hermann Waterkamp presented his findings on the social mobility of these four groups and concluded that the Polish migrants from the east did not fare as well as the Germans from the west. By comparing the occupations of the grandfathers with that of the fathers, he argued that the "East Germans," as he called the Polish migrants, were more likely to experience downward than upward social mobility. Moreover, fathers of Polish descent were more likely than other fathers to be stranded on the lower rungs of the social ladder. Waterkamp therefore concluded that migrants from the east who ended up in the Ruhr area were socially inferior.[42] This theme, clearly informed by the contemporary racialist discourse (the book was published in 1941), was picked up by Wilhelm Brepohl. In a book published in 1948, he used similar data on thirty-eight thousand schoolchildren in Gelsenkirchen to show that the children from the east clearly underachieved at school (see table 6), even when compared with children in the expulsion area.

According to Brepohl, the Ruhr area functioned as a "negative sieve." Whereas the "good" Poles got through and left after World War I to go to France and Belgium, the "bad" Poles stayed in the Ruhr because they were not able to leave, which resulted in an "accumulation of inferior people" ("Häufung der Minderwertigkeit").[43] Although Brepohl's speculative interpretation was deeply influenced by the same racialist discourse that characterized Waterkamp's study seven years earlier, it is not inconceivable that their data

*Table 6.* Highest School Level of Children (Ages 12–18) in Gelsenkirchen, 1938

| School type | West | East (Poles) | Rest | Total |
|---|---|---|---|---|
| Higher schools | 69 | 18 | 13 | 100 |
| Middle schools | 59 | 31 | 10 | 100 |
| Vocational schools | 46 | 39 | 15 | 100 |
| Elementary school (*Volksschule*) | 33 | 53 | 14 | 100 |
| Special elementary school (*Hilfsschule*) | 25 | 57 | 23 | 100 |

Source: Brepohl, *Der Aufbau,* 178.

indeed reflected the backward position of the Poles. And even if the data are biased, which is difficult to judge from the publications, it seems probable that the Poles in general did not experience much upward social mobility, if any. This conclusion is confirmed by recent research on the descendants of Poles in Bottrop, which shows that especially among the second generation, the chances for social improvement were worse for Poles than for other Germans.[44] The best data, which show how slowly the position of the Poles changed over time, is from a study on Wilhelmsburg, near Hamburg. In the period 1904–25, the proportion of unskilled Poles remained twice as large as for Germans (see table 7).

## "Pollacken" and the Prussian State

The racialist discourse used by Waterkamp and Brepohl can only be fully understood in the light of the policies initiated in 1871 by the first chancellor of the German empire, Otto von Bismarck. He tried to achieve a homogeneous German national state by discriminating against and excluding groups that he considered to be a threat to the state: Catholics, socialists, and the Polish-speaking population in the eastern part of the empire (most of whom were also Catholic). How central the "Polish problem," as it soon became known, was to Bismarck's *Kulturkampf,* his fight against the Catholic influence, is demonstrated in his memoirs, wherein he states that the "beginning of the Kulturkampf was mainly determined by its Polish side."[45] This policy of "negative integration," as the well-known German historian Hans Ulrich Wehler phrased it,[46] affected the Catholic Church (especially its internationally oriented sections such as the Jesuits),[47] the Catholic political party (*Zentrum*), and the Social Democrats. However, in the end, the Pol-

*Table 7.* Labor Market Position of Polish and German Men in Wilhelmsburg, 1904–25

|  | 1904 | | 1914 | | 1925 | |
|---|---|---|---|---|---|---|
|  | Poles | Germans | Poles | Germans | Poles | Germans |
| Unskilled | 80 | 31 | 78 | 31 | 61 | 24 |
| Skilled | 6 | 10 | 3 | 6 | 3 | 4 |
| Subtotal workers | 86 | 42 | 81 | 38 | 65 | 30 |
| Craftsmen | 7 | 26 | 9 | 26 | 13 | 27 |
| White collar | 1 | 7 | 1 | 9 | 2 | 10 |
| Entrepreneur | 3 | 10 | 3 | 10 | 3 | 10 |

Source: Hauschildt, *Polnische Arbeitsmigranten,* 238.

ish-speaking minority in Germany was the hardest hit. Initially, Bismarck and his conservative supporters considered the Polish minority in the east primarily as a territorial problem, as he believed their nationalistic aspirations were a threat to the German state. The depth of his hatred for the Poles is illustrated by a letter Bismarck wrote in 1861 to his sister: "Hit the Poles, so that they break down. If we want to exist, we have to exterminate them; the wolf can also not help it that he was created by God, and nevertheless he is being shot whenever one sees the opportunity."[48]

Bismarck and many others did not trust the Poles because, in their view, the Poles were out to create a Polish state, and they were suspected of being Prussian by name only.[49] The solution the conservatives devised was complete "Germanization," which was to be achieved primarily by furthering the German language. Once the Polish tongue was eradicated, the nationalistic fire would die out by itself, so many thought. In this way, the belief that Poles were a people with an inferior culture,[50] a conviction that was often loaded with racist undertones, could be overcome. If the Poles would only relinquish their language, the door would be opened to cultural assimilation and incorporation into the German national and cultural body, also defined as *Deutschtum*.[51]

The program of Germanization started immediately after national unification in 1870 and was initially restricted to the (north-) eastern part of the German empire where the Polish-speaking population (the term minority was deliberately avoided) lived. The first measure in 1873 was to make German the official school language, religious lessons excepted, relegating Polish to an auxiliary role.[52] This school act was followed three years later by another act, which stipulated that German was to be the sole official language. This meant that all public officials—judges, policemen, civil servants, teachers, soldiers, mailmen, and train conductors— had to speak German while on duty. By 1901, even religion had to be taught in German at schools, which led to a massive school strike during the 1906–7 school term. Finally, in 1908 a new law forbade using any other language but German at public gatherings, an ordinance that became known as the "muzzle paragraph."

The German state did not leave it at that, however; it also tried other ways to force Poles to assimilate. The primary target (apart from language) was land-ownership. Similar to the English colonization of Ireland in the seventeenth century,[53] the German states also colonized the east and southeastern areas of Europe. In the last decades of the nineteenth century, this practice was reinstated in order to Germanize the eastern provinces. By replacing

Polish landowners and farmers, the Prussian state hoped that the German-speaking population in the overwhelmingly Polish regions of the German empire would increase, thus weakening the nationalistic threat. Other measures included refusing to give the status of permanent immigrant to Poles from Russia and Austria who worked as seasonal workers in Germany, and the draconian expulsion in 1885 of thirty thousand Poles (among whom some nine thousand were Jewish). Although these Poles had lived in Germany for many years, they were expelled by force, often with only a few hours notice to pack their things, on the pretext that their nationality was unclear. Even the conservatives were shocked by this harsh approach of the Prussian state.[54]

More structural steps were taken in the next year, when an act was passed in April 1886 that made it possible for the German state to buy Polish-owned land in the east and subsequently sell or lease it to German colonists. The immediate aim was to weaken the position of the Polish-speaking nobility (the *Schlachta*) who, alongside the German *Junkers*, owned many of the large estates in the east. When it became clear that this act was a failure[55]—not in the least because the Poles reacted successfully by buying up land through their own banks—new legislation followed: a 1904 proclamation stated that whoever bought new land in the east needed official permission to use it.

The antidemocratic and unconstitutional nature of these measures was welcomed by the ultranationalistic *Ostmarkenverein* that aimed at making the eastern provinces German and reducing the Polish presence as much as possible—and in this sense foreshadowed Hitler's *Lebensraum* policy a few decades later. The *Ostmarkenverein* put up a strong lobby that led to the ultimate Germanization policy: the contentious expropriation act of 1908, by which Polish-owned land could be acquired by force. Like all the preceding acts, the impact of this policy was more ideological than practical, and because there was no money, hardly any land was purchased. However, these anti-Polish measures, known as "Hakatismus,"[56] marginalized Poles and reduced them to second-class citizens, but they heightened Polish nationalism considerably.

## The Catholic Church and Polish Nationalism in the West

Most of the measures mentioned above were aimed at the Poles living in the eastern provinces. However, their impact on the life of Polish migrants in the west, especially in the Ruhr district, was also considerable. During the first decades, nationalism among the Polish migrants was not very strong, as their numbers were still relatively small, and regional loyalties and identities (aimed at Posen, Silesia, etc.) were often stronger than a pan-Polish feeling. However, the German-speaking citizens of the host country were not aware of these regional differences and saw all Polish migrants as "Pollacken." This mechanism is often seen in migration processes.[57] Anti-Polish sentiment frequently flared up in the mines, as Poles were often seen as potential strike-breakers by their fellow miners. The Irish in Great Britain and the Italians in France did not experience these accusations as often.

A much more sensitive matter, which increased national feeling among the Poles even further, was Prussian religious policy. By May 1873, there was already an act making it obligatory for priests working in provinces *without* a Polish-speaking majority to speak German. Moreover, they were forced to complete an exam on German literature and culture. As a result, Polish migrants in the western regions, both Catholics and Protestants, simply had no Polish priests at all. Some, like the Silesians in Bottrop, occasionally managed (at Easter, for example) to smuggle in a Polish priest from the Netherlands.[58] This situation improved somewhat in the 1880s, when the *Kulturkampf* waned and Polish Masses were allowed. An important step in this direction was the reinstallation of the bishop of Paderborn in 1882; his diocese covered a large part of the Ruhr area, and one of his aims was to ensure pastoral care for the Polish immigrants. Within two years he had installed a Polish-speaking priest named Joseph Szotowski, who spent time visiting Poles in the main settlement areas and read Mass in Bochum, Dortmund, Gelsenkirchen, and Bottrop. The Catholic Church and the Catholic political party (*Zentrum*) welcomed their Catholic brethren and criticized the anti-Polish attitude of the conservative party. Soon, this religious unity faded, as the German Catholics began to feel more national solidarity. They agreed in principle with special religious facilities for the Catholic Poles, but it was considered a temporary measure.[59]

However, nationalism increased among the Poles in the west. Their nationalism was given a voice by the successor of Szotowski, Franz Liss, who came to Bochum in 1890 from West Prussia. Within a year Liss started publishing a Polish-language newspaper, the *Wiarus Polski* (the Polish Companion), which at first appeared three times a week, and then daily by 1902. Furthermore, Liss stimulated the growth of Polish associations. He believed that furthering Polish nationalism would keep the Polish workers out of the hands of the emerging socialist movement. Liss hoped that by creating a Catholic national identity, class-based loyalties would not develop. Stressing the pan-Polish consciousness was a necessary part of this policy, as illustrated by the next citation from the *Wiarus Polski* (1891):

> God has given the Poles a language and a very beautiful one. All who speak Polish have to consider themselves as Poles. When asked who they are, nevertheless some Poles view themselves as Posener, West-Prussian or Silesian, others regard themselves as Masurians etc. These, however, are bad answers. When Poland was divided, its different parts retained different names. The inhabitants may be Posener, West-Prussians etc., they still are POLES and that is how they should view themselves and at most add that they come from Posen etc. Therefore, dear friends, leave out these confusing denominations and proclaim who you are.[60]

Liss probably fueled more nationalist feeling among Polish migrants than he originally intended. In taking up this position, he found he had to defend himself on two fronts—against the German Catholic Church (and the authorities), who viewed his nationalistic aspirations with suspicion; and against followers of the Great-Polish movement in eastern Posen, which accused Liss of going too far in advocating assimilation.[61] Liss refused to give up what was considered by the authorities to be Polish politics, and he was removed from office in 1893.[62] Although the appointed successor was Polish, the authorities placed so many restrictions on his work that his position among the Polish migrants soon became untenable. From then on, the Catholic Church persevered in their assimilation policy, which stipulated that Poles had to integrate as soon as possible in existing Catholic parishes and not isolate themselves from the German Catholics.

## The Expansion of Polish Associational Life

The fight for religious autonomy also had other effects. The polarization between the Catholic Church and the Polish migrants caused the multiplication of all sorts of Polish associations. In the 1870s and 1880s there were only a few Polish organizations in the Ruhr district. The majority were local religious societies, led by the local (German) priest who also chaired local workers' associations. Over time the relationship between these priests and the Poles deteriorated as the priests succumbed to Germanization.[63] With the growing nationalism, especially from 1890 on, and at the simultaneous dissociation of the German priests, conflicts between them and the Polish associations they officially chaired multiplied, especially because they increasingly refused to consecrate images (on flags, etc.) of Polish saints and other nationalistic symbols.

Polish associations proliferated. There were seventy-five clubs with eight thousand members in the Ruhr area in 1896, but by 1910 this had increased to 660 clubs with sixty thousand members.[64] These clubs had various goals and ranged from unions to singing clubs. What they all had in common was their use of the Polish language and strong feelings of nationalism, actively supported by similar associations in the provinces of origin, especially Posen. The impressive growth of the Polish movement was further stimulated by the elections around 1900. Whereas in the early years of immigration the Catholic *Zentrum* party had been quite successful in winning Polish votes, Poles in both the west and the east were increasingly mobilized by Polish nationalist parties, voters' associations, and delegates. The associations could wield power by calling for a boycott of certain parties such as the *Zentrum,* which did not do enough to protect the minority rights of Poles.[65] The nationalistic enthusiasm of the Poles was fanned by a wide variety of Polish-language publications, ranging from literary journals to union magazines.[66]

## ZZP and the Sokoł Movement

How Polish associations arose is best illustrated by looking at the development and aims of two of the Polish unions, the *Zjednoczenie Zawodowe Polskie* (ZZP) and the ultra-nationalistic Sokoł (pronounce: so-koh) movement. At first, the Polish miners joined the new German miners' unions as they were being established in the Ruhr district in the 1860s and 1870s. These unions became powerful in the late 1880s. The two main mining unions were the socialist *Alte Verband,* founded in 1889, and the Christian socialist *Gewerkverein christlicher Bergarbeiter,* founded in 1894. These German unions, however, were not particularly committed to their Polish members. They employed no Polish staff and provided no publications in Polish. The Polish members lost faith in these unions because of two events that occurred in 1899. The first was that the unions upheld a new regulation, the so-called *Bergpolizeiverordnung,* which forbade the use of the Polish language in written and oral safety regulations. Officially, the reason was that all miners should be able to speak enough German so that accidents resulting from miscommunication could be prevented. However, most Poles—inflamed by agitation in the Polish press—saw this as yet another anti-Polish measure.[67] The second incident was the German mining unions' reaction to a spontaneous strike in Herne, where thousands of young Polish haulers refused to resume work because they opposed an increase in social security contributions. The unions dismissed this wildcat strike as "foreign" and "Polish" and refused to view it as a valid economic conflict. In the end, the military was called in and many miners lost their lives or were wounded. Later the "troublemakers" were fired.[68] It is obvious that this incident did not improve relationships between the Polish miners and their German unions.

In 1902, the ZZP, which followed a more or less sociodemocratic course, was established in Bochum. It soon attracted thousands of members and membership grew to fifty thousand in 1910, especially after cooperating with the other unions during the massive miners' strike in 1905, one of the largest strikes seen up to that time on the Continent. Over the years, the ZZP became an integrated part of the German labor movement and even entered into alliances with other miners' unions, such as the local chapters of the sociodemocratic *Alte Verband*.[69] After World War I, the ZZP adopted a more nationalistic stance, taking the position that, in principle, all migrants had to return to Poland, and therefore regarding their presence in Germany as temporary.[70] The result was that within a few years, the ZZP was reduced from being the third most powerful miners' union in Germany to an insignificant club.

Even though the ZZP was nationalistic in character, it was an important force in integrating Polish workers into German society.[71] This was less so for the ultranationalistic associations that explicitly strove for restoration of the Polish state and therefore opposed all attempts at integration or assimilation. The most well known nationalistic associations were the Sokols (Polish for "falcon"). The first Sokols were established by Czechs under Austrian rule in the 1860s. They were gymnastic societies focused on arousing nationalist feeling. Members, both men and women, wore red Garibaldi shirts, had their own flags, and wore a characteristic cap with a falcon feather.[72] One of their activities was to perform gymnastics at national rallies, showing national strength and unity through highly coordinated, large-scale exercise displays. These displays were later adopted by left- and right-wing regimes. The Czech example was imitated by the Poles in Galicia and reached Prussian Posen in 1868. It took until 1884 before the first official local Sokol association was founded in Germany, and this was followed a decade later by a national association. With Posen at the heart of nationalistic feeling, Sokol associations mushroomed both in the east and in the west of Germany. The Polish protest against the *Bergpolizeiverordnung* in 1899 gave rise to the first Sokol in Westphalia and Oberhausen, and within a few years some twenty-five Sokols had been founded.

The authorities, with Germanization high on the agenda, saw the Sokoły as the enemy, and the police were ordered to keep a close watch on these organizations. Given the strict policy of assimilation, the authorities' reaction was understandable. In 1906, the ten commandments of the Polish Sokoł were published in *Wiarus Polski*. These included "Thou shalt not have any other fatherland than the undivided Poland" and "Do not love the strange language and do not prefer it above the Polish language."[73] Moreover, the Sokoły expressed openly an ultranationalistic and militaristic rhetoric. What the German authorities considered worrying were the close ties with the epicenter of Polish nationalism: the province of Posen in the east. To escape police harassment and possible prohibitions (on the grounds of the 1908 act regarding associations), the Sokoły gathered in the Dutch border town of Winterswijk, not far from the Ruhr district. Although the Sokoły did not have a huge membership, less than five thousand members in seventy-nine clubs in 1908, they were high-profile and their ideology found wide acceptance in Polish circles (particularly among workers) and probably hampered structural assimilation.[74] As was the case for the ZZP, the rebirth of the Polish state in 1919 marked the end of the Sokoł movement.

## The Polish Threat in the Eyes of the Authorities

The Sokoły were the reason for the appointment of a special police officer, in 1906, named Goehrke. He was ordered to investigate any activities within the Polish population that could be seen as expressions of political feeling. Three years later, Goehrke became the head of a special "Poles-monitor-center" (*Polenüberwachungsstelle*) in Bochum.[75] There the police kept extensive files on Polish people and their organizations, coordinated the anti-Polish policy, and intervened whenever Polish national symbols were displayed in public. The police even interfered with intimate gatherings such as funerals if Polish flags were spotted.[76] The ban on the use of the Polish language in public in 1908, at the peak of the anti-Polish hysteria,[77] meant the police kept very busy observing and, if necessary, breaking up meetings. Official anti-Polish policy was bolstered by the western branch of the *Ostmarkenverein*, the lobby for the German colonization in the eastern provinces, which was founded in Dortmund in 1898.[78] Moreover, the German press in Westphalia further fuelled the anti-Polish fire, illustrated by the following citation from the *Kölnische Zeitung* in 1899, in response to the wildcat strike in Herne:

In towns like Herne, Bochum, Dortmund and others, especially on days of commotion such as now, you hear the Polish idiom everywhere. The Pole seldom speaks softly; this and his outward appearance, particularly the vacant or crafty, searching stare, makes him noticeable. The Polish women and girls, who almost always appear besides their better halves or their sweethearts, have none of the charming timidity or graceful amiability of the German women or German girl. One can say today that the whole Rhineland-Westphalian industrial region is thoroughly infested with Poles. They are liked nowhere, neither by the German workers nor by the business world. They are just put up with as an inescapable evil, which the rise of industry has brought with it.[79]

Many studies on the Ruhr-Poles have stressed that Germanization, at least in the short run, had a predominantly negative effect and stimulated Polish nationalism even further. This is seen not only in the activities of associations and the radicalization within Polish circles described above, but also in the proliferation of Polish banks, which responded to the Poles' desire to invest in property in the homeland, especially during the years of the colonization attempts by the German state.[80]

It is therefore interesting that in regions where the anti-Polish attitude was more subdued, Polish associations were less nationalistic and less political. This was especially true for Bremen and Oldenburg. Even the Polish journal *Brema* acknowledged in 1905 that the local authorities were very liberal in their interpretation of official policy. Likewise in 1911, the critical nationalistic Polish newspaper *Narodowiec* praised the tolerant attitude of the authorities towards the public manifestation of a Sokół club in Delmenhorst in the province of Oldenburg. In most parts of Germany, this manifestation would most certainly have been prohibited. It seems no coincidence that in Delmenhorst, although it had a substantial Polish population, Polish associational life was much less developed than in the adjoining province of Bremen.[81]

## The Fading of Polish National Fervor and Increasing Integration after 1918

With the defeat of the German army in the fall of 1918, the European states were thoroughly revised. The breakup of the Austrian-Hungarian composite empire into smaller nation-states changed the geopolitical landscape considerably. In keeping with the ethnically inspired nation-state ideology of the

American president Wilson, the Poles were rewarded for their long-standing national aspirations. Consequently, Germany lost much of the territory in the east and southeast that it had acquired at the end of the eighteenth century following the partition of the former Polish kingdom.

With the re-instatement of the Polish state after World War I, the nationalist struggle within the German Empire was solved. This was especially the case in the eastern parts (east and west Prussia and Posen) but nationalist strongholds in other parts of Germany, particularly the Ruhr district, also lost their salience. Immediately after the war, the Polish nationalist organizations in the west reached their zenith, but by the beginning of the 1920s they had almost disappeared. The immediate necessity for nationalist agitation had receded, as there was now a new Polish state to which all Poles could migrate. However, many Poles from the Ruhr area, who had deferred their nationalist claims during the war by participating in the so-called *Burgfrieden* (an internal political truce) were soon disenchanted with the new Poland. The dominance of the old Polish landed gentry (*Schlachta*) and the poor economic situation made clear that Poland was hardly a worker's paradise, and many realized that they had better prospects outside their new homeland.[82] Despite nationalistic propaganda only a small number of Poles left Germany in order to return to Poland: the overwhelming majority chose to stay and thus continued to take part in the integration process that had started in the 1880s.

During the first half of the 1920s, the nationalist fire would, however, flare up one more time, in anti-Polish propaganda and in ethno-politics among Poles themselves. The anti-Polish atmosphere was related to two factors: first, frustration about the loss of German territory to the Polish state and the fate of the German population who now found themselves living under Polish rule. This culminated in a plebiscite in 1921 to decide the geopolitical fate of Upper Silesia by ballot. This conflict resonated throughout Germany but especially within the Ruhr district, where many Poles from Upper Silesia lived. Many Poles were offered free travel to their home regions by the Polish state to cast their vote. This moved the German-organized nationalists to call for drastic measures and the expulsion of the Poles from the Ruhr area. A second factor that gave rise to anti-Polish feelings was the occupation of the Ruhr area by French and other allied troops in 1923. When the French recruited Polish miners to work in the French pits and factories, the mass exodus of Poles provoked feelings among the German authorities as well as the general population that the Poles were not to be trusted.

Although accusations of disloyalty were unjustified during the occupation, organized nationalism among the Poles in the aftermath of the war could easily give the impression that they would always be an "alien body" in Germany, as Bismarck and others had warned from the start. For example, the newly founded Polish National Workers Party (NSR) in the Ruhr district, which followed the ZZP union's moderate Christian-socialist line, warned parents not to let their children assimilate and told them to make sure that children retained their Polishness. This is illustrated by a speech at a NSR rally in 1919 in Bochum: "[I summon] all fathers and mothers to exert more control over their children. I ask the parents urgently to see to it that their sons and daughters join Polish associations, to learn to read, write and sing Polish, as well as other activities, in stead of going to the races or cinemas. The youth of our Polish brothers are often ashamed of their Polish language and customs. Beware foremost that the Poles do not lose their religion."[83]

During the Weimar republic there was a more liberal policy toward national minorities, which was in part motivated by the realization that this could guarantee similar rights for Germans in Poland. This policy supported initiatives to teach the Polish language at (private) schools where there were many Polish children, as well as initiatives to set up language courses outside the public domain. Subsequently, several books and journals were published in Polish and were often aimed at children (the journal *Maly Polka w Niemczech,* or "The Little Pole in Germany," for example).[84] Finally, special train trips were organized during the summer to send children to Poland, where they could learn the language and experience Polish culture firsthand.[85]

That in practice only a small minority of the second generation participated[86] was not so much the result of the lack of supply and the obstruction by German authorities; rather, it reflected the end of the ongoing integration process and the realization by most Poles that their future was in Germany. In the course of the 1920s, identification with the Polish cause and the desire to remain within a restricted Polish subculture decreased rapidly. This trend can be shown by the decline in Polish associational life. In 1920, in the Ruhr area, nearly 1,450 organizations flourished, but by 1926 this number had fallen to seven hundred,[87] and most of these held social events without any political or nationalistic aims. This gradual shift in orientation is also illustrated by the patterns of intermarriage and the changes in Polish surnames.

## Mixed Marriages

Because of a lack of systematic research on intergenerational changes among Poles in Germany, the patterns of intermarriage among the different generations are difficult to reconstruct. However, there is enough anecdotal evidence scattered around to allow us to piece together some of this puzzle. During the early stages of immigration in western Germany, when the number of migrants was still relatively small, mixed marriages between migrants and locals were quite common. In the Ruhr area, about 1 in 5 Poles married a local German woman.[88] This relatively large proportion of mixed marriages can be explained by the fact that there were hardly any Polish female migrants at that time. After 1890, when immigration was at its height and ethnic Polish communities emerged, mixed marriages declined considerably to 2–5 percent.[89] First-generation male migrants decided en masse to marry women from Poland and bring them to the west of Germany. By 1906, only 4 percent of all the Polish men in Herne, for example, were married to German women.[90]

A study on first-generation Polish migrants in Bremen (1943) revealed an interesting relationship between social mobility and mixed marriage.[91] It found that Polish men who married German women were more likely to be employed as white-collar workers by the end of their working life. Those who married Polish women were in these positions less often.[92] Similarly, there were fewer blue-collar Polish workers (laboring class) with a German wife. Population scholars during (and even after) the Nazi rule deduced that the Poles who married German women were of a better (racial) stock.[93] However, it could also be argued that Polish men who attained a higher social status were considered more suitable marriage partners; likewise, it could be that by marrying outside their own restricted migrant circle and entering the wider German networks, they were more likely to be promoted.

Second-generation Polish men, those born in the west between roughly 1890 and 1914, for the most part married Polish women (also from the second generation), but the proportion was significantly lower. In the 1920s, 30 percent found a spouse outside their ethnic circle,[94] signaling a clear decrease in endogamy and a further step toward assimilation. Nevertheless, the majority of the second generation still preferred a partner from their own ethnic group, and until the Second World War, more than half a century after the start of the immigration, the Poles displayed much more ethnic cohesiveness than is commonly assumed.

Marriage patterns not only diverged according to class, as shown in the Bremen case, but also according to religion. An interesting case is the Polish-speaking but Protestant and Germanized Masurian community from East Prussia. In this group, the intermarriage rates of both the first- and second-generation migrants were significantly higher,[95] supporting the accepted view that these migrants integrated more easily than the Poles. However, we should not lose sight of the fact that there were striking parallels between migrant Masurians and Poles. They were both predominantly recruited for the mining industry; they both lived in isolated places; and they both had trouble feeling at home in the local church communities. Whereas the protestant Irish migrants were immediately able to join English churches when they came to Britain, the Polish-speaking Masurians did not feel at home in the German Protestant churches and, in response, the Masurians established numerous autonomous cults in both in East Prussia and the Ruhr area.[96]

Furthermore, the German locals, unlike the authorities, did not distinguish between the protestant Masurians and the Catholic Poles because language and customs seemed similar. On the whole, Poles and Masurians were treated as foreigners, especially the first-generation migrants. The colorful head-scarves of the women and sounds of the Polish language helped the Germans identify the Protestant Masurians and the Catholic Poles whom they saw as beings from a different and alien world.[97] Both groups were labeled *Pollacken:* people of a lower cultural (if not racial) level, and people who could not be trusted.

## Assimilation Pressure and Name Changing

When the Nazi party came to power in 1933, the protection of national minorities, as instigated (albeit often halfheartedly) during the Weimar period, was abolished, and this had dire consequences for the Polish associations. The ultranationalist ideology of the Nazis did not leave much room for ethnic expressions other than German/Aryans. Having "suspect" or inferior roots, according to the Nazi worldview, made life difficult or even dangerous, as the Jewish Germans knew all too well. After 1933, the Poles, who had been seen an inferior "Slavic" people and a threat to the German nation from the very start, became increasingly the target for discrimination and exclusion. In contrast with their Jewish fellow citizens, however, they were not defined by the state as alien and were not deprived of their civil rights. Apart from a few hundred Polish leaders who were taken to concentration camps immediately after the attack on Poland in September 1939, German Poles were not persecuted and were included *de facto* in the German "Volk."

It was clear to the Poles, however, that ethnic profiling was to be avoided and that being associated with their Polish roots could have social repercussions. As the third generation grew to adulthood in the 1930s, one of the few visible characteristics by which a Pole could be "recognized" was the surname. Surnames ending with "ski" or "sko," for example, invariably pointed at Polish roots, and no matter how integrated a person was, this could have stigmatizing effects. Or, as Kasimir Przewozna from Hamburg declared in his application of July 1913: "I would not only like to change my surname but also my Christian name, because to be considered as a Pole everywhere harms my position as breadwinner."[98] Many Poles therefore decided to have their names changed. The German (Prussian) authorities used this as a tool to further the process of Germanization that had begun in 1870. A study carried out in the 1930s showed that between 1880 and 1935 in the Ruhr area some thirty thousand people were allowed to change their names.[99] Almost all of them were migrants from the east: fourteen thousand from East Prussia, mostly Masurians, followed by thirteen thousand from West Prussia and Posen, and twenty-five hundred from Silesia, whereas only five hundred applicants came from outside the German empire.[100] These almost thirty thousand applications must have affected nearly two hundred forty thousand people (the children and spouses of applicants). At that time, about eight hundred thousand to eight hundred fifty thousand people of eastern descent lived in the Ruhr district. This means that possibly about a third ended up with a German name, making it easier for them to blend into German society.

The Masurians were the largest group to change their names; the next largest group was the Poles from "mixed residential areas." Many translated their Polish name directly (Piekarz into Bäcker [=baker]), some changed the ending (Kowaler instead of Kowalski),[101] while others preferred to take on a common German name like "Müller," "Schmidt," "Wagner," or "Hofman." This confronted the authorities and ultranationalist pressure groups, like the *Alldeutscher Verband*,[102] with an interesting paradox: they had always strived for Polish assimilation, which included changing names, but when the migrants took on German names, they became less visible and more difficult to identify. As the anti-Semites in so many European countries were frustrated by the fact that the emancipation of the Jews from the end of the eighteenth century onward had made it increasingly difficult to recognize a Jew simply by his or her name, the German nationalists had trouble accepting that Poles were becoming "invisible." They therefore proposed giving them German names with endings like ". . . berger" or ". . . höfer," and this became common practice from the 1910s onward.[103]

## Conclusion

In 1882 Friedrich Engels predicted that the Poles, just like the Irish before them, "are obliged to be national before they become international."[104] Although the second part of this prediction proved to be wishful thinking, the ideological soulmate of Karl Marx was right in his assessment of the ethnopolitical developments among the German Poles. The impact of the Polish nationalism on the German host society, however, was different from that of the Irish nationalism in Great Britain. The German state felt far more threatened by the nationalist aspirations of the Polish immigrants than Britain felt about the Irish. The extreme fear of Polish nationalism is not only explained by the fragile nature of the new German state, its much more centralized rule, and the different geopolitical circumstances, but also by the "master status"[105] of the Catholic religion as a major threat to the British society and the British state.

Apart from these fundamental contextual differences, the integration processes in Germany and Britain show several interesting parallels. Perceived as alien group in the localities where they settled, coming from a lower-class background, and being allocated to inferior positions on the labor market, both the Poles and the Irish developed a separate ethnic subculture, stimulated by residential concentrations, church affiliations, and a rich associational life. Stigmatization slowed integration, and discrimination encouraged ethnic closure, both socially and politically, and so even second-generation migrants remained under the ethnic sphere of influence. This began to change only in the third generation, often more than half a century after the initial immigration. And yet, in the case of the Irish and the Poles, even at that time the master-status had not fully waned. Having an Irish or Polish name or living somewhere that was known as an Irish or Polish area could still give cause for exclusion or discrimination. After the Second World War, in Britain, as in Germany, there were still many cases of descendants of immigrants being stigmatized and considered alien. In the case of Germany this tendency to consider Poles and their offspring as different was of course very much stimulated by the pervasive racist interlude of the Nazi regime.

# 3

## A Threat to the Native Workers: Italians in France (1870–1940)

The final example of "large and problematic" immigrant groups in western Europe's past takes us to France. In the same period as the Polish-speaking Germans moved to the Ruhr area, France experienced a wave of immigration similar in size and outlook with the arrival of hundreds of thousands of un- or low-skilled, predominantly male, laborers. These were part of a massive emigration of fourteen million Italians who left their country between 1876 and 1914. Whereas the flow of migrants to overseas destinations in both North and South America (55 percent) has been thoroughly studied, the choice of European destinations (44 percent), especially Switzerland, the Austro-Hungarian empire, Germany, and France, has been broadly underestimated and less well researched.[1]

In the second half of the nineteenth century the image of (predominantly male) Italian migrants in France, but also in Switzerland and Germany, increasingly converged with that of the docile, low-paid native workers, who pursued the most dangerous and unhealthy jobs, such as the construction of roads, tunnels, and railways, and work in mines and stone quarries. This image became so dominant that there was widespread equation of Italians with Chinese coolie labor.[2] These immigrants, dubbed the "Chinese of Europe," soon bore the brunt of the native workers' ire and were accused of working for lower wages and breaking strikes. This was especially the case in France, where in the last decades of the nineteenth century hundreds of thousands of Italian migrants entered the labor market, and where brutal conflicts broke out, resulting in occasional lynchings. As we have seen in the preceding chapters, Italians were far from unique in provoking hostile reactions from native workers who felt threatened by foreign competitors. Although nationalistic and religious prejudices also played a role, the emphasis of antagonism in the public representation of the Italians in France was centered on their role as cheap labor and scabs.

## Italian Migration to France

The presence of Italians in France dates back to the Middle Ages. Italian craftsmen, traders, artists, seasonal workers, and musicians had visited France for centuries, and some of them settled down permanently. Apart from the seasonal workers in the south, who stayed only a few months,[3] the number of Italians was limited. This changed after 1870, when the size of the Italian population in France increased from about sixty thousand around 1850 to more than three hundred thousand half a century later.[4]

The numbers could be even higher, in fact, if one chooses to include the naturalized Italians (by birth or by choice), who around 1900 numbered at least fifty thousand[5] but disappeared in the census statistics.[6] As in the Polish case, the migration was initially dominated by young males, but when the Italians decided to settle down, from the 1880s onward, the proportion of women from the home country increased. It is important to note that the settlement process was not a linear process: it did not progress neatly from one stage to the next. Many Italians, especially young, unmarried men working as navvies, miners, or construction workers, were no more than a floating population and labeled by contemporaries as "nomads." They changed jobs easily whenever they could earn more somewhere else, and many traveled back to Italy frequently. Only after many years did a number of them marry and remain in France. The flux in the departures for France illustrates the often-uneven character of the migration much better than the number of Italians counted in census years, as figure 2 makes clear.

The graph more or less follows the economic tide, but it also reflects the influence of the strained political situation and the anti-Italian atmosphere in France in the 1880s and early 1890s. When diplomatic relations between Italy and France improved and labor relations became less tense around the turn of the century, with the beginning of the "belle époque," the number of Italians leaving for France increased accordingly. The often-temporary nature of the migration of Italians to other European countries as well as overseas destinations[7] also characterized the period between the wars. Thus in 1925, 145,529 Italians entered France, whereas 103,299 left the country the same year.[8]

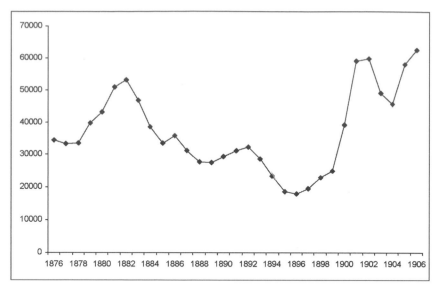

Figure 2. Number of Emigrants to France, 1876–1906
Source: Milza, *Français et Italiens*, 176–78.

During the 1920s the proportion of Italian "leavers" was almost 50 percent, which was much higher than among the Poles (16 percent), and slightly lower than among the Czechs (55 percent) and Portuguese (58 percent).[9]

Italians were by no means the only foreign migrants. In the second half of the nineteenth century, the Belgians were by far the largest group seeking a life elsewhere. Beginning in 1906, however, Italians became the largest migrating group and, notwithstanding the fast growth of the Polish community after the Great War, did not relinquish that position until the Second World War.[10] Although the image of the Italians in the second half of the nineteenth century was dominated by that of the itinerants from the southern part of Italy (especially Naples, as depicted in Hector Malot's famous 1878 novel *Sans Famille*), in reality most Italians came predominantly from the north at that time. Many more Italians migrated to France and Germany from northern regions such as those bordering Piedmont, Tuscany, Veneto, Lombardy, and Emilia Romana than from the southern area. This proportion barely changed in the interwar period. Only within the north do we see a shift in the pattern: the Veneto region (partly because of the diminishing emigration possibilities overseas) became the principal supplier of migrants, at the cost of Piedmont and Tuscany.[11]

## Settling Down

The history of Italian migration to France is much harder to summarize than that of the Irish in England or the Poles in Germany. This is due to the great variation in the geographical dispersion and variety of occupations, as well as the types of settlement. The Italians who worked as navvies in the southeast and east, for example, encountered markedly different circumstances than those who worked as agricultural laborers in the southwest, many of whom eventually started their own farms there, or those who settled with their families in Paris as artisans and construction workers. And even within these regions, differences in social position and integration of migrants could be considerable. As in the case of the Irish and the Poles, the Italians were not spread evenly over France, but were concentrated in certain parts of the country, as figure 3 indicates.

The highest concentration of Italians in France was to be found in the southeast, especially in the *départements Alpes Maritimes* (Nice) and *Bouches du Rhône* (Marseille).[12] About one-third of all Italians in France lived in Marseille district around 1900; but they could also be found in Lyon and its surroundings, in Paris, and increasingly in the metal mining area around Briey and Longwy in the northeast after 1900.

At the end of the nineteenth century the greatest chance of encountering an Italian migrant was in the cities of Nice and Marseille where, at that time, 1 in 5 inhabitants was born in Italy. In Nice many more of the migrants continued to speak Italian, because until 1859 this part of France belonged to the Italian-speaking Duchy of Savoy-Piedmont. Within these towns Italians were often concentrated in a number of neighborhoods known as "petite Naples," where the density of Italians could amount to 40 percent. With more than ninety thousand Italians within its boundaries in 1901, Marseille contained by far the largest Italian community.[13]

Less numerous, but far more isolated and concentrated, were Italian colonies in the northeast, which were established after 1900. In the region of Briey especially, Italian workers, predominantly male, were housed in so-called "cités," often poorly designed barracks in the vicinity of the factories or mines where they were employed. This housing model, which Polish migrants encountered in the Ruhr area, became widespread (beginning in 1900) in mining areas and stimulated the isolation of migrants. In the north and northeast, both Poles (coal miners) and Italians (metal miners) were segregated in this way. At the outbreak of the Great War, Briey (one hundred twenty-five thou-

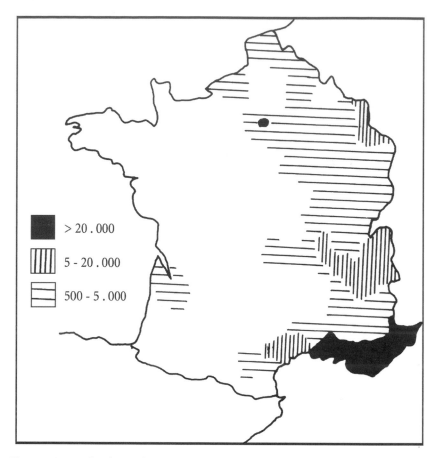

Figure 3. Geographical Distribution of Italians in France, 1896
Source: Milza, *Voyage en Ritalie*, 67.

sand inhabitants) counted forty-six thousand Italians: thirty-six thousand men, four thousand women, and six thousand children. They lived, as the Poles did in Germany, in their own colonies and had little contact with the surrounding French population.[14] This isolation only gradually began to give way in the 1920s. The inflow of foreign labor was a result of the sudden transformation of the northeast into a center of heavy industry, comparable with the Ruhr area, when it became possible to exploit one of the world's largest iron reservoirs there. Within a few years the once-rural *département Meurthe-et-Moselles* was littered with mines, blast furnaces, and metallurgic factories. This "Far West," as the French historian Gérard Noiriel has characterized it, attracted hundreds of thousands of migrants (mainly Italians and Poles), most of whom were mobile young men who often remained in one place for a short while and then moved to other destinations in France, or remigrated. This highly volatile migration pattern changed in the 1930s, when many settled down or returned to their home countries.[15] This was partly due to the anti-emigration policy of Mussolini, issued in 1927, which stimulated leftist opponents to his regime to stay in France and prompted others to return.

Paris, with a longer history of Italian settlement, was less a "pays de passage" than the northeast. Although the capital attracted a substantial share of the Italian migrants in France, its position was quite different from the areas of settlement we have discussed so far. Not only were the numbers smaller—in 1901 only 0.7 percent of the population of the *département* Seine were Italian[16]—but as 14 percent of the total foreign population they also were only one of many groups of foreigners and attracted far less attention than Italians in Marseille, Nice, or Briey. Within Paris they lived predominantly in the north and the east, but they never established dominant concentrations: job opportunities in the metropolis meant Italians in Paris were well spread over the various sectors of the labor market.

## Labor Market Position and Xenophobic Reactions

Until the end of the nineteenth century, the image of the Italians in France was dominated by conspicuous and colorful itinerant groups. Most of them were street musicians. According to the Italian consul in Paris, Luigi Cerruti, these consisted essentially of two groups: organ grinders and violin players from Parma; and musicians with bagpipes (*cornamusa*), flutes, and harps from the southern province of Basilicata, playing popular tunes (such as "O sole mio"), but also performing with animals (monkeys, groundhogs, dogs, and even bears). They attracted a lot of attention from both the public and the police. Many were poor, earned part of their living by begging, and were looked upon with a mixture of fascination and fear. The Italian *padroni* who employed young boys (ages 5–12), also known as "the little slaves of the harp,"[17] were accused of harsh exploitation deemed especially problematic. The itinerant musicians were considered a nuisance and a social problem, and the police in the large French cities regularly tried to get rid of them. Thus in 1867, the year of the big international exposition in Paris, 1,544 of them were arrested and expelled.[18]

Whereas these "nomads" continued to garner attention and were a prominent element of the popular stereotype of Italians in France,[19] the character of Italian immigration had changed fundamentally. From the 1870s on, the bulk of the newcomers were unskilled workers, attracted by the many (infrastructural) public works and building activities undertaken during the Third Republic. Inevitably, the change in the social and economic composition of the Italian migrant population also brought about changes in the relations with the native French population. Musicians on the streets may have caused irritation for some French, but the presence of large groups of unskilled workers was felt to be a direct threat by many French workers who were active in the same sectors. The Italians may have been concentrated in the least attractive and most dangerous kinds of jobs (and they soon dominated certain occupations), but they always found themselves in the company of French workers, who accused them of accepting too-low wages and breaking strikes. The English and the Germans lodged similar accusations against the Irish and the Poles, respectively. However, the tensions between the Italians and French workers led to a number of violent and bloody confrontations which, in a number of cases, resulted in large-scale manhunts ("chasse à l'Italien"), killing dozens of them and wounding many more.

These xenophobic conflicts, which were stimulated by the simultaneous international tension between France and Italy, were concentrated in the period from the 1880s to the 1890s. In her seminal work on strikes in France, Michelle Perrot counted eighty-nine xenophobic incidents between 1867 and 1893, the large majority of which occurred in the 1880s.[20] Almost all conflicts between French and Italian (male) workers occurred in the lowest segment of the labor market: construction of roads, railways and tunnels; dock work; in mines and quarries; and rather less so where Italians worked as artisans or in small firms.[21] Many French workers and their unions (including the socialist unions) accused Italians of undermining worker solidarity. To what extent the accusations were justified in general is difficult to assess. What is important is that the workers—and, more broadly speaking, the French public—fed by stories in the numerous newspapers, clearly were convinced that Italians posed an economic threat. As is so often the case with processes of negative stereotyping and stigmatization, only the evidence that corroborated these preconceived ideas was picked up and generalized. The fact that some Italians were actually recruited by contractors, the *padroni,* who paid them a wage lower than average, is a well-known example. Thus, Piedmontese workers who were recruited by the intermediaries Vani and Peraldo in 1868 only barely escaped a public lynching.[22] This system of subcontracting was immediately associated with the Chinese coolie system, which had led to the Chinese Exclusion Act (1882) in the United States, and which has been widely discussed among French scholars and politicians.[23] These comparisons were not entirely unjustified: these teams of young unskilled Italian men with little experience in industrial relations were indeed occasionally used to break strikes or to lower wages.[24] Moreover, the typical behavior of seasonal and temporary migrants, living as soberly as possible—often on polenta and water—in order to maximize their earnings, confirmed the existing suppositions even further.

The relation between Italian and French workers deteriorated further in the 1880s because of the growing political tensions between the two countries. Especially tense was the conflict about Tunisia, where the French—encouraged by Bismarck—established a protectorate in 1881, which frustrated Italy's imperialistic ambitions and would complicate the bilateral relations until the end of the nineteenth century. When Italy, headed by prime minister Crispi, joined the triple alliance the following year, allying himself with Austria-Hungary and with the despised (since the defeat of 1870) German neighbor, an era of mutual irritation and nationalistic frictions set in, which gave rise to a number of tariff wars. These conflicts fueled ultranationalist attacks in the widely distributed popular French press and thus created widespread xenophobic feelings among the French population.

It was in this strained atmosphere that serious riots broke out in Marseille in 1881, when French troops returned from Tunisia.[25] At that time, the city counted 360,000 inhabitants, 58,000 of whom were Italian nationals (apart from many thousands of naturalized Italians). Three-quarters of the Italian men and women worked in industry, mainly in dangerous and poorly paid jobs, and (only men) as dockworkers in the harbor. When the ships from Tunisia disembarked on June 18, 1881, and the troops marched through the town, cheered by the public, some spectators thought they heard disapproving whistling from the Italian club (*Club Nazionale Italiano*) and immediately after the parade the club was attacked. When some Italians reacted and stabbed a French participant to death, large-scale rioting broke out for two days, during which a real "hunt for the Italians" took place, leaving three people (one Italian) dead and twenty-one (fifteen Italians) severely wounded. As a result, some two thousand Italians left the town, afraid of the possibility of repercussions or further riots.[26]

These "Marseillian vespers," as they have become known, triggered a number of serious incidents that were rooted in a mix of economic and nationalistic grievances. The format was more or less standard: Italians were accused of lowering wages, and after some incident or other, riots broke out, during which the houses or barracks of Italians were attacked and pillaged, and people were molested, injured, or even killed. If the perpetrators of such crimes were put on trial, the French attackers often received only a minor punishment (a few months) or were simply acquitted, whereas remuneration of the damage was almost invariably denied to Italian victims. The most violent conflicts were the large-scale riots in the salt mines of Aigues Mortes in the southern Camargue, not far from Nîmes.[27] Of the three thousand workers, about one thousand were Italians, most of whom were hired to hoist the salt that had been broken in pieces by other workers. There had long been severe tensions between French and Italian workers because the Italians were deemed to be more docile and obedient. One day these mutual irritations came to a head, and a group of Italians attacked their French co-workers. As soon as other French workers heard about the incident, the situation escalated very quickly. Notwithstanding the arrival of the prefect (head of the *département*) who called for law and order, large groups of rioters roamed the streets shouting "death to the Italians" and marched towards the salt fields where some 350 Italians were working. The *gendarmerie* arrived there first and decided to escort about 80 Italians to the railway station. Returning from the station, these officials ran into the angry gang, some of whom were armed with revolvers, and in the ensuing fight the gendarmerie were unable to prevent the killing and wounding of a number of Italians. Because the authorities hesitated to call in reinforcements and troops, the attacks continued for days, and eventually at least eight Italians were killed and fifty severely injured. The death toll may even have been higher, as isolated groups of French workers hunted down Italians for several days thereafter in the surrounding marshes. The total of fifty deaths, mentioned in the *Times*, however, has never been corroborated.[28] As a result of this unrest, virtually all Italian seasonal workers left the salt mines, and when the news reached Marseille, an atmosphere of panic spread among the Italian inhabitants, and several of them fled to the harbor to embark for Italy.[29]

The last major xenophobic incident occurred only one year later in Lyon, also a center of Italian immigration, when in June 1882 an Italian anarchist murdered the French president Sadi Carnot during Carnot's visit to Lyon. The assassination sparked violent reaction from the French and resulted again in a "hunt for the Italians." Numerous Italian shops were pillaged, and Italians were attacked and beaten up indiscriminately.[30]

## Italians and French Unions

Although these incidents of violence against Italians in France were characterized by an overt and extreme form of nationalism, economic accusations always lay just below the surface, and it is no coincidence that most riots occurred in those areas (predominantly the southeast) where the competition by unskilled Italian workers was felt most intensely. At the end of the nineteenth century, the xenophobic atmosphere in France waned. Three factors seem to be responsible for this change: international relations between Italy and France improved considerably after 1898; Italian workers, as well as French unions, became increasingly aware that it was important to organize themselves; and, paradoxically, a campaign in the last decades of the nineteenth century to protect the national labor market in France against foreigners ameliorated tensions between Italian migrants and French workers and softened economic grievances.

Whereas French unions and labor parties had been very hostile towards Italians in the 1880s, as is clear from the often spiteful newspaper articles about the Italian migrants, it soon became clear that the Italians needed only a little time to learn the union ropes. In 1882 Italians already participated in the strikes of sugar refiners in Paris, and a year later (two years after the "Vespers") Italians joined French dockworkers in a strike at the harbor of Marseille.[31] Stimulated by the active involvement of Italian socialist union leaders like Luigi Campolonghi, who were deliberately sent to France to organize their compatriots, Italians revealed themselves to be active and combative workers who even took the lead in a number of strikes from the 1890s on.[32] In contrast to the Poles in Germany, who successfully established their own union, the Italian socialist "missionaries" like Campolonghi encouraged migrants to join French unions. As the French "syndicates" took a positive stance, stimulated by the massive support of Italian migrants in various strikes, this policy was very successful. Jules Guesde, the well-known socialist leader who had denounced the Italians in the mid-1880s as an "invasion of sarrazins," was praising his Italian comrades just a few years later. In Marseille the relations between native and Italian workers were even turned around when, during the great dockworkers strike of 1901, French workers, organized in the "yellow" *Syndicat français*, were called in by their employers to break the strike started by the socialist *Syndicat international*, whose members were predominantly Italian.[33] In the northeast metal region of Briey and Longwy, harsh and violent conflicts between French workers (backed up by

Belgians and Luxembourgers) and Italians continued until the beginning of the twentieth century. But when Italian socialists like Cavallazzi were brought in to show their compatriots how to organize a strike, the foundation was laid for a long period of collaboration and integration between Italian and French workers.[34] Although the image of Italians as scabs and as responsible for lowering wages did not disappear entirely, the burgeoning Italian class consciousness around 1900 marks the beginning of a new phase in the relations between Italian and French workers.

## Protection of the Labor Market and Naturalizations

A thorn in the side of the French workers was the massive presence of Italians in the public sector, where jobs were allotted by both the local authority and the state. This dominance of Italians and other foreign workers in the public sector was very much resented by French workers and the nationalist press, who demanded measures restricting the percentage of foreigners in these jobs. It is striking, however, that the discussions about the necessity and effects of foreign labor were largely symbolic. Most participants in the debate, often economists and law students, agreed that French workers faced unfair competition, but only few of them thought that curtailing the immigration ("invasion," as the title of a popular 1907 novel by Louis Bertrand reads), or taking legal measures offered a solution.[35]

A good example is the frequently cited study by Albert Blanc, published in 1901, in which Blanc warned of the danger of industrial espionage by foreign workers and underlined other negative effects of the large-scale labor migration, such as criminality and unfair competition.[36] Not surprisingly, the Italians were portrayed as scabs and hot-tempered individuals who were quick on the draw with a knife. Many, he asserted, would lapse into poverty and become financially dependent on the French state. Finally, Blanc accused foreign nations of provoking strikes and thus weakening French industry by sending their workers to France. In short, he concocted a peculiar mix of arguments that supported the reigning idea that something should be done about foreigners in the labor market. He therefore supported local initiatives, as had been enacted in Paris, Béziers, Marseille, and Dijon, to limit the numbers of foreigners employed in the public sector. Blanc welcomed a similar national decree issued in 1899 but opposed instituting a fixed percentage, as he realized that for certain jobs, such as municipality laborers, almost no French workers could be found.[37]

The parliamentary initiatives in the 1880s and 1890s also reveal that the xenophobic discourse of the time, from which the Italians suffered far more than others, was mainly symbolic. Dozens of bills were introduced to curtail foreign labor, but only very few were enacted. As a result, no effective measures were taken to stop or control foreign immigration. Apart from the fact that the state was not yet sufficiently powerful to introduce such a policy,[38] the main reason for failing to introduce restrictive measures was the peculiar French demographic situation. In contrast to other European states, the growth of the French population was slow, and the expanding economy was in desperate need of labor, heightening the need for and importance of large-scale immigration. In 1897 the famous statistician Jacques Bertillon, who founded the International Statistical Institute in 1885, explicitly warned of a demographic catastrophe in his *Problème de la dépopulation*, which drew a lot of attention.[39] This fear of depopulation also explains why the xenophobic and populist campaign (in the form of the Boulangist movement, for example) in the 1880s against a generous naturalization act founded on the principle of *ius soli* (those born in France are French citizens) was not successful in the end.[40] The nationality act of 1889 made it easy for foreigners to naturalize, whereas their children born on French soil almost automatically became French citizens. The demographic fear—of a dwindling population—also explains the support, even by Albert Blanc, for a smooth naturalization policy.[41] By becoming French, it was assumed that migrants would identify with French values and become incorporated in French institutions, including the unions. By sharing the same obligations (such as the draft), unfair competition would be ruled out.

Thanks to the nationality act of 1889 the process of becoming French, as advocated by Blanc and others, paid off: in 1881, some 78,000 inhabitants of France were naturalized citizens; this number had tripled by 1911, when their numbers reached beyond 250,000, of whom about one-third were former Italians or their children born in France.[42] The motives for Italian-born migrants to apply for naturalization varied. A number of them married French citizens and thus became more motivated to acquire the French nationality; but it seems that most Italians hoped that in becoming French, they would face less discrimination. This is supported both by quantitative and qualitative data. First, it is no coincidence that the culmination point of the naturalizations coincided with the strained political and social relations present during the first half of the 1890s.[43] Furthermore, a study of naturalization dossiers in the *département* Rhône shows that, for many Italians, the anti-Italian and anti-foreigner climate at the end of the nineteenth century was an important incentive to make themselves less visible and less vulnerable. Once a migrant had become a French citizen, he could no longer be excluded from the labor market on the basis of nationality, and this was especially relevant for those who aspired to become civil servants or functionaries in the public service, such as in the railroads and the postal services. As well, after the assassination in 1894 of French president Carnot by an Italian anarchist in Lyon, many were especially afraid of losing their jobs and pressed for naturalization.[44] Finally, it is interesting to compare the annual naturalization rates of the Italians with those of other nationality groups, which shows that Italians were naturalizing at above-average levels, especially in the interwar years: in the 1920s alone, 144,000 Italians were naturalized.[45]

## Social Mobility and Group Formation until 1914

The integration process of the Italians in France cannot be assessed by naturalization rates and the evolution of stereotypes alone. We also need to understand to what extent and at what pace migrants were able to rise from the lower ranks of the labor market and how their children participated in the French educational system. The answers to these questions are by necessity incomplete and sometimes inconclusive because no real systematic research has ever been performed in these fields, especially not for the period up until the First World War. Moreover, general judgments are also impossible, because it is essential to differentiate between the various regions in which Italians settled and the variations in their social status.

Notwithstanding these caveats, however, it is not too bold to claim that most Italian migrants after 1870 were unskilled and entered the French labor market at the lowest level. The example *par excellence* is the navvies, who specialized in constructing roads, railways, and tunnels throughout Europe. Teams of young men moved from one public project to another earning money by hard labor (digging and hewing) and in harsh circumstances. It is unclear what proportion of these people eventually returned to Italy or took up other (industrial) jobs elsewhere in France, but it seems reasonable to assume that most of them were not upwardly mobile, and that their children did not fare much better. This would imply that a large proportion of the Italians in the south and southeast, where about 50 percent of the men were employed in construction work at the time, fit into this category.[46] Furthermore, Italians who were less "nomadic" and who settled with their families in big cities like Marseille, Nice, and Lyon were predominantly confined to unskilled jobs in the harbor (as dockworkers) and in the "grande industrie," such as chemicals, foods, and metals, whereas women worked as domestics or in the clothing and textile sectors. Living a more settled life in cities with a varied opportunity structure may have offered more openings to Italian migrants than were available to their fellow countrymen who toiled in the large construction works, and who were far more isolated, as were the Italians in quarries and salt mines, like Aiges Mortes.

The prospects for Italians in the building sector (masons, plasterers, carpenters) may have been somewhat more favorable. In Paris and the surrounding Seine *département*, where many such jobs were concentrated, the occupational differentiation was much greater than in other parts of France. Due to the specific character of the French capital, with its manifold economic functions and rich cultural and political infrastructure, it also attracted a lot of educated and skilled migrants, Italians among them. Indeed, Paris had the largest Italian elite and middle class in France, in addition to a relatively low proportion of unskilled workers. Apart from intellectuals, artists and the well-to-do, Paris housed a relatively large group of artisans (cabinetmakers, hatters, shoemakers, etc.) and a number of café, hotel, and restaurant owners, as well as shopkeepers. Outside the city boundary, the proportion of workers was higher, but also here the differentiation was more pronounced than elsewhere. Italians worked as skilled or semiskilled workers in smaller factories and workshops, in the building industry (23 percent), as office workers (11 percent), and were well represented in the budding automobile and other mechanical industries.[47] This relatively large occupational diversity is typical for Paris, but it was also true of other big cities like Lyon and Nice, where the size of the lower-middle class was more pronounced, compared to the massive numbers of unskilled workers elsewhere (except for the agricultural southwest).[48]

The settlements of Italians in northeast France present yet another variant. As we saw earlier, the settlement pattern around Briey and Longwy diverged markedly from that in the metropolis. In the northeast we see a typical colony model, except that in the French far west, compared to the Ruhr area in Germany, the quality of the housing was worse and living conditions far more primitive. To what extent the children of the Italians who eventually remained and married (often Italian women) were able to obtain better positions in the metal-mining area is hard to surmise. Gérard Noiriel's claim that the second generation of these miners moved on to skilled positions—and the majority of the third generation even moved out of the working class entirely[49]—is not substantiated by empirical research and seems a rather optimistic claim. It is more likely that Italians in this region followed a slower and more gradual path, similar to that of the Polish miners in the Ruhr area and also that of many native workers.

## Looking for "Little Italys"

With the Irish and Polish case studies and the well-known ethnic community formation in the United States in mind, and also given the considerable number of Italians in various French cities and regions, one would expect the formation of a large number of "little Italys." Strikingly, however, this is not the case. Where Italians were concentrated, some sort of ethnic infrastructure, in the form of shops and cafés, did emerge, but this certainly did not resemble the close-knit communities of other nationalities we encounter elsewhere. This is all the more remarkable, given the fact that one could expect that the widespread stereotyping and overt racism at the end of the nineteenth century would lead to a greater group cohesion and a more defensive attitude. The contrary is true, however: ethnic institutions were rather weak in France, and many Italians chose to become invisible (by naturalization, for example) instead of highlighting their ethnicity or nationality. The intriguing question remains: How do we explain this pattern?

Contemporaries, especially Italian consuls throughout France around 1900 who, for nationalistic reasons, tried to create Italian colonies and thus keep the *Italianità* alive, complained constantly about the lack of cohesion and the absence of interest in the nationalistic project. Interest in joining Italian associations, often supported by the Italian state, or attending private Italian-language schools was low and often even absent.[50] According to the consuls—and this point has been reproduced by the French historiography[51]—this has to be explained by the lack of a substantive elite and middle class. Although they were right in pointing out the one-sided social composition of the Italian population in France, it is doubtful that this explains the failure to build a community, because such a composition did not hinder the Irish in England or the Poles in Germany, who had an even more proletarian outlook.

The absence of a strong feeling of nationalism among Italians in France, a feeling so central for many Irish and Polish migrants, is closely linked to the Italian process of state formation and nation building. When Italy became a unitary state in 1870, the state-seeking project was completed. More important, however, is the fact that the lower classes in Italy identified primarily with their village or region and not with the nation-state, which was considered to be an invention of the elites and was mistrusted. Nationalism therefore played a very different role for Italians than it did for the Polish and Irish migrants. This, however, does not explain the difference between the weak community building in France and the proliferation of little Italys in cities like Boston, New York, Philadelphia, and Chicago. Paradoxically, the difference may be explained by the absence of other migrant groups in France. At the end of the nineteenth century, Italians were often the only substantial foreign group in the areas of settlement (in Nice and Marseille, for example). Although there was also a large number of Belgians in France, and a considerably smaller number of Germans and Spaniards, these groups were more or less restricted to their own geographical strongholds: Belgians in the northwest and Spaniards in the southwest. This did not apply to Paris (and the northeast), where immigrants were more mixed. This implies that the multi-ethnic dimension which characterized most American cities, and which gave way to a more ethnically stratified society, did not emerge in France. In contrast, the French state stressed the importance of the ideal of the Republic and the necessity of assimilation through naturalization (the act of 1889) and the central education system.[52]

As a result, contemporaries and historians alike have characterized the residential pattern of Italians in French cities using terms such as "atomization" and "dispersal," with few organizations and low membership rates in Italian associations that did exist.[53] Even the Italian colonies in Lorraine, often highly concentrated, lacked the organizational and associational vibrancy that characterized the Polish and Irish communities at the time. This does not imply that communal life was totally absent, of course. In all cities with a substantial Italian presence, small associations were engaged in cultural, social, and political activities. Moreover, there were sometimes considerable differences between towns. In Nice, for example, the ethnic bond seems to have been stronger than in Marseille. Both places had roughly the same proportion of Italians (1 in 5) and were close to the Italian border. Nevertheless, three times as many Italian newspapers were sold in Nice than in Marseille. In 1896 *La Stampa* sold thirty-six hundred copies a day; *Il Caffaro*, twenty-five hundred; and *Il Secolo XIX*, two thousand. Taken together, this represented more than seven thousand copies a day for a population of almost thirty-two thousand Italian residents, an extraordinarily high number, even if we realize that Nice welcomed many more temporary migrants. In Marseille, with almost one hundred thousand Italians in 1900, there appeared almost thirty Italian newspapers in the era 1870–1914,[54] but most of these were only short-lived and had a restricted readership. Attempts to establish a local Italian newspaper produced in France amounted to a marginal and short-lived weekly (*L'Eco d'Italia*), which appeared for only one year, in 1911. According to Pierre Milza, the difference between the two main gateways of Italian immigration in southern France can be explained by the fact that Italians in Marseille were a much more homogeneous working-class group, whereas in Nice the lower-middle class (hotel and café owners, clerks, and shopkeepers) was much more prominent.[55] But even in Nice, there was no vibrant associational life among Italian migrants, and most attempts of the Italian consulate to foster this, whether through schools or poor relief, did not bear much fruit.

## The Waning of the Stereotype and Integration after 1918

Soon after the end of the Great War, the Italian state resumed its attempts to stimulate community life among emigrants abroad following nationalist guidelines. The doctrine of organizing Italians into colonies with a direct line to the fatherland was given high priority after the "March on Rome" on October 29, 1922, when Mussolini and his fascist party assumed power.[56] These dramatic social and political developments led to fascist-dominated communities abroad, while at the same time provoked a strong anti-fascist movement, both among the Italian workers already in France (many of whom after 1900 had been deeply influenced by socialist and syndicalist ideology) and also among the new migrants, some of whom had fled Italy for (at least partly) political reasons. The result of the fascist emigration doctrine was therefore not so much the creation of a unitary Italian nationalist movement in France but a highly politicized atmosphere with fiercely opposing factions. Both sides were often interwoven with regular French institutions, such as political parties and unions, which Italian migrants had joined from the end of the nineteenth century onward. Most Italians, however, seem to have remained aloof from politics and kept their distance from both blocs.

The First World War signaled a breach with the past in at least two other respects. First, migration to France (and other countries) surged dramatically, almost doubling the Italian population in France within a decade. France could use these men and women very well, because the existing demographic crisis had been deepened by the huge losses during the war: 1.3 million dead and 1.1 million seriously wounded of an active population of only twenty million. An extension of the country and of its colonies (protectorates) as well made the need for manpower even more acute than before the war.[57] The second change in the postwar period is closely linked to the demand for immigrants and signifies the expansion of the state into the social and economic domain, especially where the labor market was concerned. For the first time in the history of the French Republic, the central state slowly but decidedly began to monitor labor migration, albeit partly through private agencies.[58] To achieve this aim, France created an office for regulating and steering labor migration and at the same time concluded a number of bilateral agreements with donor countries, so to speak, of which Italy, Poland, and Czechoslovakia were the most important.[59] This new policy was not simply the result of the specific scarcity of labor in France. Other European countries and the United States had become aware that the state had a stake in protecting and regulating the national labor market, demarcating through passports and forms of registration (far more clearly than before the war) the difference between natives and foreigners.[60] In the case of France, this interference with international geographical mobility implied not so much restricting immigration—as was the case in the United States—but stimulating immigration and actively importing labor.[61] In practice, recruitment was left to the employers (both agricultural and industrial) who were organized in the *Société Général de l'Immigration* (SGI), whereas the state took responsibility for the diplomatic aspects of the process.

By far the largest group of immigrants in the 1920s was the Italians, who settled in France by the hundreds of thousands, predominantly in the traditional regions (southeast, east, northeast, and Paris), but also heading in new directions (southwest). Although this massive immigration doubled the already sizeable Italian presence, it did not invigorate the old anti-Italian prejudices. Instead, during the interwar period Italians ceased to be regarded as a threat and slowly became a respected immigrant group. A number of factors explain this development. To start with, it is important to realize that France, unlike most other countries, had deliberately embarked upon a policy of immigration, somewhat similar to the United States before 1914. Immigration, at least until the depression of the 1930s, was officially considered as a good thing. Anti-immigrant discourse did not simply disappear, but its impact was much more restricted than in countries that followed a restrictive course. Second, in contrast to the period before the Great War, the official regulation of labor migration implied that, in close consultation with the unions, minimum wages and standard social arrangements were agreed upon so that the danger of strike breaking and the undercutting of wages—the key accusation in the recent past—was eliminated. Also, the Italians were not the only emigrants to France, and after 1918 the existing xenophobic feelings were directed more heavily to new groups, such as the Poles and Spaniards, but predominantly to migrants from Greece, Armenia, and especially from Algeria and Morocco. Italian newcomers benefited from the fact that the French population had become accustomed to migrants from the peninsula and that they were compared positively with those later migrants from elsewhere who were regarded as much more alien in both racial and cultural terms. In the otherwise solid study of immigration by Georges Mauco, published in 1932, these new migrants were negatively juxtaposed with what he called the white race (*la race blanche*), which included the Italians. Finally, a substantial proportion of the Italians were able to benefit from contacts with established compatriots, often possessing French nationality, who acted as employers and co-workers. These contacts with established Italian communities, many of whom were characterized by specific chain migrations, made the integration of this new wave of Italians easier than for new groups without predecessors to pave the way.

## How the Italians Lost Their Stigma

The Italians in France were never generally perceived and stereotyped as "black" or as being fundamentally different from the physical aspect, as was the case with their compatriots in the United States, and also the Irish in the United States.[62] Nevertheless, at least until the First World War they ranked very low in public esteem compared to other foreigners in France. This impression gradually changed in the twentieth century, and by the interwar years the Italians had risen from the lowest to an intermediary position, behind the Belgians and the Swiss but ahead of the more recent migrants. According to the prefects of the French *départements* in 1925, the assimilation of the Italians, with the exception of the migrants in the southern regions, went smoothly and the state therefore anticipated no problems.[63] Except for isolated periods, such as during the economic crisis in the 1930s, when anti-Italian agitation as it related to job competition re-emerged to some extent (in the hotel sector in Southern France, for example),[64] Italians had become an established and accepted part of the French population.

Apart from the fact that integration efforts had started to bear fruit, the more favorable image Italians enjoyed was caused by the increasingly sedentary nature of Italian immigration. The fact that many Italian workers decided to bring over their families was considered an especially positive sign, as it was interpreted as a proof of putting France first. Although family reunion was a problem in countries with restrictive policies concerning aliens, this situation differed in states that considered immigration as beneficial. At the time, both in France and the in United States, the absence of family members and the "nomadic" behavior of Italian migrants, including the widespread return migrations, was seen as a sign of non-integration and was therefore criticized. As the French economist Henri Peyret wrote in his dissertation on the Italians in Gascogne, published in 1928, immigration with complete families would positively influence stability, tie migrants to the soil (a well-known French *topos*),[65] and speed up assimilation.[66] Finally, Italians profited from the "competition" more recent immigrant groups imposed.

The aforementioned study by Georges Mauco on immigration in France is useful in mapping public opinion about various immigrant groups. Using various contemporaneous surveys, Mauco concluded that the Swiss, Belgians, Luxembourgers, and the Italians were very much valued by French industry because, among these groups, specialized workers were far more abundant than among the rest. Deemed less valuable in this respect were the Spaniards and the Portuguese, whereas the "Levantines" (Greeks, Armenians, Lebanese), Africans (Algerians and Moroccans), and Asians were at the bottom of the ladder, lacking physical strength and the "right attitude."[67] As the work of Mauco clearly breathes the reigning prejudices of the day,[68]—especially against the Algerians and Moroccans, who had been working in considerable numbers (about one hundred thousand) in France already since the First World War[69]—it probably satisfactorily reflects the contemporaneous public opinion. In a critical and more elaborate study, Ralph Schor arrives at a similar ranking, without reproducing racist notions.[70]

From these studies it is very clear that after 1918, Italians were no longer the most heavily stigmatized of the immigrant groups. Italians were still looked upon as having more primitive morals than the Swiss and the Belgians; in the eye of the public they were far inferior in this respect than other foreign immigrants. The same is true with regard to criminality. According to statistical overviews in the mid-1930s, Italians were four times as likely to commit a crime as the French, just as they were thirty years earlier.[71] The difference with the early period, however, was that by the 1930s other groups, mainly the North Africans and Poles, had even higher rates of crime. How important this image may have been, it is doubtful that it influenced the integration process greatly. When one looks more closely at the basis of these statistics, it appears that a considerable portion of the crimes consists of breaches of the special regulations for aliens. If we control for this factor, the differences between foreigners and Frenchmen crumble to a rather insignificant level.[72]

## Mixed Marriages

Given the patchy nature of available research, it is impossible to determine the patterns of intermarriage among Italians in France. Nevertheless, a number of interesting results enables us to gain at least some insights in its development through time. Most information is related to Paris and the Seine basin, which is by no means representative of the whole of France, but neither can any single region be considered representative of the whole nation. According to Pierre Milza, the leading expert in the field, during the early years of the Italian migration, intermarriage was more common than it was later because of the highly unbalanced sex ratio (177 men to every 100 women) among the Italians in that period. Initially, there were so few Italian women that the Italian men who were looking for a marriage partner and who did not prefer a spouse from their home country were largely dependent on the French marriage market. In the Seine *département* between 1882 and 1891, almost 75 percent of the Italian men married French women, but in the following decade this proportion had decreased to 43 percent.[73] The main reason for this decline was probably the growing number of Italian women who settled in the Paris region, but it is conceivable also that the growing numbers of naturalizations within the migrant generation played a role.[74] Marriages between former Italians, who were now French citizens, with native French partners were no longer counted as "mixed."

Nevertheless, the intermarriage rate was rather high, especially considering the negative image of Italians at the time, and in order to explain this we can turn to an interesting recent comparison between Italian neighborhoods in Paris and New York by Judith Rainhorn.[75] In her study, Rainhorn tries to explain the large differences in intermarriage rates between these cities. In New York, Italians predominantly married compatriots; Paris at the end of the nineteenth century resembles more of a melting-pot model. Focusing on the two core areas of Italian settlement (the XIXth district, La Villette, in Paris, and East Harlem in New York) Rainhorn shows that the divergent development is not so much caused by differences in origin. Although more Southern Italians settled in New York and were more inclined to marry fellow Italians, that factor carries too little weight. Neither is the difference explained by the nature of the city itself, because in the gateway of America other European groups scored much higher on the intermarriage scale. All things considered, Rainhorn convincingly shows that the most important variable is the size of the community and the density of the settlement. In La Villette, Italians constituted only 7 to 8 percent of the total population and consisted of a few thousand, whereas in East Harlem, where the size of the community was much larger (forty thousand), they were far more concentrated (33 percent). Italians in New York therefore had a greater chance of running into a marriage partner of their own ethnic background and had a wider choice than their countrymen in the French capital. Public spaces, such as parks, streets, cafés, and shops were much more diverse in La Villette, increasing the chances of meeting native Frenchwomen. This is confirmed by the rising number of Italians in Paris, especially after 1918, and the sinking intermarriage rate.[76]

No matter how interesting these results are, population percentages and sex ratios do not solve this puzzle entirely. Italians could have returned to Italy to marry, or they could have brought over a marriage partner, as many Turks and Moroccans in present-day Europe did (and still do). Moreover, in migration studies, examples are available of small groups which nevertheless keep their distance from outsiders by remaining closed to members of other ethnic groups, like gypsies and groups involved in certain economic niches (Chinese restaurant owners, for example). Notwithstanding the Italophobic atmosphere at the end of the nineteenth century, the cultural gap between Italians and French was apparently not as great as one would expect, and the negative stereotype in practice at the time was not strong enough to prevent intimate interrelationships and intermarriage. Only in some cases (people coming from the Ciociaria region of southern Italy, for example) was endogamy dominant, showing how chain migrations, tying specific local and regional migration streams to (often) concentrated settlement at destination, could reverse the main pattern.

These specific niches of endogamy did not die out in the twentieth century, as the seminal study of the Italians in twentieth-century Paris by Marie-Claude Blanc-Chaléard shows. Whereas after the turn of the century intermarriage rates on the whole slowly increased in Paris, this was not the case in the working class area of Nogent. In this *Rocca-sur-Seine,* as it was called in 1911, of the 157 marriages recorded, only 12 percent were mixed. Most Italian men worked as masons and were employed by fellow Italians. Moreover, as with the Ciociara connection in La Villette, Nogent was also characterized by strong chain-migration networks, especially linking Nogent with the Ferriere region in the Appenines. In this male-dominated environment, new migrants were recruited by Paris-based, small construction and building firms whose owners had come from the same area.[77] Women's worlds of work were separated from those of the men, and they worked either in local households or in the textile industry.[78]

Such examples show that, even in Paris, it is impossible to discern one master pattern of marriages. Time, space, and ethnic niches determined the extent of intermarriage, and variations could be huge. Considerable numbers of Italian migrants, mostly men, married French women, whereas others chose their marriage partner from within their ethnic circles.[79] It is important to note, however, that there was no fundamental barrier to intermarriage, notwithstanding the anti-Italian stereotype. This inclination to mix with other ethnic groups can be illustrated by comparing the proportion of mixed marriages among foreigners in the 1920s. On average, the Belgians were most exogamous, compared with their share in the total foreign population: more than 7 in 10 Belgian men married French women. The Italian figures were slightly lower, followed closely by the Spaniards and Russians. The Poles, however, lagged far behind in this respect, a pattern that had not changed much immediately after the Second World War.[80] The percentage of foreign women choosing French spouses was lower, but we see more or less the same ranking, whereas it is striking that Italian women, most of whom arrived in France already married to Italian men, increasingly preferred French men.[81]

Such data have to be treated with some caution, however, because they do not allow us to understand fully the social reality hidden behind the numbers. It is conceivable, for example, that some of the Italians with French spouses consisted of naturalized or second-generation Italians. For the Poles, this was virtually out of the question, as there were very few Poles in France when the mass migration took off after the Great War. The gap between Italians and Poles in this respect could therefore have been smaller than data suggest. Furthermore, the effect of intermarriage on integration is less unambiguous than is often assumed.[82] Thus it is important to know whether marriages lasted and to what extent the native partner was drawn into the ethnic milieu. All things considered, however, the trend toward increasing integration of Italians in the interwar years, which is supported by a variety of other data in numerous studies, seems to be real and irrevocable.

## Social Mobility in the Interwar Period

The integration of the Italians can, in the end, be illustrated by their slow but steady rise on the social ladder. Before concentrating on the status level, let us first look at their distribution within the labor market, compared with other foreign immigrants in 1926 (see table 8).

The position of the Italians (men and women combined) is quite similar to that of the Belgians and the Spaniards: they represent the majority in industry, a marginal role in mining, and a sizeable minority in agriculture. The position of the Poles was quite different. Concentrated in the coal mines and in agriculture, their occupational activities were not only less diverse, they were also activities characterized by inferior status. Most of these low-wage jobs attracted unskilled labor and represented the classical second segment of the labor market. Many Italians could also be found in these low-level jobs (albeit on average less extensively), but the "escape" from the second segment was easier for them because of the presence of a considerable number of fellow countrymen who had established (mostly small) industrial firms, especially in the building trade.[83] The much more diversified labor market position of Italians, as well as the possibilities of their acquiring upward so-

*Table 8.* Occupational Distribution of Four Groups of Immigrants in France, 1926

|                       | Italians | Spaniards | Poles   | Belgians |
|-----------------------|----------|-----------|---------|----------|
| Agriculture           | 15       | 29        | 17      | 20       |
| Mining                | 6        | 6         | 42      | 3        |
| Industry              | 57       | 43        | 32      | 53       |
|   building[a]    | 21       | 11        | 3       | 8        |
|   heavy metal   | 7        | 8         | 11      | 14       |
|   light metal   | 4        |           | 3       | 4        |
|   ceramics/glass | 4       | 3         | ?       | ?        |
|   textile       | 4        | 3         | 3       | 13       |
|   clothing      | 4        | 3         | 4       | 4        |
|   other         | 10       | 12        | 8       | 10       |
| Transportation        | 5        | 6         | 1       | 3        |
| Commerce/banking      | 10       | 11        | 5       | 12       |
| Liberal professions   | 1        | 1         | 1       | 3        |
| Domestic service      | 5        | 4         | 3       | 5        |
| Public services       | 0.4      | 0.4       | 0.2     | 0.4      |
| N = [b]               | 438,221  | 175,819   | 169,569 | 188,784  |

[a] Including infrastructural groundwork
[b] Restricted to the economically active men and women
Source: Olivier Milza, "Les Italiens," 87–88.

cial mobility through their own occupational networks, reflects their higher social status compared with most other foreign immigrants.

Whereas the Italian had been the prototype of the unskilled proletarian immigrant before World War I, after 1918 this position was taken over by the North Africans—predominantly male Algerians, but also Moroccans and Tunisians.[84] Like many Italians before them (and like the later guest workers of the 1960s), they came to France with the aim of earning as much money as possible and then returning home. This implied that that they were content with low-status jobs and bad housing conditions as long as they could save enough money from their efforts. The only sector they shunned was agriculture, because of the low wages, harsh treatment, and racist attitudes of most farmers. Instead, they went to the well-known "Italian" regions: the southeast, the northwest, and Paris. Within these regions they performed the most filthy, unhealthy, and dangerous jobs—jobs in which very few French workers were to be found. Most of them were employed in the metal sector (car production), the chemical industry, and mining.[85] Whereas the Italians, who were also well represented in these sectors, had gradually managed to rise to more specialized positions, the North Africans were condemned to unhealthy work involving great heat, toxic gases, acids, dust, hot metals, and dyes.[86]

## Conclusion

The Italian immigration in France constitutes an intriguing example of the history of immigration and integration in western Europe. Faced with a rather hostile receiving society and made up largely of unskilled workers, Italian immigrants found that these rather unfavorable conditions did not form a major obstacle to their integration, not even in the short term. While Italian workers were being chased and killed by furious French workers in the salt fields of Aigues Mortes, naturalization figures were nevertheless rising, and mixed marriages between Italians and French were quite common. This two-sided nature of Italian integration demonstrates the need for a differentiated form of analysis. To understand these seemingly opposing tendencies, it is first of all essential to realize that there was no such thing as *the* Italian immigration. Experiences differed from region to region and from class to class. Moreover, it makes sense to speak of at least two types of Italian immigrants: on the one hand is the male, nomadic proletarian who worked in the lowest segments of the labor market and who generated the stereotype of blackleg and scab; on the other hand we find Italian immigrants who also belonged to the proletarian class but who decided to settle down, marry, and lead a more sedentary life. The latter category, which increased after 1880, attracted far less negative attention and was able to integrate slowly but surely, while remaining out of the public eye. Thus the two processes of xenophobia and integration coexisted and were far from mutually exclusive. As soon as the threat, alleged or not, to the labor market position of native workers began to wither through symbolic legislation, Italians in greater numbers tended to settle down and enter the French labor movement, precipitating a significant reduction in the xenophobic attitude within French society and a noticeable rise in the integration of Italians.

This in itself, however, does not explain why a fairly large group of low-skilled immigrants could integrate much more quickly than the Poles and Irish, with whom they had so much in common. It seems that in the case of France, much weight should be attributed to the much more factorable stance of the state towards immigration and the absence of an ideological threat, be it religious or nationalistic. The French state needed immigrants and was aware of its demographic problem from the second half of the nineteenth century onward. The state itself did not therefore stimulate a stigmatizing offensive against foreigners in general or Italians in particular, notwithstanding the symbolic restriction acts of the 1890s. The welcoming attitude was reflected in the nationality act of 1889, which gave a significant boost to the number of naturalizations for decades to come, and in the deliberate labor recruitment policy during the First World War and the 1920s. Furthermore, the Republican ideal of citizenship based on choice and the *égalité* forged by the educational system further helped to facilitate the integration process. Finally, the ongoing mass immigration, with the arrival of new groups who were regarded as more foreign than the Italians (especially the "Arabs" and the North Africans), reduced the anti-Italian stereotype and enabled Italian immigrants to present themselves as much more French than the later immigrants.

# 4

# Old Threats, New Threats: Conclusion and Preview

The large-scale immigration of Irish, Polish, and Italian immigrants in various western European countries during the second half of the nineteenth century resulted in an oftentimes tense relationship with the receiving society, both the state and segments of the population. All three groups were perceived to be threats because of their religious, political, and social characteristics. These groups had a lot in common, especially their size, their sudden immigration, and their low social status. It is therefore not surprising that the xenophobic reactions to their arrival and subsequent settlement converged in a number of aspects.

In all three cases accusations of unfair competition in the labor market played a role.[1] Religion was not only important in the Irish case, but also for the Poles; even the Italian Catholics were looked upon somewhat suspiciously, in part because of anticlerical tendencies among the French population but also because French Catholics occasionally raised their eyebrows when confronted with "exotic" Italians' Catholic practices. Nationalism, the third important bone of contention, was omnipresent for all three populations. The Irish fight for an independent Ireland, or at least home rule, did not improve the image of this despised migrant group in Great Britain—certainly not when radical elements organized in secret societies and occasionally resorted to violence. For the German state, the threat that the nationalist movement among the Poles could eventually lead to the loss of the eastern region of the newly founded empire (or at least destabilize the fragile national unity) is crucial in understanding the repressive policy. The Italophobia in France, finally, which was rooted primarily in workers' resentment about unfair competition in the labor market, was greatly enhanced by the heated conflict over the colonies between France and Italy in the last decades of the nineteenth century and may even explain the sometimes extreme violence against Italians.

Although it is impossible to truly separate the three threats or to explain neatly how they interacted, it is clear that in each of the three case studies one element dominated. Religion played no role whatsoever in the violent conflicts in Marseille (1881), Aigues Mortes (1893), or Lyon (1894), whereas the inciting lectures by people like William Murphy in the heartland of Irish settlement were one long diatribe against the detested Catholic faith. Nationalist hatred against the Italians undisputedly inspired many French for their "chasse à l'Italien," but it is revealing that it went hand in hand with accusations of wage lowering. Moreover, it seems no coincidence that the large majority of these incidents were concentrated in the southeast of France, where the "nomadic" and unskilled Italian workers were concentrated. In Paris, for example, with its much more diversified Italian population and few labor disputes between Italian and French workers (irrespective of the nationalist atmosphere), no such incidents were reported. And then there are the Poles: it is true that the Prussian authorities in the Ruhr area looked with a suspicious eye toward the predominantly Catholic newcomers, especially considering the anti-Catholic nature of the *Kulturkampf* Bismarck initiated in the 1870s to limit the influence of the Catholic Church and thus carry out his politics of "negative integration."[2] The primary motive for the anti-Polish policy, however, was focused on the nationalist aspects of the Polish presence, particularly symbolized by the use of the Polish language, their nationalist societies, and their refusal to integrate, at least in the eyes of the authorities. It leaves no doubt that the fight against the Polish ethno-nationalist group formation overshadowed the anti-Catholicism, which had lost its momentum already in the 1880s. The Polish priest Franz Liss, who arrived in Bochum in 1890 to coordinate religious life among the Polish miners, was not forced to leave the Ruhr area three years later because of his religious work, but because his *moderate* nationalism was regarded as too great a risk.

To a large extent, this three-headed threat bares a number of important similarities to those experienced by many inhabitants of western Europe in the last decades of the twentieth century. It becomes clear, as we shall see, that the fear of the Islam, the idea that many immigrants deliberately refuse to integrate, and the link between immigration and social problems, so prominent in the discussion today, are not as new as one might think. The key question is whether these seemingly obvious similarities justify the conclusion that there is not much new under the sun.

What is clear already is that the integration experience of earlier "large and problematic" immigrant groups also diverged to some extent from what European countries experience nowadays. These differences can be mapped out in two ways: first by looking at the various national paths of integration in England, Germany, and France, and second by focusing on a number of aspects that all three cases have in common.

## Paths of Integration

Italians, Poles, and Irish all faced harsh discrimination and exclusion in and by the societies where they chose to settle. Furthermore, they had a number of characteristics, such as a low social status, in common. Nevertheless, these similarities did not produce a uniform integration path in the long term. Comparing the three cases, it is clear that the Italians integrated much faster than the Poles and the Irish. Their overall rates of intermarriage were much higher, already in the first generation, and they lacked the group cohesion and vibrant ethnicity that we encounter with the Poles and the Irish. As a result, the integration in French society went relatively smoothly, especially for the second and third generation. The Poles—and this is true probably even more so for the Irish—faced a much more closed receiving society; on the other hand, however, they imported their own nationalism, the expression of a vibrant state-seeking project. The popularity of the Irish ethno-politics in Britain was greatly enhanced by the refusal of the British government to give in to nationalist demands. This explosive mixture gained even more force by the virulent anti-Catholicism, which then resulted in a considerable slowing down of the integration process, blocking both intermarriage and social mobility to a large extent. Finally, it is notable that the anti-Irish stereotype lingered much longer than those associated with the Italians and even the Poles. Until after the Second World War, Irish migrants were still confronted with widespread prejudice and exclusion, while by that time Italians in France and even the Poles in Germany had become accepted groups not considered to be a menace any longer.

The much longer-lived anti-Irish threat should not lead us to think, however, that their integration was entirely blocked. The problem in measuring integration over generations is that it is difficult for historical researchers to trace systematically the descendants of migrants. This is true for both the Irish and the Poles, who in the first place were not foreigners and therefore were often not registered and classified (in censuses) separately. To a large extent the Italians also "vanished" because many of them had naturalized already in the first generation, whereas their children more or less became French citizens automatically.

Apart from this legal aspect, there are also social effects that should be considered. Irishness was not only determined by recognizably Irish surnames, religion, and ethno-political beliefs, but also by social status. Those who were able to rise from the poor working class milieu became in this manner less Irish in the eyes of the receiving society. This mechanism of passing into the dominant society and becoming invisible is a rather general phenomenon and even can apply to groups with distinct different phenotypical characteristics, like Africans and Asians. As a result, it is difficult to assess what part of the second and third generation has left the confinement of their migrant milieu. This selectivity easily leads in the long run to distorted conclusions about the intergenerational integration process by creating the impression that integration is blocked, whereas this conclusion is based upon the observation of only some of the immigrants and their descendants—a mechanism, by the way, that also plays tricks on us in the present.[3]

Notwithstanding the distorting effects of the selectivity of the sources, it is clear that the Irish (and the Poles to a lesser extent) had greater trouble being accepted, and they integrated much more slowly than the Italians in France. The explanation for the relative Italian "success" is twofold: on the one hand, the socioeconomic threat they posed to the French was much more superficial than the religious and national gap that separated the other two groups from their surroundings. Working for lower wages and breaking strikes was only a transitory phenomenon and much more easily overcome and forgotten than the religious and nationalist characteristics, which were associated with innate, sometimes even racialized, features of the Irish and Poles. On the other hand, Irish Catholicism in Great Britain and Polish nationalism in Germany were felt as much more fundamental—and long-lasting—threats than the labor conflicts of Italians in France. In this sense the Irish and the Poles seem to foreshadow the anti-immigrant atmosphere at the end of the twentieth century, when religion (Islam) and nationalism, now in the guise of transnationalism, are once again in the center of attention.

## Domains of Integration: Shape and Intensity

From the Middle Ages onward societies that experienced immigration were worried about the possible costs these newcomers could pose. For this reason, cities (the crucial entity until the era of the nation state) monitored the settlement of "aliens" and either refused to accept poor and destitute immigrants or sent the bill for the poor relief to the place of origin. Moreover, many new residents were only gradually granted rights to access welfare systems, so aliens were for a long period dependent on their own ethnic or religious group, like the Jewish immigrants in England in the nineteenth century.[4] The same system was more or less continued after the Napoleonic wars, only with more emphasis at the national level, as indirect rule had to give way to direct rule.[5] When aliens were defined as non-nationals, the state and its representatives could then voice fears concerning the financial costs of immigration, which resulted in various "aliens" acts in the nineteenth century in Europe, as well as in the United States.[6] Because welfare relief was rather marginal until the First World War, with aliens often excluded (at least temporarily), it was therefore mainly the labor market that directed migration streams. Whether this guaranteed the selection of the most suited migrants in the past is debatable,[7] but one could argue that the self-selecting mechanism among old migrants was stronger than among the new migrants, not only because the new migrants, just like natives, could profit more from the welfare state and are afraid to lose these rights, even in the United States,[8] but also because the option of return is more problematic as a result of restrictive immigration acts.

Whereas until the Great War the state was not very interested in controlling and restricting immigration, this changed on a worldwide scale after 1918, albeit haltingly. In the main, nineteenth-century welfare arrangements were still very modest or nonexistent, which implied that citizens as well as migrants were primarily dependent on their own revenues and therefore on the ups and downs of the labor market. When things went wrong and few jobs were available, migrants stayed away, moved elsewhere or, as was often the case, returned to their region of origin. In theory, under this "laissez-faire regime" those migrants who eventually stayed were a select group and therefore fit better in the receiving societies.

It is unclear, however, to what extent this neoclassical expectation of the survival of the "most fit" migrant reflects reality. Little systematic research exists regarding the processes of selection in the past. Not only are we virtually ignorant about who emigrated from and who remained in the sending regions, the same holds true for selection after arrival. Who stayed for good? Who returned home? Who moved along? These are important questions that still await answers. Although it has been established in many studies that it was not the poorest people who migrated, and that those who decided to migrate were not the desperate and down-and-out members of society,[9] this conclusion is still very rough. Research on selectivity, often using life-course analyses on the individual level, has so far focused primarily on internal migrants in France, Great Britain, and the Netherlands.[10]

Of the three old migrant groups in this book, we can only say that all of them had the opportunity of returning home and until 1914 were not hindered from re entry to give migration another try. Although Irish and Italians could be sent back in case of poverty,[11] expulsions were relatively insignificant considering the large scale of the immigration. Whether migrants themselves returned home when things went less well than expected is unclear. We know that young Italian men were very mobile and often returned home temporarily, but how this influenced selectivity remains to be answered. For all three groups, the alternative of returning home was not very enticing because their regions of origin offered little in terms of income or jobs—their primary reason for migrating in the first place. In short, the evidence about migrants' selectivity is inconclusive, and it is too early to decide whether the old migrants differed fundamentally from the new migrants in this respect.

## Racism and Color

In the discussion about old and new American migrants, Nancy Foner has forcefully argued that it is misleading to think that present-day immigrants have a more difficult time integrating because they are perceived and categorized as more different. New immigrants may be darker, more exotic, and of different phenotypes (Asian, African); but in the past, immigrants who are now seen as "white" and integrated, like the Eastern European Jews, the Irish, and the Italians, were also often regarded as culturally and biologically different and confronted with harsh racism.[12]

This also holds true for Europe's old migrants. The Irish were often pictured as a wild Celtic tribe whose morals and values differed fundamentally from the British, and many doubted whether these innate traits would ever change over time. In the anti-Irish stereotype cultural, biologistic and religious elements were inextricably bound.

The idea of a low cultural level (*eine tiefe Kulturstufe*) dominated the discourse about Poles among German elites, including famous scholars like Max Weber.[13] Until the 1930s Poles were characterized as a Slavic people that differed considerably from the Germans. The idea of "Slavs" as having a "collective" mentality instead of being individualistic, as docile instead of adventurous and enterprising, was widespread and also voiced by contemporary French scholars like Georges Mauco.[14] Interestingly enough, in Germany (even during the Nazi era) this stereotype did not rule out the possibility of assimilation. In the Polish case, mixing with Germans—which was considered so detrimental when Jews and gypsies were involved—was even considered a good thing, because this would reduce Polish nationalism and exceptionalism.

The Italians also received their share of discrimination. The "macaronis" were considered to be rough, brutal, and violent—aspects they shared with the lower working classes in general and a picture which bears many similarities to the discourse on the nineteenth-century *classes dangereuses*, who, like the Italians, were seen as permanent nomads.[15] In contrast to the Irish and Poles, however, there are no indications that this general stereotype of an alien *Lumpenproletariat* prevented a speedy integration process, as evidenced by the high naturalization and intermarriage rates already among the first generation. The only Italians who were looked upon as somewhat racially and culturally different were those from southern Italy, simply referred as Neapolitans. They made up only a small proportion of the Italian immigrants in France, and we may conclude in hindsight that this stereotype did not become dominant.

The differences in the long-term effects between the Irish and the Italians make clear that proof of stereotyping and racialization in the past is in itself insufficient to demonstrate that, in this respect, there is nothing new under the sun. Only after a thorough comparison of the intensity and depth of the stereotyping of old migrants with that of present-day migrants can we establish whether factors as color, religion, and perceived cultural distance of the new migrants really are different and create more stumbling blocks on the road of integration.

## Gender and Generation

When we talk about the various threats the old migrants posed, we have to recognize first of all that these threats involved primarily male migrants. This was not only because in most cases the migration was initially heavily dominated by men (especially with the Italians and the Poles), but also because the negative image was inextricably linked to these men (especially with the Italians and the Irish). Conflicts about strikes and wages were to a large extent restricted to navvies and dockworkers, exclusively male domains. Women were either not active in the labor market, or they remained in sectors where they did not pose a competitive threat (clothing, textiles, domestic service). Moreover, men in the unskilled segments of the labor market were mostly single, and their nomadic behavior strengthened the fear for violent and unpredictable behavior. This positioned them much more as outsiders than Italians who settled down with their families. It was therefore family reunification (often precipitated by the arrival of spouses and sometimes children from the home country) that was welcomed by the French as a sign of stability and a firm choice for France. It is an argument that we also encounter in the United States in relation to Italians, as well as other immigrant groups.[16]

From a present-day perspective, this interpretation is somewhat surprising, because (especially in contemporary western European states) family reunification and family formation by the new "large and problematic groups" is seen as a detrimental effect of the initial recruitment of the "guest workers" in the 1960s and early 1970s. Women and children from the same ethnic group are considered as a twofold threat: they increase unanticipated and unwanted immigration, and they slow down the already difficult integration process by marrying partners from the countries of origin. This assumption remains to be proven, but the restriction of migration has been put forward as an explanation of the "whitening process" of old migrants in the United States.[17] Especially the immigration restriction by the 1924 quota act, which put an end to the ongoing increase of Southern Europeans, would have helped them to become accepted as "white."

One could object that the difference in appreciation of family migration is not so much explained by the time period but linked more to the attitude of states toward immigration in general. In the past, France viewed itself explicitly as an immigration country (like the United States) and therefore had no trouble with the arrival of family members, particularly women and children. Contemporary western European countries have denied for decades (and some for longer than that), that they are immigrant countries, defying reality and thus trying to limit the inflow as much as possible. The right to family reunion of former guest workers was respected, reluctantly at best.

Although this is true, there seem to be fundamental differences in the way the second generation is looked upon in the past and the present. While conflicts in the past focused on the first (often male) generation, this has moved, or at least spread, to the second. One of the reasons is that the new immigrants are accused of importing values that contradict those shared in the West, especially core values like the separation of church and state, individual responsibility, and the emancipation of women and homosexuals. There are some parallels in the past, such as the allegedly violent and primitive Italian and Irish culture, and the stereotyped herd instinct of the Poles, but these seem to be much more superficial and less relevant to the core values of the receiving society. What comes closest are the paranoid diatribes against Irish Catholicism, particularly against the detrimental patriarchal power of the Catholic (Irish) priests over the female members of the family, which would thus interfere with the women's own responsibility. In this case, however, the worries were not that Catholic priests would block the emancipation of women, but that they put themselves between husband and wife and thus would threaten the power of the male heads of the household.

Another reason that the predominantly male members of the second generation are regarded as a problem is directly related to the social problems they pose. Again, this was not completely absent in the past, as has been illustrated in chapter 2 by the research into the school attainment of second-generation Poles in the Ruhr area in the 1930s, but again the scale and intensity of the problematization seems to be wider and deeper. Contemporary migrants from "large and problematic groups" are seen as much more difficult than their old predecessors: social problems like school dropout rates, criminality, unemployment, and even identification with global Islam are seen as the first step on the road of the formation of an ethnic underclass.

## Integration and the State

It is clear that the state was, historically, not absolutely absent in the field of integration, with its use of naturalization procedures and applications for name changes (in the case of Poles), but in general it did not really interfere. Integration was, deliberately or not, left to the people themselves and to intermediary institutions, like the church, charity organizations, and unions. Only after the Second World War did the state invade and partly monopolize this domain, which meant that integration became an increasingly public and political issue. To a large extent, this expansion of the state into the public social domain is the effect of the welfare state, which has made itself responsible for offering a safety net for its citizens and has furthermore positioned itself to fight poverty and ignorance, and to further equal opportunities. This policy was first aimed at the working class and has inspired many attempts to eradicate antisocial behavior. Those who in the perception of the state did not want to become equal (gypsies are a good example here) were accused of sabotaging the policy of equality and rejecting the ideals of the welfare

state.[18] When immigrants arrived in large numbers and the second generation grew up, their social deprivation soon became the center of discussion,
research, and policy, and it now forms the focal point of public debates about
the "failed integration" in various western European countries.

# PART 2

# New Migrants

# 5

## The Discomfort of Color: Caribbean Migrants in Great Britain (1948–2002)

On June 22, 1948, the *Empire Windrush* arrived at Tilbury Docks in London. The ship's 492 passengers consisted mainly of Jamaican men who were returning to Great Britain, where they had worked during the war in munitions factories and as ground crew in the Royal Air Force.[1] Although it was not the first ship to arrive carrying immigrants from the West Indies, the disembarkation of its passengers led to a great deal of publicity in English newspapers and signaled the start of a new chapter in western Europe's history of immigration and integration, because it marked the beginning of colored settlement on a large scale in an almost entirely white area of the world.

Migrants from non-European regions had made their appearance from the early modern period onward, albeit in small numbers. Most of them came from the European colonies in Asia, Africa, or the Caribbean, as was the case with West African and Arab sailors who were regular visitors to British ports, especially Liverpool. In the last decades of the nineteenth century, in the wake of the scramble for Africa, colored students from India, Africa, and the West Indies began arriving in Britain, most of them gravitating to London.[2] Much larger numbers entered Europe during the Great War, when both France and Great Britain were short of manpower and both countries recruited hundreds of thousands of workers and soldiers from their colonies. Some 220,000 Algerians and Indo-Chinese were put to work in factories and on the land, while more than half a million soldiers were recruited from countries like Senegal (181,000) and Algeria (170,000).[3] Most of the soldiers returned as soon as the war was over, but a few Africans and Chinese stayed on. Moreover, the Algerian presence in France increased in the interwar years to more than one hundred thousand, complemented by a smaller number of Moroccans. In the Netherlands, the third colonial power in western Europe, the number of colored immigrants remained low. Apart from a few hundred Indonesian students, immigrants in the Netherlands were mainly female servants working for Dutch colonial families who spent their long annual leave in the mother country, taking their entourage with them. Because these women worked in private houses, they were for the most part absent from the public domain and attracted little attention. This was not the case with men from Suriname, for although they were few in number, they were much more visible, especially those who worked as musicians and unskilled laborers. These men were regarded as highly problematic because the police, who kept files of most of them, suspected them of seducing white girls, although in practice it was more likely to be the other way around.[4] As we will see later, this fear also influenced public opinion in Great Britain in the 1950s.

Apart from the large numbers of North Africans in France, the black presence in western Europe was numerically insignificant before the outbreak of World War II. This changed fundamentally in the second half of the twentieth century, especially in Great Britain, France, and the Netherlands. For most contemporaries, the settlement of colored migrants came as a complete surprise, and the prevailing opinion in Great Britain, where the Caribbean presence increased considerably during the 1950s and early 1960s, was that assimilation would be very difficult, if not impossible. The increasing number of blacks was viewed as highly problematic and undesirable, to say the least, and would soon lead to violent and racist reactions.

Although most white Europeans have gradually become accustomed to the permanent presence of black fellow citizens, many believe that with their arrival the integration landscape changed for good. In contrast to past experience, this new wave of colored immigration is seen to differ fundamentally from earlier patterns in at least three respects. First, most black newcomers are believed to have a culture of their own, one which is only partly compatible with that of the native population; second, even if blacks assimilate culturally, their skin color singles them out as different. Unlike the descendants of the Irish, Poles, and Italians, who were barely distinguishable after two or three generations (especially when they changed their names), the offspring of black immigrants remain recognizable as such. Finally, many fear that when color is conflated with social problems and low socioeconomic status, a caste system determined primarily by color will emerge. In this respect many are convinced that the position of black immigrants will become very similar to that of African Americans and other black immigrants in the United States who, through a process of segmented assimilation, end up sequestered in the same "colored quarter."[5] As soon as racial tensions arose in western European countries, resulting either from the formation of a color line or from all-out riots, contemporaries immediately labeled these developments as "typical American situations."

The central question in this chapter is whether color indeed poses a much greater barrier to integration than western European states have experienced so far. The reason for selecting the West Indians, instead of looking at *all* colored immigrants, is that it makes the analysis less complicated. Concentrating on one group with roughly the same social, economic, and cultural background and mapping the integration process over a longer period of time allow us to make a more precisely structured comparison with the earlier integration experiences in western Europe. Moreover, the West Indian migrants are far more suited for use in a case study than, for example, immigrants from India, Pakistan, and Bangladesh, who differ considerably from the native population in the "mother country" in both their culture and religion. Thus by choosing West Indians—who were almost entirely Christian—we are not forced to deal with the problem of disentangling two kinds of alleged threats, color *and* religion, which makes our analysis more straightforward and less ambiguous. This is also the reason that *within* the group of West Indian migrants, I limited myself to the descendants of former African slaves, many of whom, over the course of time, have mixed with European migrants, resulting in a wide skin-color spectrum that ranges from white to black. The small minority of Indians who were the offspring of contract laborers (many of whom were brought to Trinidad and Guyana) has not been included in the research.[6] A final reason for choosing the Caribbean migrants, in contrast to many other colored migrants, is that they have been living in Britain now for almost half a century, which provides some scope for the historical analysis of the course of the integration process.

The reason for concentrating on the Caribbean migrants in the United Kingdom rather than those in France or the Netherlands is double edged. Not only were they the first immigrants to arrive in large numbers whose history can be traced over almost three generations, but it is also the case that nowhere else did the native population feel so direly threatened as on the British Isles. The experiences of newcomers from Guadeloupe and Martinique in France, and the Surinamese and Antilleans in the Low Countries, are dealt with very briefly in the conclusion to show how specific the British case is and to what extent the outcomes can be generalized for western Europe as a whole when considering the role of color in the integration process.

## Colonial Migrants and the Perception of "Race"

Viewed from a French or Dutch perspective, it is striking that, in Great Britain, "color" (swiftly replaced by the term "race") soon dominated the debate, much more than any other of these migrants' characteristics. If we ignore the morally loaded accounts provided by social workers during the interwar period who voiced concerns about mixed relationships and the "half-caste" offspring, the first phase of the debate started in the 1950s and involved studies by social scientists whose work dealt primarily with the "color problem." Sociologists like Michael Banton, Anthony Richmond, and, somewhat later, Sheila Patterson, as well as anthropologists and Africa specialists like Kenneth Little, were preoccupied with the role of color in the integration process.[7] Undoubtedly influenced by the horrors of the racist Nazi regime and the generally prevailing anti-discriminatory atmosphere after World War II, their studies breathed a spirit of optimism, focusing on color as a feature of immigration that the native white population would have to get used to and one that would not prove to be a durable obstacle in the long term. Considering that not all of these pioneers who undertook field work among colored immigrants in Liverpool, Birmingham, Cardiff, and London were free from racial prejudice,[8] most case studies—especially those by Banton, Little, and Richmond—made subtle distinctions and offered interesting insights into the relationship between West Indians and the native English population. As opposition to colored immigration from the Caribbean, India, and Pakistan increased and tensions in the settlement areas reached the surface, the tone of scholarly studies became less confident. As a reaction to violent conflicts and riots at the end of the 1950s, many observers started to focus on discrimination and on (what soon became known as) "race relations," a phrase that was to replace "color" as the key term.[9] The theoretical foundations of the "race relations school," laid by John Rex, were challenged in the 1980s from two sides, first by a new generation of critical Marxist scholars like Robert Miles, Annie Phizacklea, and John Solomos, who stressed that the race-relations approach unwillingly reified "race" as an essentialist and biological concept. Furthermore, they argued that the race-relations school paid too little attention to the power structures that support and uphold racial discrimination. Instead, they chose to focus on the "social construct" of race and color, and they sought to disclose the racist, imperialistic, and colonial roots of the discourse about "race" used by scholars and politicians.[10]

The second wave of criticism aimed at the race-relations school came from radical scholars (some of whom were black) who focused on the political mobilization of "black Britons." Foreshadowing the later post-modernist fixation on "identity," scholars like Stuart Hall stressed the importance of the articulation of race as part of the struggle of black groups against discrimination. They argued that blacks in Britain, instead of striving to maintain "good race relations," would do better to emancipate of their own accord and use their black consciousness in the process. Thus, not only did these radical scholars clash with the race-relations school, but they also took issue with Robert Miles *cum suis*, whose Marxist approach, with its emphasis on class struggle, ignored and denied this form of political black consciousness.[11]

Notwithstanding the sometimes fundamental differences in the approaches advocated by scholars like Banton, Rex, Miles, and Hall, they all share the conviction that Great Britain is a pervasive racist society in which black immigrants, especially those of African descent, are reduced to the level of second-class citizens, very similar to the position African Americans find themselves in. All four scholars are primarily interested in the role of color (or race) as a social construct in postwar British society and in how racism, in the form of stigmatization, violent conflicts, and discrimination, has influenced the integration process of both Caribbean and Asian immigrants. Due to this preoccupation with "race," much less attention has been paid to the actual integration process. What actually happened to the Caribbean migrants and their offspring? How did they fare in the labor market and in education, and to what extent did they mix with "whites" in the marriage market? These questions, if not embedded in studies primarily interested in discrimination, were much less prominent on the research agenda.

One exception is the demographic and anthropological work carried out by American migration scholars like Ceri Peach, Nancy Foner, and (recently) Susan Model, whose starting point was the general migration and settlement process. Being relative outsiders (disciplinary and national) to the "race approach," their work has centered on issues like migration motives, migrant networks, social mobility, and intermarriage.[12] Given the focus of this book, I will draw extensively upon their work and reserve the mainly British literature on discrimination and "discourse" for an analysis of the development of stereotypes and institutional barriers to integration.

## Trading Jamaica for Brixton

As was the case in France and the Netherlands, small contingents of students and other—mostly male—colonial migrants came to the "mother country" starting at the beginning of the twentieth century. Soon, however, these small numbers were to increase dramatically, resulting in a large-scale West Indian settlement in Britain (see table 9).

The seeds of mass migration were planted during World War II. The idea of bringing over Caribbean men to fill vacancies in Britain—vacancies brought about by the large-scale military mobilization of the male population—first met with resistance from the Colonial Office. They were afraid of racial conflicts and questioned the suitability of colored workers. Eventually, small groups of mainly Jamaican men were recruited (some eight thousand) as ground crew in the Royal Air Force, and a few hundred were brought on as machine workers in ammunition factories in the northwest, along with men from British Honduras who were employed in the forestry service in Scotland. Most of them were housed in isolated barracks, and they were soon confronted with the "color line," which regularly barred them from dancehalls and restaurants and also lead to conflicts at work.[13] Notwithstanding the confrontation with British racism (which came as a shock to many West Indians, who had a very positive image of British culture), the war experience would trigger a much larger migration, of which the arrival of the *Empire Windrush* in 1948 was the symbolic start.

The significance of the larger geopolitical context as it applies to migration from the Caribbean to the British Isles is a heavily debated topic. Scholars refer to the structural dependency of the colonies in general (and of the West

*Table 9.* Caribbean Ethnic Population of Great Britain, 1951–91

| Year | Caribbean born | U.K. born | Total |
|------|---------------|-----------|-------|
| 1951 | 18,000 | 10,000 | 28,000 |
| 1961 | 174,000 | 35,000 | 209,000 |
| 1966 | 269,000 | 133,000 | 402,000 |
| 1971 | 304,000 | 163,000 | 467,000 |
| 1981 | 295,000 | 251,000 | 546,000 |
| 1991[a] | 265,000 | 268,000–326,000 | 500,000–558,000 |

[a] In the 1991 census, 58,106 categorized themselves as "Black British," most of them having a Caribbean background. Peach, "Trends in Levels of Caribbean Segregation," 204.
Source: Peach, "Trends in Levels of Caribbean Segregation."

Indies in particular) as an explanation for the migration from the so-called periphery to the core area. The main argument of this "dependency" theory is that the dominant core zone of capitalist development sustains its own wealth and economic development by using the materials and human resources of the periphery as cheaply as possible.[14] This theory has also been applied to the relationship between Great Britain and its former colonies, which—like the relationship with the West Indies—is characterized by the extension of citizenship and resulting access to the metropolis.[15] Colonial power profits when cultural racism limits upward social mobility of certain groups, thereby insuring a relatively large pool of low-wage workers who are more or less permanently confined to the lowest segment of the labor market.

There are, however, a number of flaws in this global variant of the split labor-market theory. First, there was little organized recruitment of migrants after World War II; in fact, only London Transport, British Rail, and National Health Service hospitals explicitly targeted Caribbean men and women when they were short of manpower.[16] Moreover, as Ceri Peach points out, it was not so much the centers of capitalism that tried to lure West Indian migrants, but rather it was the "flagging social services and the weaker parts of the industrial economy which used migration as a prop."[17] Finally, it soon became clear that colored migration was totally unexpected and on the whole deemed undesirable by large parts of metropolitan society after World War II. As French prime minister Pierre Mesmer declared in an interview with *Le Monde* in 1973,[18] the unprecedented and unexpected colonial migration was "a trap set by history."[19] An even better example is the sudden and unexpected exodus of migrants from Suriname to the Netherlands after 1973, where any link with recruitment or labor-market demands was wholly absent.[20]

A more plausible explanation for this sudden migration to Great Britain can be found in the "push" hypothesis, which is made up of various facets, one of which has to do with traditional male migration from the West Indies, dating from the middle of the nineteenth century. It started with the building of railways in Panama in the 1850s, after which Costa Rica, Mexico, Venezuela, and Haiti were to attract tens of thousands of British West Indians, mainly from Jamaica—men who later (at the beginning of the twentieth century) were drawn to the United States. The construction of the Panama Canal alone pulled in some eighty-four thousand Jamaican men and enticed another fifteen thousand from various West Indian islands.[21] When migration to the United States was suddenly frustrated by the McCarren-Walter Act in 1952, which reduced West Indian immigration to the United States from sixty-five thousand to eight hundred per year, Great Britain remained one of the few alternatives.[22] As a "modern colony," as Ramón Grosfoguel labeled it, inhabitants of the British West Indies had free access to Britain.

This right was safeguarded in the British Nationality Act of 1948, which granted all inhabitants of the countries within the New Commonwealth the right of free entry. This act was primarily a reaction to Canada's plan, launched in 1946, to introduce a separate Canadian citizenship that automatically implied British subjecthood. This thwarted the traditional Britain-centered imperial concept of subjecthood, which can be defined as a uniform relationship between Britain and its imperial dominions guaranteeing free movement within the commonwealth. Threatened by the unilateral Canadian move, which would have interfered with this principle, the basically "backward looking" 1948 Nationality Act, to quote Randall Hansen, reaffirmed the link between Britain and the Empire, without a distinction between the Old (countries like Canada, Australia, and New Zealand) and the New Commonwealth.[23] This new definition of the traditional *civis Britannicus sum* ("I am a British citizen") now extended to the New Commonwealth, making unlimited entry possible for West Indians, West Africans, Pakistanis, and Indians until the 1962 Commonwealth Immigrants Act put an end to this free colonial migration.

Although the combination of facets, such as a longstanding migration tradition, poverty in the West Indies, the closure of the United States labor markets, and the opening up of Great Britain to New Commonwealth migrants, offers a more plausible explanation for the sudden flood of immigrants in the 1950s than does the *dependency theory,* its emphasis on "push" factors is too one sided. This becomes clear when we look at each island's contribution to the migration stream in relation to the others (see table 10).

Contrary to the expected outcome of the push theory, there is no clear relationship between the scale of the migration to Great Britain and factors such as unemployment, poverty, and population pressure on the islands—all of which did in all likelihood play a role, but they fail to explain the sometimes-striking differences between the separate islands. Therefore, to supplement a more balanced explanatory framework, Ceri Peach suggests that the general *pull* of the British labor market *and* the functioning of migrant networks in the form of chain migration be included.[24] It is apparent, for example, that the annual variations in immigration are closely linked to the rhythm of employment and unemployment on the British Isles.[25] Furthermore, anthropologists have unearthed numerous chain-migration patterns between specific islands and can even pinpoint the localities on the islands and the neighborhoods in England's cities where people settled. The clas-

*Table 10.* Relative Share of the Migrating Population to Great Britain, 1961

| Island | % of population that migrated | Total number |
|---|---|---|
| Jamaica | 9.2 | 148,000 |
| Barbados | 8.1 | 19,000 |
| Trinidad | 1.2 | 9,600 |
| British Guyana | 1.3 | 7,141 |
| Leeward Islands | 13.0 | 16,025 |
|    Antigua | 8.7 | 4,687 |
|    Montserrat | 31.5 | 3,835 |
|    St. Kitts and Nevis | 13.2 | 7,503 |
| Windward Islands | 8.6 | 27,154 |
|    Dominica | 10.0 | 7,915 |
|    Grenada | 8.6 | 7,663 |
|    St. Lucia | 8.5 | 7,291 |
|    St. Vincent | 5.3 | 4,285 |

Source: Peach, *West Indian Migration,* 15.

sic seminal study on this topic is that of Stuart Philpot on the Montserrats in London. As table 10 shows, inhabitants of the small island of Montserrat were more than six times as likely to migrate than those of the equally small St. Vincent. They did not settle in great numbers in London itself—in the traditional Brixton area, where most Jamaicans lived—but instead showed a preference for Hackney and Finsbury Park. Moreover, they displayed a strong tendency toward "island endogamy," and they resented Jamaicans.[26] How the migratory process got underway is less certain, but it is clear that strong networks and information exchange between pioneers and those who were to follow were crucial elements in determining specific migration and settlement patterns. Margaret Byron found a similar trend among migrants from Antigua and Nevis in Leicester, pointing out: "The significance of the island/village/kinship-based network in the accommodation search for the arriving Nevisians cannot be over-emphasised. The network diagram reveals that few Nevisian migrants to Leicester were not recruited by a relation or a friend in the city."[27]

## The "Color Problem"

In the Caribbean, West Indians saw themselves as British Commonwealth citizens and the British queen's subjects. Just as in the French and Dutch

Caribbean, they created a distinctive Creole culture, a mix of African and European elements, but the dominance of the colonial power meant that they were deeply influenced by the alleged superior language and culture of the colonizer, characterized by notions of fair play and equality. The few white English people they met in the West Indies were mostly high-ranking officials and businessmen who were treated with great respect. This does not imply that racism or preoccupation with color was absent in the West Indies: far from it. The very fact that status was linked to color produced a society that, like most colonial societies, was obsessed with color consciousness. People of mixed parentage or with light skin had a greater chance of acquiring a higher status. At the same time, *within* this colonial context one could also rise socially by achieving economic success. Black West Indians who did well could afford to send their children to school and thus secure the next generation's status. Despite pervasive racism and color obsession, culture and money did "whiten."

This background explains why many West Indians who migrated to Great Britain after World War II were shocked when they realized they would not be treated as equal citizens.[28] Although many immigrants initially played down the racism experienced at work and in the public domain as a temporary phase, they soon realized that racism in Great Britain was far more deeply rooted than they had expected. This became apparent on the labor market, where many skilled male workers felt that their skills were not valued. Labor exchanges regularly refused to offer jobs to black immigrants because employers (especially shopkeepers) were afraid that black employees would put off the white clientele.[29] But in some factories, too, white workers might refuse to work alongside West Indians.[30]

## Race Awareness in the Interwar Period

This racist attitude was ingrained in the British history of colonialism and imperialism.[31] The first time racist stereotypes were apparent on a large scale *within* the British Isles was immediately after the First World War, when conflicts arose between colored seamen and native English sailors. At that time small numbers of Arab, Chinese, West Indian, and West African sailors employed on British ships formed communities in harbor towns like London, Cardiff, Liverpool, Glasgow, and Newport. A crisis in global shipping meant that many of them lost their jobs and were considered a threat by English sailors. The National Union of Seamen, especially, took open action against what they saw as unfair and undesirable competition. Most of the colored seamen, however, were British subjects and therefore could not be expelled.[32] The frustration of the native sailors soon led to attacks on the "coloreds." Such was the incident in Cardiff in June 1919, when houses were ransacked and torched, and three migrants were killed. Similar riots broke out in other towns, the most serious one in Liverpool.[33] During the First World War, the Liverpool community of almost entirely black male sailors had increased to about five thousand. Because of the military mobilization, these men had no trouble finding employment in the merchant marine. When the war was over, however, black sailors were expected to give up their jobs so that returning "heroes of war" could fill the vacancies. When work was scarce, tensions soon soared, and attacks on blacks became a part of everyday life. As in Cardiff, colored seamen were assaulted in the street and their houses set on fire. The most dramatic event was the drowning of the young sailor Charles Wootton, who suffered the blows of a large crowd and was eventually thrown into the water. During the days that followed, "chasing negroes" (echoing the "chasse à l'Italien" in France three decades earlier) almost became a normal activity, as the following quote from a police report illustrates: "On the ninth and tenth [of June 1919] a well-organized gang, consisting principally of youths and young men, soldiers and sailors, ages of most of them ranging from six-teen to thirty years and who split up into different gangs, savagely attacking, beating, and stabbing every Negro they could find in the street, many of the Negroes had to be removed under police escort to Great George Street fire station for their own safety. When no more Negroes were seen on the street these gangs began to attack the Negroes houses . . . and in some cases they completely wrecked them."[34]

Competition for work was not the only factor to cause white workers to bear a grudge against the blacks: the role of gender was significant as well. As the example above makes clear, the immigrant threat was mostly a "male" phenomenon. As in the case of the Italians in France at the end of the nine-teenth century, the conflict arose between male migrants and male native workers. Moreover, the fact that several of them had married white women during the war constituted a serious threat to the status quo in many people's minds. Fears about miscegenation were further stimulated by newspaper reports that spread the notion that these marriages were not only morally but also genetically wrong.[35]

One of the effects of these race riots in British ports was the introduction of the Coloured Seaman's Order of 1925, which made it obligatory for un-documented colored sailors (most of whom came from British colonies) to register as aliens, in order to facilitate eventual repatriation.[36] While many could not be deported and formed small communities, in the 1930s the center of attention shifted to relationships between colored men and white women. This miscegenation was deemed particularly undesirable and worrying because of the "half-caste" offspring it would produce, and it did not take long before welfare associations were established with the explicit aim of helping these children.

From this short sketch one might have the erroneous impression that colonial migrants from various origins were just passive and powerless victims. Especially the well-educated professionals and students among them reacted by establishing organizations to counter discrimination, such as the Colonial Defence League, the West African Students Union, and the League of Coloured People, presided over by the West Indian physician Harold A. Moody, who not only protested against the "color line" experienced by the black elite, but also interceded on behalf of the less privileged, albeit with little success.

During World War II, along with work issues and mixed-race relationships, housing developed as a third domain of friction between the native white population and the colored immigrants, as conflicts over municipal housing projects for "colored youths" in Cardiff in 1944 reveal.[37] So although the presence of colored (male) immigrants was insignificant in the interwar period, they attracted a lot of attention and were seen by many as unwanted and threatening, both from an economic and a moral point of view.

## Here to Stay

The interwar experience explains why the passengers of the *Empire Windrush* and the thousands who were to follow were not received with open arms, and why dormant discriminatory attitudes were easily rekindled. Whereas the first groups of West Indians, mainly men, were looked upon with a mixture of curiosity and benign interest, as soon as it was clear that they were the forerunners of immigration on a far larger scale, attitudes changed. The size of the group of immigrants was also seen as a threat because West Indians were not the only colored immigrants in the 1950s who profited from the free movement of persons within the commonwealth: West Africans, Indians, and Pakistani found their way to Great Britain, too. There was a sharp rise in numbers from 1954 onward: while the total number of colored immigrants amounted to some twenty thousand in the beginning of the

1950s, by 1958 this number had multiplied tenfold to about 210,000, among whom 115,000 were West Indians, 25,000 were West Africans, and 55,000 were Indians and Pakistanis.[38] By that time the West Indian population included a large number of women, who were concentrated mainly in London (Brixton), Birmingham, and Manchester.

In the course of the 1950s, resentment, especially among the white English working class, had built up about what they perceived as a massive and ongoing invasion of "blacks."[39] Conflicts focused on the same domains as before the war: the labor, housing, and marriage markets, and the primary targets were young black males. Although white workers and unions voiced concern about black immigrants on the labor market, the main focal point was the competition for houses and women. Housing was especially troublesome, because the war had dramatically depleted the housing stock in the poorer parts of working-class neighborhoods in cities like London and Birmingham. Anger about "them taking our houses" was clearly greater than "them taking our jobs." Moreover, white citizens blamed the newcomers for the deterioration of their neighborhood, although migrants had little choice than to move into the cities' crowded, dilapidated Victorian houses.[40]

Resentment among the (lower) white working class in the areas of black settlement increased in the 1950s, and aggression against Cypriots ("Cyps"), West Indians ("niggers"), Pakistanis ("Pakis"), and Indians, especially by young white male hooligans known as "Teddy Boys," soon became endemic. Despite the structural and organized nature of the violence against black immigrants, the riots in August 1958 did come as a surprise. Trouble started in Nottingham, where large crowds attacked both West Indians and the police.[41] These recurring street fights and attacks on houses and pubs frequented by West Indians became national news and almost immediately spread to the Notting Hill district in London, where the "Teddy Boys" played a leading role in attacking blacks in the street, setting houses on fire, and pillaging cafés frequented by West Indians. Racist motives were unmistakable as crowds shouted "let's lynch the niggers," "kill the niggers," and "let's burn their houses." The extreme right (the White Defence League, the National Labor Party, and Mosley's Union Movement) was well represented, and most rioters blamed the black immigrants for the housing problem, as one of them made quite clear to a journalist: "Just tell your readers we've got a bad enough housing shortage around here without them moving in. Keep Britain white."[42] The police had great difficulty in curbing the riots, and it took more than a week to restore order.

Although nobody was killed and the damage was minor compared to the riots in the 1980s, these events came as a shock, especially to politicians and bureaucrats, and they influenced the backstage discussion among policy makers and ministries about the desirability of introducing a restrictive immigration act. After years of fights between the Colonial Office (against restrictions) and the Ministry of Labor (a staunch restrictions advocate), the conservative government introduced the Commonwealth Immigrants Act in 1962. The overall Citizenship of the United Kingdom and the Colonies (CUKC) remained in place, but the act differentiated between the places where passports were issued. Only CUKCs with passports issued under the authority of London were exempt from immigration control. All others, both from the colonies and New Commonwealth countries like India and Pakistan, could immigrate only if they had a special permit, in the form of a voucher, from the Ministry of Labor.[43]

The primary effect of the 1962 act on migration from the West Indies was a steep rise in immigration by those who wanted "to beat the ban." Whereas the annual number of entries in 1958 and 1959 was around 15,000, immigration increased sharply to 50,000 in 1960 and reached an all-time high at 66,000 in 1961. Thereafter immigration continued in the reduced form of family reunion, adding another 130,000 to the 170,000 Caribbean-born immigrants who lived in Britain in 1961. From 1970 onward the numbers of immigrants dwindled as migration came to a virtual halt.[44]

## Rivers of Blood

Contrary to the hopes of many in Great Britain, the Commonwealth Immigrants Act did not stop the flow of immigration from New Commonwealth countries. Apart from the "dependants," unforeseen developments in newly independent Kenya (1968) and Uganda (1972), where the Indian communities became increasingly marginalized due to the "Africanization" ideology, sparked a new sort of immigration to Great Britain, leading eventually to more restrictive legislation.[45] A prominent catalyst in this xenophobic mood was the Conservative member of parliament Enoch Powell, whose populist, anti-immigrant campaign made him extremely popular among many in Britain. His apocalyptic speech delivered on April 20, 1968, at the annual general meeting of the West Midlands Area Conservative Political Center in Birmingham became widely known:

As I look ahead, I am filled with foreboding. Like the Roman, I seem to see "the River Tiber foaming with much blood." That tragic and intractable phenomenon, which we watch with horror on the other side of the Atlantic but which there is interwoven with the history and existence of the States itself, is coming upon us here by our own volition and our own neglect. Indeed, it has all but come. In numerical terms, it will be of American proportions long before the end of the century. One resolute and urgent action will avert it even now. Whether there will be the public will to demand and obtain that action, I do not know. All I know is that to see, and not to speak, would be the great betrayal.[46]

Powell not only challenged the Conservative leadership, but he also put the Labor party, which was finding it very difficult to appease its traditional voters, under great pressure, as the popular racist slogan "If you want a nigger neighbor, vote labor" testifies.[47] It comes as no surprise that, in this climate, the attitude toward the West Indians did not improve. The Race Relations Bill, for example, introduced under a Labor government in 1965 and meant to prohibit discrimination in public places and the dissemination of abusive and insulting utterances, seems not to have been very effective in combating institutional racism in the labor and housing markets.

## The "Black Problem" and the 1980s Riots

Whereas at the end of the 1960s crime rates among recent Irish migrants were higher than those of West Indians, juvenile crime rates among the West Indians were already starting to worry policymakers.[48] In the 1970s this trend persisted, and the negative image of colored immigrants in general (and that of West Indians in particular) changed, in the sense that second-generation youngsters, especially males, were increasingly regarded as a criminal problem. Many of them became involved in visible street crime, particularly robbery under threat of violence, commonly referred to as "mugging," which spread rapidly. Some scholars have interpreted this criminal behavior as a form of social protest against their exclusion from white society and have linked criminal patterns to emerging cultural and political transnational movements like the Rastafarians and Black Power.[49] Others focus on the systematic exclusion of "blacks" from equal participation but focus more on the social construct of "blackness" and the problematization of the "black youth" by government officials, the media, and, not in the least, the police.[50]

These perspectives are important, but do not provide a full picture of the multifaceted reality and the differences within and between colored immigrants. There are, for example, huge differences in crime rates between the Caribbean and Asian groups. In the second half of the 1980s, criminal behavior among Caribbean men was four times higher than crime rates for Indians and Pakistanis.[51] If we assume that these crime rates were indeed much higher among West Indian young men than among whites or Asians, it is not so surprising that the police kept a closer watch on them and used skin color as a primary distinguishing feature. The result, however, was that it turned virtually all West Indian young men into suspects and quickly increased frustration, anger, and outrage among both the guilty and the innocent, confirming their sense of exclusion and second-rate citizenship. This was compounded by the fact that many police officers made no secret of their racial prejudice.

This "racial profiling" intensified when the police started to use the Vagrancy Act of 1824 to arrest people on suspicion of "loitering with intent to commit an arrestable offence," commonly known as "sus"—an abbreviation for "suspicious persons."[52] It is indisputable that the police used this clause to harass black youngsters in a systematic way. According to a Home Office study published in 1979, blacks were fifteen times more likely to be arrested as "suspicious persons" than whites.[53] It was this policy that was largely responsible for the outbreak of large-scale riots in the inner cities of London and Birmingham in the first half of the 1980s.[54]

It is important to note that these riots were quite different from those in 1958. Instead of white men attacking colored immigrants, the riots in the 1980s were to a certain extent a mirror image, set off most often by an incident in which the police arrested a colored youth or used violence considered unwarranted and excessive. In reaction, West Indians (but also Asians), joined by a minority of their white peers, would attack the police; for the most part, these street fights ended in the large-scale pillaging of shops, arson, and hooliganism. Troubles started in 1980 in the St Paul's district of Bristol, but the most well-known riots erupted a year later in London (Brixton and Tottenham districts) and in Liverpool (Toxteth district), almost invariably as a reaction to major police operations in which hundreds of people were stopped and arrested. By far the largest outbreak of violence aimed at the police and resulting in large-scale arson and looting occurred in 1985 in Handsworth, Birmingham. The reaction to this unprecedented urban violence was mixed. Initially, government reports focused on the deprivation of the black population and oppressive policing, but after the Birmingham riots, the tone changed. Most observers now blamed the rioters and stressed the pathological black culture of poverty and crime, downplaying more structural causes like unemployment, poverty, and police actions.[55]

Many observers have noted that around 1990 the image of West Indians became less tarnished, especially after the commotion surrounding Salmon Rushdie's novel *The Satanic Verses*. This event showed Muslim migrants (from Pakistan and Bangladesh) in a bad light and shifted the debate on integration (in part) from the racial to the cultural domain.[56] This shift in focus from color to religion was less sudden than the reaction to the Rushdie affair suggests. Islam had already become the focus of collective fears in the West since the start of the Islamic revolution in Iran, led by Ayatollah Khomeini in 1979, but perhaps even more important was the widely felt cultural gap between Britons and migrants from the Indian subcontinent, especially those with an Islamic background. As early as the 1970s, especially in the heyday of the National Front, migrants from Pakistan and Bangladesh had a much greater chance of becoming victims of racial attacks than West Indians did. And since the late 1990s, West Indians have even "surpassed" the Indians in this respect.[57] The notion that, in cultural terms, the offspring of Caribbean migrants are much closer to the native population than the Asian minorities became even more rooted after the attack on the World Trade Center buildings in New York by Islamic terrorists in September 2001 and the subsequent military intervention in Afghanistan and the war against Iraq initiated by American and British forces in the spring of 2003.

Notwithstanding these changes in the image of the West Indians, their social position is still worrisome, as is illustrated by the depressing crime and unemployment statistics. Moreover, racial discrimination is far from dead, although it is more subdued than in earlier decades. One is therefore tempted to think that color indeed proved to be a much greater barrier to integration than, for example, Catholicism (Irish) or nationalism (Polish), which is congruent with the claim by the renowned American scholar Ira Katznelson in his 1973 study that the American and British liberal regimes share an underlying racist structure.[58] To substantiate such a conclusion, however, the information offered in the mainstream studies on "black" immigrants in Great Britain, which concentrate on racism and discrimination, is insufficient, having little to offer with respect to the changes over time in terms of position in the labor market, educational attainments, and patterns of intermarriage. If the idea that the integration process of colored, non-European migrants differs fundamentally from that of European migrants in the past is to be properly tested, these domains will have to be examined systematically.

## West Indians on the Labor Market

In the booming era of the 1950s and 1960s, most West Indian men and women found jobs quite easily, although the large majority worked as unskilled or semiskilled laborers. Men were employed predominantly in industry and the low-wage segment of the service sector, while women were able to secure somewhat better positions in nursing and secretarial jobs. As "starting at the bottom" is the fate of most immigrant groups we encounter in this book, this circumstance need not in itself lead to the formation of an underclass. The rough economic climate prevalent in the 1980s and early 1990s, however, seems to have led to a deterioration in the position of these immigrants, and what is especially troubling is that the second generation is not catching up, at least if we look at the unemployment rates in 2001 (see table 11).

When we compare these figures to those from the past, it becomes clear that, when compared to whites, the gap for these immigrants did not close in the last two decades of the twentieth century.[59] Unemployment remains roughly double that for whites and is only slightly lower than among Pakistanis and Bangladeshis, who migrated later (see figure 4).

For the West Indians the only good news is that the gap that widened dramatically between whites and blacks in the early 1990s has been reduced to 1980s proportions, and that the fall in unemployment among blacks is sharper than among Pakistanis and Bangladeshis.

It would be wrong, though, to conclude from this that underclass formation as predicted by the Marxist school (*dependency* driven or not), locking the black West Indians in the second and bleak segment of the labor market, is actually underway. While it is true to say that the first generation was confronted with discrimination in the labor market, this illuminates only part

*Table 11.* Unemployment Rates of Ethnic Groups in Great Britain, 2001

|             | All ages | 16–24 |
|-------------|----------|-------|
| White       | 4.7      | 10.9  |
| Indian      | 7.3      | 18.4  |
| Caribbean   | 11.6     | 23.7  |
| African     | 14.1     | 24.1  |
| Pakistani   | 16.1     | 24.9  |
| Bangladeshi | 21.3     | 36.9  |

Source: www.statistics.gov.uk/statbase/expodata

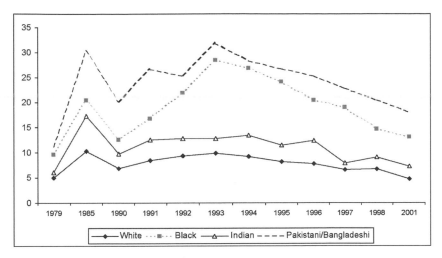

Figure 4. Unemployment Rates in Great Britain by Ethnic Origin, 1979–2001
Note: The rates for 2001 are a bit problematic for "Blacks," because Nickell did not differentiate between Caribbean and other Blacks or between Pakistani and Bangladeshi. Looking at the size of these groups, I have therefore made an estimate using the much more differentiated data in 2001 produced by the National Bureau of Statistics.
Source: Nickell, "Unemployment in Britain," 17; www.statistics.gov.uk/statbase/expodata.

of the picture.[60] The fact is that the majority of the migrants, especially men, simply did not have the required skills to enter the more promising sectors of the economy and were therefore concentrated in sectors and industries that provide few chances of social mobility, such as manufacturing (cars) and transportation, which contributed to their low position.[61] In this sense they were to a certain extent a "replacement population," filling in the vacancies at the lower end of the labor market because the native population had moved up (a situation very similar to the position of the "guest workers" in continental western Europe).[62] And even if it is true that "the majority were denied the opportunity to express their skills and talents through employment," being confined to jobs designated as "suitable through racialized and gendered constructions of identity," as a scholar recently stated,[63] the key question is whether and to what extent this pattern of discrimination has been continued into the second generation.

So far, the available evidence supports the underclass thesis only partially. Although West Indians still face discrimination in the labor market,[64] with unemployment rocketing, this has not prevented the offspring of West Indians from improving their position. Whereas their parents held mainly unskilled and semiskilled positions, the second generation is better represented in higher-status jobs. And what is more, this is not only due to the effect of the restructuring of British industry, which has reduced the proportion of jobs at the bottom end of the market.[65] This upward social mobility was already apparent in the 1980s (see tables 12 and 13).

These tables make clear that, despite the gap that still exists between Caribbean and white Britons, the former group is catching up fast, and differences in job levels are decreasing. This is especially the case for Caribbean women, who hardly differ from their white counterparts anymore, which again underlines the importance of gender as an analytical tool. Moreover, we have to keep in mind that if we had been able to differentiate between the first and the second generation in tables 12 and 13, we would have seen that the second generation was the main beneficiary of the improvement in overall job levels. The assumption that upward social mobility for West Indians is blocked as a result of some kind of "color bar" may have been true in the 1950s and 1960s, but the notion can no longer be sustained for the last decades of the twentieth century, especially not for the position of women.[66] This picture did not change dramatically in the 1990s, except that the gap closed even further and that Caribbean women achieved parity with white female Britons (see table 14).

*Table 12.* Change in Job Levels of Caribbean Men, 1982–90

|  | 1982 Carib. | 1982 White | 1990 Carib. | 1990 White | % change Carib. | % change White |
|---|---|---|---|---|---|---|
| Professional | 5 | 19 | 8 | 20 | +60 | +5 |
| Other non-manual | 10 | 23 | 23 | 27 | +130 | +17 |
| Skilled manual | 48 | 42 | 39 | 33 | −19 | -26 |
| Semi-skilled | 26 | 13 | 23 | 15 | −12 | +15 |
| Unskilled | 9 | 3 | 6 | 4 | −33 | +33 |

Sources: Brown, *Black and White Britain,* 197–98; Jones, *Britain's Ethnic Minorities,* 99–100.

*Table 13.* Change in Job Levels of Caribbean Women, 1982–90

|  | 1982 Carib. | 1982 White | 1990 Carib. | 1990 White | % change Carib. | % change White |
|---|---|---|---|---|---|---|
| Professional | 1 | 7 | 7 | 10 | +600 | +42 |
| Other non-manual | 52 | 55 | 55 | 57 | +6 | +4 |
| Skilled manual | 4 | 5 | 4 | 5 | 0 | 0 |
| Semi-skilled | 36 | 21 | 25 | 22 | −31 | +5 |
| Unskilled | 7 | 11 | 9 | 7 | +29 | -36 |

Sources: Brown, *Black and White Britain,* 197–98; Jones, *Britain's Ethnic Minorities,* 99–100.

*Table 14.* Qualifications of People of Working Age by Ethnic Group and Gender in Great Britain, 1997–99

|  | Men | | | Women | | |
|---|---|---|---|---|---|---|
|  | Higher qual. (%) | Other (%) | No (%) | Higher qual. (%) | Other (%) | No (%) |
| Indian | 28 | 55 | 16 | 18 | 56 | 24 |
| White | 22 | 62 | 14 | 21 | 59 | 20 |
| Caribbean | 16 | 59 | 23 | 22 | 59 | 18 |
| Pakistani | 17 | 52 | 29 | 10 | 49 | 40 |
| Bangladeshi | 8 | 52 | 40 | 6 | 41 | 53 |

Source: Pathak, *Race Research for the Future,* 16 (based on the *Labor Force Survey*).

This rather optimistic trend, certainly in a long-term perspective, leaves one important question unanswered, however. Considering their gradual rise to the first segment of the labor market, why is it that unemployment rates remain much higher for black than for white Britons, and why is this gap not closing? That the rate *is* higher is to be expected, because the chance of being unemployed is far greater for manual workers, especially males. In 1998 unskilled and semiskilled men were five times more likely to be unemployed than high-skilled men.[67] Their position in the labor market, however, can only explain some of the differences in levels of unemployment. If this were the sole indicator, we would expect much smaller differences between white and Caribbean women, as well as lower rates of unemployment for the young, who are second or in some cases third generation. Apparently, the discrimination recorded throughout the 1990s has still not disappeared entirely.

Less clear is how exclusion—or self-exclusion—is distributed over the group as whole. It is conceivable, for example, that as far as Caribbean migrants and their descendants are concerned, at least two different types of integration paths can be distinguished: one upwardly mobile, for those who have managed to acquire middle- and upper-class jobs and who have moved out of the inner cities; the other a downward path for those who were less lucky when it came to acquiring good jobs and who are stuck in a ghetto-like situation, surrounded by high unemployment, crime, and few positive role models.[68] Within these neighborhoods subcultures can easily develop, producing exclusion as well as self-exclusion from mainstream society. Such an explanation, which is often associated with Oscar Lewis's "culture of poverty concept,"[69] does not imply that this culture is a law unto itself, but that such a strategy of self-exclusion is a defensive answer to structures of inequality.[70] Recent studies on social trends show that these structures seem to be determined more by class than by color or minority status. Thus in the labor market, unqualified members of minority groups fare a great deal worse than comparable British-born whites, whereas those with a good education or professional schooling are not nearly so disadvantaged as the unqualified members of their group.[71] In other words, when color is conflated with a lower-class social position, as in the inner cities, West Indians and other colored migrants face much higher "race penalties" than white Britons do. Education and residential patterns are relevant testing grounds to measure the differentiation in integration paths.

## Education and Segregation

When West Indians arrived in Great Britain, their level of schooling was quite modest and, given the fact that they started work immediately, it was to be expected that the gap in educational attainment would only start to close by the time the second generation left education. This process of catching up was not as straightforward as it might seem, and it did not run particularly smoothly. Studies in the 1970s and 1980s focus on the difficult position of Caribbean children in British schools and report that teachers systematically underestimated the children's capacities.[72] This was not simply a matter of color: children of Asian migrants did much better, outpacing even white Britons. Malcolm Cross and Mark Johnson have argued that whereas Asians experienced much more *popular* racism (confirmed by their greater risks of being victims of the racist assaults mentioned earlier), Caribbean children suffered more from *institutional* racism, characterized by culturalist perceptions of their abilities. In general, schools and teachers perceive them more frequently as being underachievers and disruptive, so they therefore expect less of these children and channel their energy into noncognitive activities such as sports.[73]

Recent research on educational qualifications of second-generation men and women who were active on the labor market in the 1990s shows that these problems did not prevent them from attaining better results than one might have expected from the depressing studies on discrimination at schools. Working Caribbean women have indeed almost closed the gap between themselves and their white peers. And again, the results for the second-generation are better than for the group as a whole, shown in table 14.[74] We have to be careful, though, as these conclusions refer only to those immigrants who are active on the labor market. By leaving out the permanently unemployed, significant numbers of the second-generation Caribbean immigrants are being ignored—and it is exactly this category that is most likely to be influenced by the oppositional culture in the inner cities, which mushroomed to a much greater extent among West Indians than among Asians. That the boys growing up in these environments *are* indeed more disruptive and unruly is highly probable and is confirmed by the high dropout rates and permanent expulsions from schools among Caribbean pupils in 1999 (38 in every 10,000), compared to 13 in 10,000 for whites and only 3 in 10,000 for Indians.[75] The problems of Caribbean boys at school are also reflected in their academic results. The proportion of West Indians (age 16) who attain the highest levels in school is much lower than that for white pupils, with boys faring much worse than girls.

One could argue that those children who underachieve at school or drop out run a great risk of taking the downward integration path, whereas those who are able to avoid or break loose from the oppositional school culture, which also flourished among lower-class whites,[76] have a much brighter future. It would be interesting to know more about this watershed, and about the relationship between underachievement and social background. As long as systematic and more detailed studies focusing on the world behind the aggregated survey data are lacking, this question cannot be dealt with satisfactorily. For the moment we adhere to a two-road integration model, assuming that there is a clear link between an oppositional school culture, segregation, unstable families, crime, and unemployment on the one hand, and upward social mobility and rising school levels for those West Indians who have managed to detach themselves from the inner city on the other.

## Segregation

As we have seen, West Indian migrants settled in substantial numbers in only a few cities. The large majority settled in London, with a second large cluster in Birmingham and smaller concentrations in Manchester, Leeds, and Bradford. Most West Indians found housing in the cheaper areas of the inner cities, following the pattern of most low-skilled migrants both in Europe and the United States. Within these areas, the West Indians clustered in particularly squalid areas, like Brixton and Notting Hill in West London. Their segregation can be measured by using the *segregation index,* which expresses the percentage of people from a certain social or ethnic group that would have to move to different neighborhoods to make it nonsegregated (0 = no segregation, and 100 = total segregation). Compared with the situation in the

United States, segregation among West Indians was moderate and decreased in the late twentieth century, with the index of segregation for London falling from 64 in 1971 to 49 in 1991, and from 50 to 40 for Birmingham in the same period.[77] These levels are about half those found among African Americans in the United States. It is equally interesting to compare segregation rates with the extent of ghettoization among European immigrants in the United States half a century earlier. Compared with other immigrant groups in 1991 London, West Indians have the lowest group percentage in terms of ghetto populations at the enumeration-district level.[78] The fear of creating "new Harlems," as voiced in the 1950s, clearly did not materialize.[79]

Comparisons with other immigrant groups in London are especially salient because they show that segregation itself does not predict underclass formation or social pathologies. Indians, for example, are doing very well both in the labor market and at school, but they live much closer to one another than do the Caribbean immigrants. This suggests that it is not so much their spatial distribution as it is the nature of the ethnic group and the characteristics of the district (quality of the houses and schools, levels of crime) that matter. Following the two-road integration model, this implies that those Caribbean immigrants who were unable to escape the "ghetto" are confronted with a host of social problems, such as long-term unemployment, bad schools, widespread crime, and broken families. Those who moved into more middle-class areas with much lower concentrations of weak social groups (minorities or not) represent the upwardly mobile integration path. Due to a lack of systematic comparative studies, we can only guess at the underlying factors explaining upward social mobility within the West Indian group. It is plausible, however, that migrants (and their offspring) with low social capital and who come from broken and unstable families have a much greater chance of following a downward path than those with more positive role models and a higher social position in the country of origin.

## Intermarriage

If one wants to know whether the "color line," to use this now old-fashioned expression, does indeed prevent or at least alter integration in the long run, studying the occurrence of mixed relationships (both marriage and cohabitation) through time is of utmost importance. Not that one can simply equate a high level of intermarriage with integration—we know that life is more complicated than that—but such analysis provides a crude measure of the acceptance of migrants, as well as the salience and perception of ethnic and racial differences. Or, in the words of Richard Alba: "A high rate of intermarriage signals that individuals of putatively different ethnic backgrounds no longer perceive social and cultural differences significant enough to create a barrier to a long-term union. In this sense, intermarriage could be said to test the salience, and even the existence of a social boundary between ethnic categories."[80]

In view of the widespread racial prejudice toward West Indians in British society, one would expect such bias would be a barrier to a high level of intermarriage. The scholarly literature on the Caribbean migrants in Britain has stressed the importance of how structural racism affects colored immigrants, especially West Indians, and rightly so. It is undeniable that racism in the housing and labor market as well as at schools was—and still is to some extent—a pervasive aspect of everyday life. On the other hand, we have seen that the salience of color (or "race") has not prevented part of the second generation from climbing the social ladder and moving out of the traditional immigrant ghettos. Clearly, racism was not so strong that it could keep the West Indians in a dead-end segment of British society. When we then look at patterns of intimacy between the West Indians and white Britons, these appear to follow roughly the general course of social mobility among West Indians. This means that mixed marriages and cohabitation have become much more usual in recent decades—far more commonplace than many would have predicted.

Expectations about intermarriage in Britain have a peculiar history. As we have seen, before World War II, relations between black men and white women were regarded as undesirable and were regularly the immediate cause of race riots. "Interracial" marriages and their "half-caste" offspring were highly problematized and became objects of deeply felt social concern. Many saw black men as "predatory creatures," white women as victims, and their children as the regrettable and unassimilable product.[81] After the war these stereotypes were still in force, but they could be expressed less openly due to the taboo surrounding racism. At the same time, social scientists such as Michael Banton, Anthony Richmond, and Kenneth Little, who studied the "negro" or "colored" immigrants, rejected the racist and eugenic assumptions related to mixing and expected that color would become insignificant because of increased levels of intermarriage, among other factors.[82] It would just be a matter of time before the native British population would accept colored immigrants. In the words of Michael Banton, "familiarity banishes fear."[83]

This optimism faded when immigration from the Caribbean shot up around 1960. Subsequently, scholarly literature used the low rates of inter-marriage primarily to illustrate the significance of racial discrimination.[84] The explanation for the decreasing intermarriage rates is double edged. On the one hand, the sex ratio within the West Indian group achieved a greater balance, so men could find a partner much more easily than in the early days. On the other hand, from the end of the 1950s onward, attitudes towards colored migrants (from the West Indies, Africa, India, and Pakistan) became increasingly negative. In the 1960s almost 80 percent of the British people were against interracial mixing and regarded it as a serious social problem.[85] In the 1970s there were signs that endogamy among the West Indians was slowly decreasing, but to scholars it was not clear whether this meant that the second generation was really marrying outside their group, because in the census, only birthplace and not ethnicity was registered. Moreover, given this preoc-cupation with and focus on racism and discrimination (which dominated the literature well into the 1990s),[86] most scholars were not very interested in interracial relationships, probably assuming that the numbers would remain insignificant; so it is understandable that the gradual increase in intermar-riage rates, which had already started in the 1970s, was largely ignored.

The first reliable data to use intermarriage as a sort of "litmus test" for integration are present in the 1991 census.[87] Compared to the sparse infor-mation available a decade earlier, this census shows that the percentage of colored people married to native-born white partners increased considerably in the 1980s, especially among West Indians, whereas endogamy remained very high among immigrants from India, Pakistan, and Bangladesh. In 1981, 15 percent of all married West Indians had a white partner, compared to only 4 percent for the Asian groups; these rates had increased to about 24 and 6 percent, respectively, ten years later.[88]

In view of the role assigned to "race" and "color" in the debate on old and new migrants in the United States, it is interesting to compare the intermar-riage patterns of West Indians in Britain with that of "blacks" in the United States in 1991. Whereas in the United States only 4 percent of the African American men had a white partner, the intermarriage rate for Caribbean men born in the United Kingdom reached 40 percent. For women the share was much lower (1 percent and 24 percent, respectively), but the gap was even wider.[89] This shows that intermarriage between West Indians and "whites" is much more common in Great Britain than with African Americans and whites in the United States, and also that West Indians as a population are more exogamous than African Americans. A third important conclusion we can extract is the difference between foreign and native born, or roughly between first- and second-generation migrants. In contrast to what some observers expected, we see an impressive increase in mixed marriages among the second and third generations (albeit to a lesser extent with the third). In Britain in 1991, 2 out of 5 young Caribbean immigrants chose a white native-born partner, a number that is expected to rise to 50 percent into the first decade of the twenty-first century. Finally, it is clear that black men are more likely than black women to choose a white partner. At least in Great Britain, however, the black women seem to be closing the gap, which could be explained by the fact that Caribbean women are doing better in school and in the labor market, which would correspond with the finding that intermarriage is most common among more highly educated Caribbean immigrants. Moreover, whites and blacks in Britain are much more positive about intermarriage; the proportion of the population which declares it has no problem with such unions is 20 percent higher than in the United States.[90] The period in which Anthony Richmond wrote that "mixed marriages between colored and white people evokes greater antipathy than any other aspect of colored colonial immigration to Britain" seems to be largely over.[91]

The striking differences between intermarriage patterns in the United States and Great Britain calls for an explanation and sheds an interesting light on developments in Great Britain. Let us first look at the divergence *within* the United States, between African Americans on the one hand and West Indians on the other. That the latter are more exogamous demonstrates that color in itself only offers a partial explanation for social segregation and discrimination. Apparently, white Americans perceive Afro-Caribbean immigrants as different from native blacks. This difference in perception is mainly explained by social factors. West Indians migrated from West Africa to the New World as slaves, just like the African Americans, but they were socialized very differently. Instead of being a minority, they constituted the bulk of the population on the Caribbean islands. Once slavery was abolished, a highly color-conscious society developed wherein marriages with whites or people with a lighter skin color enhanced blacks' upward social mobility. Skin color clearly functioned as a "master status" but in a different way than in United States, where until the 1960s the "color line" dominated social relations between African Americans and native whites. When West Indian immigrants settled in the United States, they were treated as a homogeneous black group for the first time and put on a par with native blacks. Many West Indians have therefore distanced themselves from the native black minority and have tried to present themselves as different by (among other things) cultivating their more colorful English, but also by expending some of their cultural capital. This makes them less threatening in the eyes of whites, and they are therefore associated to a lesser degree with the social (ghetto) problems of native blacks.[92]

This "comfort factor," as Mary Waters called it,[93] also applies in a different way to the situation in Britain, only there it is used not to distinguish West Indians from native blacks, who are absent, but to distinguish *within* the Caribbean group between the "problematic," poorly educated, inner-city Caribbean immigrants and the more successful ones who have jobs, a (fairly) good education, and who have moved out of their original residential areas with high black concentrations. This brings us to the second interesting comparison: West Indians in the United States versus those in Great Britain. A comparison with the United States shows that the color line for West Indians is much less relevant in Britain. This can be proved not only by the much higher intermarriage rates, but also because, on average, Caribbean migrants in the United States are better educated and have more appropriate skills, although the difference with African Americans is less than often assumed.[94] This implies that if we were to adjust the figures and take education into account, the British rates of intermarriage would be even higher than they are already.

The different salience of race and color between Great Britain and the United States is perhaps best explained by the absence of an internal slavery tradition *in* western Europe and the subsequent politics of segregation and racial discrimination, which in the United States lasted until the civil rights movement of the 1960s.[95] Although, in Europe, negative stereotypes of Africans and other blacks were widespread and part of the collective consciousness, the influence this categorization had on social relations between black immigrants and the native white population appeared to be much less pervasive and lasting than the legacy of centuries of slavery and segregation *inside* American society. Instead, West Indians, not only in Great Britain but also in the Netherlands and France, were perceived as being less alien than the more physically similar immigrants from Asian colonies (India, Pakistan, and Bangladesh) because of their similarities where religion, language, and other cultural markers were concerned.

## Conclusion

In contrast to what many people often assume, and reinforced by the pre-occupation of most studies with racism, exclusion, and discrimination, the adaptation of West Indians to white British society has not been blocked in the long run, and there are clear indications and trends that warrant optimism that the color line will be largely overcome in the near future. Given the initial widespread hostile reactions to colored immigration in general and to West Indian immigrants in particular, this conclusion refutes the idea that "color" in itself is a fundamental obstacle for new migrants in western Europe. Having said this, it is true that not all descendants of Caribbean migrants fared well, and apart from a group that has experienced upward mobility, decent housing, and high intermarriage rates, there was also a significant number of Caribbean Britons who were less fortunate and who were confronted with unemployment, bad housing, and racism.

This two-road integration model in itself is not new, but the role played by gender and color is. This connects to broader discussions in the field of social history about the interaction between the three master categories—class, gender, and ethnicity.[96] In the case of the West Indians, *class* seems to be the most important factor in determining the long-term development of the integration process. The largely rural and semiskilled background of most migrants explains their initially low starting point in English society with respect to work and housing. Moreover, in the first phase of the settlement process, the negative stereotyping by the native population had fixed this position and partly blocked upward social mobility. In this sense West Indians very much resemble the Irish and, to a somewhat lesser extent, the Poles and the Italians.

Within the given class structure, *gender* is essential to an understanding of the divergent paths taken by men and women. As in the case of many other recent immigrant groups, women have better opportunities for upward social mobility due to better school results, and women are less susceptible to opposing youth cultures and less likely to engage in criminal behavior. The reason for their different attitude lies in the semi-independent role of women in the West Indies, where many were wage earners and, at least temporarily, experienced raising their children without the presence and support of their male partner.[97] This matrifocal role model explains why women in the West Indies had already taken an interest in good education and why a considerable number of them, especially trained nurses, did not start at the bottom of the British labor market. Judging from their position in the British labor market, the daughters (and granddaughters) of the immigrants have exploited their cultural capital quite well. They perform better in school, have significantly lower rates of unemployment, and are viewed by whites as less threatening; their chances of taking the "right road" are therefore much greater than for men.

The settlement history of the West Indians has made it clear that the perception of "colored" immigrants as being undesirable and problematic has delayed their integration. The first generation, especially, felt this slowing-down effect and experienced discrimination in the labor and housing markets, as well as in the public domain. But their children, too, were confronted with negative attitudes that reduced their chances both at school and in the job market. Moreover, color was, and still is, a serious handicap for those at the bottom of the social ladder, those who live primarily in the inner-city areas. Although whites in the same position are disadvantaged as well, being black does not help, making it much harder to escape the underclass. However, those who are more fortunate (women more than men) and manage to finish secondary school, get a job, and fan out into predominantly white residential areas are not only much better off economically, but for them color is much less a burden. This is reflected especially in the positive correlation between high rates of intermarriage on the one hand, and higher education plus residential spreading on the other. Given the spectacular rise in overall intermarriage rates, it seems not too far-fetched to say that for this segment of the Caribbean population, the primary importance of color is a thing of the past.

It is instructive to put the Caribbean migration to Britain in a western European perspective. Apart from the British Isles, France and the Netherlands also received large groups of migrants from the Caribbean. France started to recruit people from its overseas *départements* Guadeloupe and Martinique from the early 1960s onward, offering them jobs in the lower ranks of the French civil service (postal services, ministries, public transport, hospitals). Numbering some three hundred fifty thousand, they are the fifth-largest immigrant group in France. The Surinamese in the Netherlands came roughly a decade later. They were not recruited, but rather they flocked to the Netherlands because of the uncertain situation during the chaotic period leading up to Suriname's independence (1975). By 2000 there are almost as many Surinamese in the Netherlands (three hundred thousand) as in Suriname itself (four hundred thousand).

Given the fact that colored immigrants who arrived in western Europe initially encountered much more blatant racial discrimination in Great Britain than, for example, in the Netherlands or in France, and observing that in fifty years' time this threat has lost much of its salience, we may assume that Caribbean immigrants in France and the Netherlands will experience even fewer obstacles on their road to integration. This expectation cannot be tested in full, as migration to these countries occurred later than in Britain, but nevertheless a number of trends point in the expected direction.[98]

Although there are a number of differences in the contexts of both the migration and the reception in the so-called "mother countries," it is striking that all of the West Indian migrants concentrated in the metropolitan areas (London, Paris, and Amsterdam) and that many of them ended up in government jobs, often in the service sector.[99] Moreover, Caribbean migrants, due to their familiarity with the language and culture of the "mother country," are perceived as much less threatening than the almost-white Muslim immigrants, like the Turks. This is reflected in their position in the labor market (where they experience lower unemployment rates than other immigrant groups),[100] in academic achievement, and in high rates of intermarriage. The latter is especially true for African-Caribbean immigrants, as the example of the Netherlands shows: the Netherlands is the only country with a substantial number of former Indian contract workers among its Caribbean immigrants. The "Creoles" (of African descent) have much higher intermarriage rates than the "Hindustans," and their socioeconomic position is also better on average, although the Indians have been catching up since the 1990s.[101] To conclude, although the timing, composition, and context of the migration was quite different for Caribbean migrants in the three countries, the most important lesson to be learned (in light of the core questions in this book) is that color itself does not seem to constitute a basic barrier to integration in western Europe, and that in this respect the integration prospects for colored immigrants do not seem to differ fundamentally from other large and problematic groups in the past.

# 6

# Foreigners Within?
# Turks in Germany
# (1960–2002)

The large-scale riots in Brixton and Birmingham in the 1980s and the racist attacks by the English National Front were not the only violent conflicts between migrants and indigenous populations that made the headlines of the international press in western Europe. Attacks on asylum seekers in Germany caused even more outrage, especially in the years following unification (1990). Firebombs and hails of stones on centers for asylum seekers in the first half of the 1990s, and on the houses of Turkish inhabitants, who had in many cases lived in Germany for a considerable number of years, aroused waves of protest and indignation, both at home and abroad. Moreover, the violence stimulated the public as well as the scholarly debate on the peculiar German stance toward foreigners. Although this wave of xenophobia was clearly linked to the dramatic increase in the number of asylum seekers during the Bosnian crisis, many observers pointed to more structural, political, and ideological causes.[1] The ethno-national character of the German nationality law was especially singled out, being part and parcel of the typical German conception of nationality and nationhood that made it quite difficult for foreigners, as well as their children, to acquire German citizenship.[2] However, not all foreign population groups, which around 1980 amounted to some 6 percent of the total population and increased to almost 10 percent at the turn of the century, were considered a problem. Immigrants coming from western Europe especially, but also increasingly the southern Europeans, were looked upon rather benignly. In practice, the negative term "foreigners" (*Ausländer*) was mainly reserved for the Turkish population, which had grown from an almost negligible number in 1960 to more than two million at the beginning of the twenty-first century. Due to the Turks' perceived alien culture and religion, many Germans, including conservative political parties, viewed them as a semipermanent foreign element (*Fremdkörper*) in German society.[3] As in other western European countries, the Turks—but also other Islamic migrants and former "guest workers" such as the Moroccans in the Netherlands and Belgium and the Algerians in France—were considered unassimilable, because of their allegedly unbridgeable cultural differences. According to some observers, this gulf has become even wider since the fall of the Berlin Wall (November 1989) and the ensuing reunification, which has made the Turks the ultimate outsiders for both "Ossies" and "Wessies."[4]

The combination of this German ethno-national self-definition and the large-scale settlement of Islamic migrants make the Turks in Germany a highly interesting group for testing the assumptions surrounding the integration process of new migrants in western Europe. The central question is: To what extent did the exclusion of Turks from the imagined German national community, in addition to the discrimination and stigmatization they encountered, influence or slow down their long-term intergenerational integration process? In my study I will, however, test the assumptions shared by many who see a clear link between the self-definition of "Germanhood" and the exclusion of the Turks from German society.

## Migration

Great Britain was not the only country after the Second World War to receive millions of migrants from its former colonies, as well as considerable contingents of Irish and so-called "displaced persons" from the European mainland: other western European countries experienced large-scale immigration as well. In France and the Netherlands, the first to move in were colonial migrants, whereas in Germany the millions of newcomers in the late 1940s and 1950s consisted of so-called refugees and *Aussiedler,* people of German stock who used to live in central and eastern Europe.[5] In all cases, these migrants were considered citizens and could not be refused entry. Moreover, the receiving states stressed that these people belonged to the nation and had to be welcomed as such, although some were more welcoming than others.[6] Notwithstanding the huge inflow, the economy of western Europe was doing so well that, as early as the 1950s, demand for labor increased dramatically, leading to a situation of almost full employment. Indeed, there arose a structural shortage of workers in certain segments of the labor market, with a particular need for unskilled workers in the industrial sector.

Beginning in the mid-1950s, Germany was one of the first countries to initiate an active recruitment policy. The goal was to find additional labor in southern Europe—first in Italy, where unemployment was very high at that time. Although the motives for the "guest-worker" scheme were primarily economic, political considerations played a role as well. From the perspective of foreign policy in the heyday of the cold-war era, stimulating labor migration from southern Europe (also from Greece and Spain) was seen as a means to stabilize the insecure political situation, especially in Italy, and thus counterbalance communist influences. Germany also viewed relations with Turkey as vital in securing Germany's membership in the North Atlantic Treaty Organization (NATO). Moreover, many German officials did their utmost to avoid any associations between migrant labor and the forced-labor policy employed during the Nazi era. The desire to maintain good bilateral and international relations therefore impeded the implementation of harsh and restrictive rules concerning the stay and permanent (or semi-permanent) settlement of these guest workers. As a result, many of them stayed on much longer than their hosts had intended.[7]

The German recruitment teams were quite successful and soon released a stream of thousands of guest workers into the booming German economy. But southern Europe could not provide enough workers, in part because Belgium, France, the Netherlands, and Sweden were fishing in the same guest-worker pool. The Germans therefore cast the net more widely to include North Africa and Turkey; they concluded bilateral treaties with the sending countries, ensuring equal pay, benefits, housing, medical tests, and costs of transportation. Turks soon became the largest guest-worker group;[8] indeed, by 1973 the Turks had become the largest group of all foreign workers, with about an 18 percent share, and their percentage would increase to 32 percent by the mid-1980s, as these workers' families joined them. As a result of a huge inflow of asylum seekers, especially from former Yugoslavia in the first half of the 1990s, along with an increasing number of naturalizations,[9] the proportion of Turkish nationals decreased and stabilized at 27 percent (some two million people) around the year 2000. Hence the development of Germany as "Turkey's 68th province."[10]

## Causes of Migration

The mass migration of Turkish workers from the beginning of the 1960s was caused, on the one hand, by the interplay of high population growth and mass unemployment within Turkey, and by the demand for labor in northwest Europe on the other. As always, however, push factors alone are not sufficient to explain why people actually leave their home countries.[11] The general economic imbalance between Turkey and western Europe does not account for the particular *direction*, or for the exact *timing*, of this emigration stream. To understand the phenomenon of the Turkish guest worker we must first take into account the traditional (diplomatic and military) ties between Turkey and Germany, which go back to the First World War and the Kemalist revolution. Apart from these historical ties, the new Turkish constitution of 1960 gave its citizens the right to move around freely. Thus unemployment could be exported, and (even better) the Turkish state would profit from the expected remittances from receiving countries.[12] This convergence of Turkish and German national interests led to the recruitment treaty of 1961, making Germany the prime host country for Turkish "guest workers." In 1973, 80 percent of the Turks in western Europe lived in Germany, and although this share had decreased to 70 percent by 1990, Germany remained by far the most important country of settlement for this group.

The general image of Turkish guest workers is very distorted. To begin with, the group did not consist solely of men. Most of the guest workers were (married) men, but there were also a substantial number of women guest workers, and between 1967 and 1973 especially, the number of female guest workers increased. For instance, of the 135,820 workers who arrived in 1973, almost 30,000 were women, most of whom ended up employed in the textile, food processing, and electronics industries.[13] Moreover, there is a widespread misconception that the average Turkish guest worker was unskilled, illiterate, and came predominantly from the backward rural regions, such as the province of Anatolia. This "Anatolian image" is largely false: two-thirds came from the western urban region of Turkey, with Istanbul as the most important city of origin, although there are indications that many of them (or their parents) had not been city dwellers for very long, having moved from the countryside to the urban centers in the decades preceding the guest-worker migration.[14] They were almost all literate, and many of them were skilled or semiskilled workers who had experience with factory work or cottage industries in Turkey.[15] In this sense, the guest workers were a select group not representative of the Turkish population, of whom in the 1960s only one-quarter lived in cities and three-quarters remained employed in the agricultural sector.[16]

Most guest workers, Turks as well as Italians, were convinced that they would only stay in the host country temporarily and sooner or later would return to their homeland to build a new life for themselves with the money they had earned in the West. They sent enormous amounts of money back home: in the 1970s their annual money orders amounted to almost 3 percent of Turkey's gross national product.[17] To many Turks, Germany seemed like a "little America," with its high wages and seemingly unlimited supply of jobs. The expectation that these workers would return home was strengthened by their work contracts, which foreclosed family reunification and were in principle limited to two years. Although this rotation principle never materialized, mobility among Turks, as well as Italians,[18] remained high and followed (in part) the peaks in the business cycle, as can be seen in figure 5.

Thus during the mini recession of 1966–67, the number of Turks leaving Germany immediately increased; the effects of the first oil crisis in the years following 1973 are also visible. The last upsurge in departures, between 1981 and 1984, was caused by mass unemployment in Germany and the policy

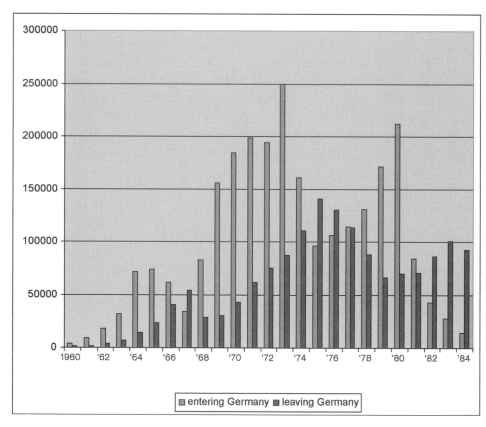

Figure 5. Annual Number of Turks Entering and Leaving Germany, 1960–84
Source: Cepni, *Türkische Arbeitnehmer,* 20; Sezer, "Zur Geschichte," 243.

of giving remigration bonuses to Turks who were willing to return to their homeland for good. This policy, carried out in accordance with the unions, was meant not only to reduce the number of Turks in Germany, but also to divert the cost of industrial restructuring onto guest workers. This "export of unemployment" was therefore specifically aimed at guest workers, predominantly Turks, working in heavy metal industries and mining.[19] In 1984 and 1985 alone, some one hundred thousand Turkish workers and their families left Germany.[20] Ultimately, however, the number of migrants who returned to Turkey remained relatively small and did not stop the burgeoning of the Turkish population in Germany.

Not all the trends in figure 5, however, can be attributed to cyclical economic effects. The rise in immigration in the second half of the 1970s was the result of a combination of factors, primarily the unforeseen consequences of the prolonged stay of many guest workers. Although the initial work agreements stipulated a limited stay, the employers did not want to lose their workers once they had learned the ropes, so employers pushed for the renewal of annual work permits time and again. Furthermore, politicians, especially on the Left, were afraid that the rotation principle (which never materialized) would be bad for Germany's image abroad—an image that had become a very sensitive issue after the Second World War.[21] As well, the more or less simultaneous introduction of the welfare state had its own unintended effects. Throughout Europe the unions had accepted the guest-worker program on the condition that these temporary migrants earned the same wages and contributed to the social security schemes,[22] but the guest workers thereby silently and often unknowingly acquired what James Hollifield called "embedded rights."[23] Turks and others may have been foreigners and as such were excluded from the receiving nation-state, but they were treated as equals in the "nationality blind" welfare state. Moreover, the prolonged sojourn also gave them greater residential rights and the opportunity to bring over their families.[24] Finally, and ironically, the decision by all western European governments to end recruitment and adopt a restrictive immigration policy during the oil crisis of 1973 had rather adverse effects: most (former) guest workers decided to stay on, because leaving meant that it would become very difficult for them to reenter—especially those from countries with stagnant economies, such as Turkey, Tunisia, and Morocco, who had settled and were joined by their partners (mostly women) and children. Thus, due to increased social and legal rights of the immigrants already in Germany, the government's change to the restrictive "aliens" policy in 1973 sparked an unexpected follow-on family reunification that was many times larger than the initial guest workers' migration. Other decisions taken to restrict immigration had similar unwanted effects: the 1975 measure limiting the amount of money paid out in family allowances for children residing abroad had the effect of stimulating family reunification in Germany even further.[25]

## Asylum Seekers

Until the military coup d'état in 1980, virtually all Turks entering Germany had arrived under the auspices of the guest-worker program, although it was clear that a number of them had political or religious reasons for leaving Turkey as well. This was the case with the communist activists, members of minority Muslim sects (such as the Alevites), and the Kurds. When the military abolished democracy in Turkey in 1980 and started a straightforward repressive policy, the number of asylum seekers increased rapidly (see table 15). This was all the more so because the "guest-worker counter" had been closed six years earlier, and the asylum/refugee ticket was the only possible way to enter Germany legally for those who did not qualify as family members of already established Turks.

One of the results of the increased refugee migration from Turkey in the 1980s was that the number of Kurds increased to about one-quarter of the total Turkish population in Germany,[26] laying the foundations for large scale intragroup violence in the 1990s, as we will see further on.

*Table 15.* Asylum Seekers in Germany, 1980–90

| Year | Number | Only from Turkey |
| --- | --- | --- |
| 1980 | 108,000 | 57,913 |
| 1981 | 49,391 | n/a |
| 1982 | 37,423 | n/a |
| 1983 | 19,737 | 1,548 |
| 1984 | 35,278 | 4,180 |
| 1985 | 73,832 | 7,528 |
| 1986 | 99,650 | 8,693 |
| 1987 | 57,379 | 11,426 |
| 1988 | 103,076 | 14,873 |
| 1989 | 121,318 | n/a |
| 1990 | 193,063 | 22,000 |

n/a = not available
Source: Herbert, *Geschichte der Ausländerpolitik,* table 24; Manfrass, *Türken in der Bundesrepublik,* 320–33.

## The Türkenproblem

It is easy to forget that during the 1960s guest workers, both southern Europeans and Turks, were viewed in a positive light in continental western Europe, apart from the ritual minor conflicts between the native population and male youths—Italian male youths in particular—whose courting of local women was frowned upon.[27] In Germany, this rather benign image was fed by paternalistic stereotypes about the "southern man" (*Südländer*) and served partly to stress the superiority of the German people. In general, however, the guest workers (then still predominantly Italian) were not seen as a threat to German society.[28] A characteristic event was the official and cheerful welcome of Ermando Rodrigues from Portugal in September 1964: as the one-millionth guest worker, he was honored with a big reception at the train station in Cologne and received a motorcycle as a sign of German gratitude. In those days—and this has also been largely forgotten—there was an open discussion as to whether, and how, some of these guest workers could become German citizens.[29]

The image of guest workers slowly deteriorated during the brief economic slump of 1966–67.[30] At that time, however, the problematization was caused primarily by the fear of economic competition and much less by the concern that, through large-scale immigration, Germans would lose their national identity. When it became clear that the guest workers would stay, and that family reunions were multiplying the foreign population, *Überfremdung* ("over-foreignization") became a dominant theme. At the same time, Turks became the prime target of anti-foreigner sentiment in German society. In fact, the "foreigner problem," as the presence of the alien population was more and more commonly referred to, was largely, and (to many) solely, a "Turkish problem" (*Türkenproblem*).[31] That Turks were singled out can be explained by a combination of their large numbers, their high concentrations in certain city quarters, and their adherence to the Islamic faith, which in the eyes of the German population made them much more alien culturally than, for instance, the Italians or Yugoslavs.

Central to the stigmatization of the Turkish population in Germany were the primordial conceptions about their culture, which often had the same connotations as "race" before and during the war (the term "race," however, had been so discredited by the end of the Nazi era that its use was banned after 1945). The ethno-national ideology was particularly strong among the members of the powerful Christian Democratic party (CDU), and its southern counterpart, the Christian Socialist party (CSU), which had its stronghold in Bavaria. Thus, in 1981 a number of scholars published the *Heidelberger Manifest*, in which they stressed the "biological and cultural" threat the immigrants (read: Turks) posed to the German people; some Social Democrats (SPD) even characterized Turks as a "minority people" (*völkische Minderheit*) who were unable to assimilate.[32]

When unemployment rose in the 1980s, anti-foreigner sentiment became even more intense, and the newly elected center-right government in 1982, lead by CDU politician Helmut Kohl, continued to stress that the cultural differences between "foreigners" (read: Turks) and Germans were unbridgeable, and that giving them equal civil and political rights was undesirable. Instead, the government deliberately played up the likelihood that the immigrants would return home, thus blocking the route to naturalization for the second generation and complicating the process of family reunion. Moreover, the Kohl government devised a policy to entice former guest workers to return. In the perception of conservative political parties, the frightening prospect of a multiethnic state (*Vielvölkerstaat*) could thus be averted. The conviction that no one wanted culturally alien people to merge was also defended by asserting that the Turks themselves were also opposed to becoming German citizens, and that therefore the exclusionary policy was in their own interest as well—an argument put forward by the minister of the interior, Friedrich Zimmermann.[33] It would be wrong to interpret this statement *solely* as veiled racism or a mere expression of anti-Turkish sentiments.[34] Many conservatives were convinced that it was wrong to "take away" other people's nationality and sincerely believed that people instinctively preferred to live among their "own kind." This also partly explains the educational policy in the conservative southern states of Bavaria and Württemberg, where children of various foreign nationalities were instructed in their native languages with the explicit argument that it was wrong to immerse Turkish, Italian, or Greek pupils in the German language.[35] This protest against "Germanification" is even more interesting when we contrast it with the endless efforts one century earlier to turn the Polish-speaking internal migrants into Germans. The big difference is probably that most Germans assumed that the guest workers would eventually go back, whereas the Poles were German citizens who could not be expelled and were probably not contemplating return.

At the end of the 1980s the public and political attention shifted somewhat away from the Turks to the fast-growing stream of asylum seekers, triggered above all by the Kosovo crisis, the ensuing Yugoslavian civil war, and the 1989 ouster of the Ceauşescu regime in Romania. Hundreds of thousands of refugees fled the former Yugoslavia, and a flood of asylum seekers (especially gypsies) left Romania, arriving in Germany in large numbers. The popularity of Germany among these migrants is explained in part by the very generous provision made for them in the asylum section (Article 16) of the German constitution, which under the Geneva convention guaranteed refugees an almost unhindered entry. The steep increase in the number of asylum seekers from the end of the 1980s onward triggered one of the most polemic public debates in postwar Germany. The discussion boiled down to the desirability of the extremely liberal asylum legislation and the motives of the asylum seekers. Right-wing politicians from the CDU and CSU, supported by the tabloid press (*Bild Zeitung*), considered most asylum seekers as frauds who would only settle in Germany to collect social benefits and thereby destroy the welfare state.

The debate became even more polarized after German reunification in 1990. Stimulated by the public debate in which asylum seekers were highly problematized, young German males, especially—but not solely—in the eastern part of the newly unified country, started attacking asylum seekers. In the years 1991–93, thousands of xenophobic (and anti-Semitic) incidents were reported. Chancellor Helmut Kohl even labeled the wave of anti-foreigner violence a "national emergency situation" in 1992. Centers for asylum seekers were set on fire, often with the consent of bystanders, and foreign-looking people were attacked in the street. Although asylum seekers were the prime targets, other migrants (primarily Turks) also fell victim to the attacks. The most atrocious excesses were the arson attacks in Mölln in November 1992, when a Turkish mother and her two daughters were burned alive in their own house. A similar murderous attack occurred in Solingen a year later, when a Turkish family of five, including three children, died after their house was set on fire. These deaths brought the total of foreigners killed intentionally to forty-nine, counting from the start of the xenophobic rage in 1990.[36]

In the meantime, the two major political players, the Social Democrats and the Christian Democrats, were engaged in a battle over a new immigration act, which was meant first and foremost to curtail the stream of asylum seekers and resulted in a political compromise in December 1992. The modified asylum law did not abolish the contentious Article 16, but the change made it much more difficult for asylum seekers to apply for asylum under the "third state principle." This implied that those who, before reaching Germany, had passed through a "safe" country (which meant all states bordering Germany) could not ask for asylum in Germany and had to be sent back to their point of departure. Only asylum seekers who arrived by air from an "unsafe country" were allowed to follow the German procedure. The act did not immediately put a stop to the xenophobic attacks (the Solingen incident was still to come), but in the long run it clearly neutralized the explosive public climate.

## A German "Sonderweg"?

It is tempting to explain the anti-foreigner sentiments—as well as the refusal of subsequent German governments to grant citizenship to the children of immigrants—as being part of a particular ethno-national German tradition. One of the most cited books on this topic, *Citizenship and Nationhood,* published in 1992 by American sociologist Rogers Brubaker, juxtaposed the French Republican tradition, stressing as it did *ius soli* (those born on French soil automatically become French citizens), with the ethno-national German tradition, which he traced back to the nineteenth century Romanticism of Herder and others. According to Brubaker, the idealized view of the German nation as a homogeneous cultural and biological entity fundamentally influenced the Germans' view of themselves as a nation and their ideas about who belonged to it.

When we take a closer look, however, such a claim is far too deterministic and simplistic. First, we have to realize that Germany has taken in many more immigrants in the postwar period than any other European country, starting with the twelve million *Aussiedler* in the 1950s and 1960s, and that its asylum legislation had been one of the most liberal in the world until 1993. Furthermore, as Klaus Bade has argued, German society does not consist solely of extreme right hooligans or demagogic populists. Such a one-sided view ignores the fundamental attempts by churches, unions, scholars, and politicians to integrate immigrants, among whom were many Turks, from the 1960s onward.[37]

A more specific argument against the Brubaker thesis is that the *ius sanguinis* principle (citizenship in principle restricted to the offspring of citizens) is by no means typically German but can be found in the legislations of most European countries. The 1913 Nationality Act, for example, which is always mentioned as the basis for the exclusionary German citizenship rules, contains no ethnic criteria and by no means makes naturalization of foreigners impossible. Furthermore, since 1990 the rules have been expanded in Germany, whereas in France, more restricting *ius sanguinis* elements have been introduced. In 1993 naturalization in Germany became automatic for those who met the criteria. As a result, the naturalization rates of Germany in the 1990s reached the European average.[38] Finally, it has been argued that as early as the 1990s, the CDU government led by Helmut Kohl started to impose considerable restrictions on the immigration of "ethnic" Germans, while allowing Jews from eastern Europe to enter freely.[39]

The most important argument against the idea of a German *Sonderweg* is that this focus on the public debates, xenophobia, and racism[40] severely clouds the ongoing integration process, which is quite similar to what we saw with the Caribbean migrants in United Kingdom. In an illuminating analysis, two leading German migration scholars, Klaus Bade and Michael Bommes, have argued that below the hectic and anti-immigrant surface of German politics from the 1970s onward, a *de facto* structural integration policy has developed and that, in a sense, the mantra of successive German governments that "Germany is not an immigration country" was necessary to divert the attention of the German public from what was really happening on the ground.[41] They and others show that despite the fact that inclusion of foreigners and their children in the nation-state was frustrated until the 1990s, Turks and other guest workers were structurally integrated in the social fabric of the German welfare state from the very start (as well as during the Kohl governments after 1982), and that various social institutions made great efforts to include them. By granting former guest workers and their families a permanent residence status, and thanks to the help of the "social partners" (employers and unions), the integration of Turks in schools, the housing market, and the workplace was even more successful than in the Netherlands, Germany's progressive, multicultural neighbor.[42]

A good illustration of social integration is the position of guest workers in the workplace. As early as 1952 workers could, irrespective of their nationality, have a say in the politics of their company and could elect representatives to defend their interests in a company council. Foreign workers were entitled to vote, and from 1972 on, they could also run for office. As a result, thousands of immigrants, including many Turks, were elected to company councils, which made decisions on matters like hiring, firing, and promotions. This occasionally led to ethno-politics on the part of the foreign representatives, defending the interests of their fellow nationals, but above all else it had the effect of creating greater homogeneity among the working class. The company councils, in cooperation with the unions (like *IG Metall*), have stimulated the enactment of antidiscrimination policies within a number of companies, mainly in the metallurgy sector.[43]

## New Threats: Illegal Immigrants and Islam

When the anti-foreigner storm had blown over in the second half of the 1990s, two new themes replaced it as the focus of attention: illegal immigrants[44] and Islam. I will restrict this discussion to the way in which the anti-Islamic attitudes gained momentum from the mid-1980s onward and changed the image of the Turks in German society. Throughout western Europe the institutionalization of Islam, visible in the building of mosques, fueled discussions about the illiberal elements of Islam and the barriers such elements could pose to integration. This debate was further stimulated by the international aspirations of the Khomeini regime in Iran and the Rushdie affair, reaching a climax in the terrorist attacks on the World Trade Center in New York in 2001. In Germany, France, England, Belgium, the Netherlands, and Scandinavia, migrants from Islamic countries and their children were increasingly viewed as Muslims instead of Turks or Moroccans. Thus in the case of Germany, it was the Turks, 85 percent of whom adhere to one of the versions of Islam,[45] who became the focal point of the discussion on integration. Whereas in the 1970s and early 1980s the Turks' culture in general was invoked as a barrier to integration, later on it was their religion that was considered to be a threat to what was labeled the German "*Leitkultur*" (leading culture). Islam, seen mostly as static and homogeneous, would contradict this *Leitkultur,* because Islam was illiberal and undemocratic.[46] Therefore, so the argument continued, Islamic migrants (read: Turks) could never really integrate into German society, and due to their large numbers, would threaten the very essence of the German way of life in the near future. This anti-foreigner rhetoric, often infused with thinly veiled anti-Islamic overtones, was not restricted to Germany but became a Europe-wide phenomenon.[47]

Based on historical developments so far, some central questions remain: What integration scenario is likely to develop now? Will Turks remain second-class citizens who are viewed as essentially different? In reaction, will they retreat into a sort of "parallel society"?[48] Or has the structural social integration in the welfare state (in the labor market and education) that began in the 1970s made the Turks already much more German than they and the indigenous German population realize? In the end, might this structural integration also lead to a stronger identification with Germany and the Western world in general?

## Turkish Organizations and the Role of Islam

In the eyes of the indigenous population, one of the most visible signs of persistent ethnicity and ethnic distance is the rapid diffusion of thousands of mosques throughout western Europe, especially in the 1990s. Once they realized that their stay would be more or less permanent, North Africans, Turks, and migrants from Pakistan, to mention the largest groups, established their own places of worship and thereby defined their place in society in a cultural way. For most members of the first generation, the increasing value attached to religion and the frequent visits to mosques are clearly a way of dealing with their changed prospects (staying instead of returning) and the failure of the initial aims of the migration project. Also, migrants' fears that their children will become too Westernized can be seen as an important motive for their clinging on to conservative religious values. In this sense the "Islamization" of many Turkish, Moroccan, and Pakistani first-generation migrants seems to be primarily explained as an attempt on their part to preserve ethnic and familial cohesiveness. In the case of Turks, they feel that their own values, "solidarity, honor and the Islamic faith," are better than those they witnessed in German society, namely "egoism, laxity, and Christianity."[49]

The Islamic faith was used as a rallying point in the development of organizational networks aimed at recruiting Turks, and thus "Islam . . . emerged as a common core of Turkish identity and gained a prominence which it had not possessed when migration into Germany first began."[50] There was a short period in which most Turkish organizations in Germany were more or less copies of political parties in Turkey, such as the leftist *Göcmen Dernekleri Federasyonu* (SDF) and the extreme nationalistic *Milliyetçi Hareket Partisi* (MHP). Soon, however, Islamic organizations became dominant, and in 1995 more than two thousand Turkish-Islamic organizations were established with one hundred thousand (almost exclusively male) members, who, when we include their family members, represent roughly one-quarter of the total Turkish population in Germany. Most of these organizations are affiliated with the DITIB (German Diyanet) mosques controlled by the Turkish state; in addition, the Islamist *Milli Görüs* movement (AMGT) is still growing. Militant fundamentalists, joined together in fifty organizations throughout Germany, represent only a tiny fraction of the Turkish Muslims.[51]

As the second generation gradually takes over the running of the mosques' governing bodies, it is striking to witness Islamic organizations adopting European rallying calls as they strive for human rights and religious freedom, which are under threat in their home country. Moreover, the *Milli Görüs* movement stimulates their members to opt for German citizenship and clearly sees a future for the Turks in Germany, where they will become German Muslims, as Osman Yumakogullari, president of the AMGT, declared at a congress of his organization in June 1995:[52] "The expectation that Turkish Islam in Europe will develop into a moderate version of the faith, focused on integration into western European society, therefore seems not at all far-fetched."[53]

## The Kurds

German Turks are not only divided politically and religiously, they also have important ethnic differences. The most salient conflict within the Turkish state is that with the Kurds, who are striving for political and cultural autonomy, and even their own state (Kurdistan), uniting Kurds living in Turkey, Iraq, Iran, Syria, Armenia, and Georgia. Although other old immigrant groups such as the Irish and the Poles were also divided (Catholic majority and Protestant minority), the rift never led to deep and violent intergroup confrontations in the countries of settlement. When the migratory process started the Kurds were barely visible; indeed, many Kurds only became aware of their identity after they had migrated to Europe, mainly because their culture had long been repressed in Turkey. Furthermore, the forbidden Kurdistan (Stalinist) Workers Party (PKK), established in 1978, soon declared Germany as its "second front," while the Turkish government strove for a military "solution" to the Kurdish problem.[54] The military coup d'état in 1980, which induced a stream of mainly Kurdish refugees from Turkey, set the stage for the conflicts that were soon to break out on German soil. The PKK may only represent a small minority of the Kurds, yet its nine thousand activists and fifty thousand sympathizers (10 percent of the Kurds in Germany) are loud and militant enough to make themselves heard. They established many branch organizations, and in the first half of the 1990s, when Germany was torn by anti-foreigner violence, the PKK waged a small "civil war" with hundreds of arson attacks on Turkish banks, shops, travel agencies, and organizations. Others started hunger strikes and burned themselves to death to win support for their struggle in Turkey. The media coverage of this conflict in Germany, especially by the tabloid press, and the prominence of the PKK should not blind us to the fact that Kurds are a very heterogeneous group, religiously, politically, linguistically, and culturally.[55]

Notwithstanding the many divisions within the Turkish population, many Germans still see them as a homogeneous, nationalistic, and fundamentalist group whose integration is highly problematic, if not totally impossible.

## Housing and Segregation

Turks in Germany are, as one might expect, concentrated predominantly in urban centers. Currently, about 60 percent of Turkish immigrants in Germany live in cities with more than five hundred thousand inhabitants: Berlin, Duisburg, and Cologne in the Ruhr area; Hanover, Hamburg, Frankfurt, Stuttgart, and Munich in the south. In comparison with the West Indians in England, however, urban concentrations are much less pronounced, and at least a quarter of the Turks live in smaller towns.[56]

During the phase of family reunification, most Turks rented cheap, poor-quality accommodation in working-class quarters of German towns. They subsequently moved to specific neighborhoods where they were concentrated in large numbers. In the 1990s more Turks started buying houses, predominantly in the neighborhoods where they were already living. This coincided with a decrease in remittances sent to Turkey (although at the end of the twentieth century, Turkey was still the world's third-largest receiver of remittances by former citizens) and with a growing awareness that their future lay in Germany.[57]

One of the topics in the current European discussion on integration is that of ghettoization. Often the American image of ethnic ghettos is used to describe the spatial concentration of "large and problematic" newcomers in western Europe. Geographers and scholars from other disciplines, however, have shown that this label is misleading. Whereas the segregation index for African Americans in the United States is around 81, the highest levels in western Europe are around 68 (immigrants from Bangladesh living in London), and for most groups the index is below 50.[58] For Turks in Germany, then, this segregation index ranged from 20 to 40 around 1995.[59] Moreover, in most cities with large Turkish populations, the index decreased between 1984 and 1994, though not significantly.[60] Within specific neighborhoods, however, Turks tend to be concentrated in certain areas. A good example is Marxloh, an area in the Ruhr city of Duisburg with about twenty-two thousand inhabitants. In this industrial town, about 11 percent of the population was of Turkish descent around the turn of the century. In Marxloh, however, the share was 25 percent; but *inside* this neighborhood, they are clustered in the eastern section, where Turkish concentrations can reach almost 90 percent.[61]

Given that these pockets are limited in scale, and given the Turks' relatively moderate segregation index, it would be an exaggeration to label the settlement of Turks as a form of ghettoization or to interpret their concentrations as comprising a tight ethnic network. Apart from the fact that living in concentrations was not a question of choice, city quarters with high percentages of Turks include a number of immigrants from other countries. Moreover, important religious, political, and ethnic differences will neutralize the ghetto effect to some extent.[62]

It has been all too easy to interpret this residential pattern, and the stagnating decrease of the segregation in the 1990s, solely as the expression of an ethnic predisposition. Such an interpretation ignores the fact that most migrants had virtually no choices in housing and that these concentrations are a direct reflection of immigrants' weak labor-market position and the availability of inexpensive (social) housing.[63] Nevertheless, an ethnic preference of Turks to live among people like themselves seems also to have played a role.

Although the majority stated over the years that it did not really matter to them with whom they shared a neighborhood, Turks, and to a lesser extent Greeks, have increasingly expressed a desire to live among immigrants, probably people from their own culture (see table 16). (Apparently, the xenophobic outburst in the first half of the 1990s has had a considerable effect.) It remains to be seen, however, whether this is a structural development. It is quite likely that those who would like to live in a homogeneous Turkish environment are predominantly members of the first generation, who in their declining years have given up making an effort to integrate any further. This phenomenon is widespread among first-generation migrants in other countries.

*Table 16.* Ethnic Residential Preferences (Percentages) of Greeks and Turks, 1980–2001

|  | Greeks | | | | Turks | | | |
|---|---|---|---|---|---|---|---|---|
|  | 1980 | 1985 | 1995 | 2001 | 1980 | 1985 | 1995 | 2001 |
| With foreigners | 9 | 12 | 6 | 12 | 11 | 11 | 17 | 25 |
| With Germans | 24 | 14 | 23 | 23 | 35 | 26 | 20 | 13 |
| No preference | 67 | 74 | 70 | 64 | 55 | 63 | 62 | 61 |

Source: Venema and Grimm, *Arbeitnehmer,* table 6.3.

## Turks in the German Labor Market

The vicissitudes of Turkish migrants in the German labor market are similar to those of other guest workers. The Turks were recruited primarily for unskilled or semiskilled work in the labor-intensive industries like metallurgy, mining, and textiles, and although many Turks were rather skilled, they had to accept the dangerous and tiring jobs at the bottom end of the labor market. Many of them entered jobs that led to downward social mobility, not only because they had little choice, but also because their primary interest was in making money to send back to their home country and not in "making it" in Germany. This does not imply that they were docile and accepted all working conditions. Their contracts may have tied them to specific jobs and industries, but in practice many of them moved as soon as they could find better-paying jobs.[64]

Almost 90 percent of the Turkish male guest workers performed unskilled and semiskilled industrial work in car manufacturing, mining, and textiles. A small percentage of the men were able to obtain skilled factory jobs, but in general their position in the labor market during the early period was rather weak, locked as they were into the secondary labor force with few possibilities for upward social mobility.[65] This was strengthened by the fact that many of these workers were concentrated in industries that were ripe for reconstruction and that were the centers of mass redundancies in the 1980s. The position of female guest workers was, to a large extent, similar to that of the men. They, too, worked as unskilled or semiskilled laborers in the industrial sector, in textile and electronics factories, with only a minority of them finding jobs in the service sector.

While the economy offered abundant jobs until 1973, the recession of the 1980s saw many positions swiftly disappear; from 1981 onward, unemployment skyrocketed (see figure 6). That the unemployment rates among the former guest workers were twice as high as among Germans is not surprising, in the light of the guest workers' position in the labor market. What is striking in the long term is that the Turks, who were, on average, better skilled than other guest workers,[66] should perform worse in terms of employment opportunity and mobility.

Compared with other western European countries, however, Germany is not doing so badly. In the Netherlands, for example, unemployment among Turks is *four* times higher than for the Dutch workforce as a whole.[67] The

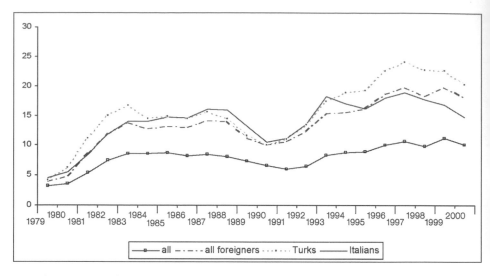

Figure 6. Unemployment among Guest Workers and Germans, 1979–2000
Source: *Daten und Fakten*, 57.

explanation for the difference between Germany and the Netherlands may be found in a mix of factors:[68] the faster restructuring of Dutch industry, the "export" of unemployed Turks in Germany through the remigration schemes, and the lower incidence of discrimination in the labor market, according to a 1995 study by the *International Labor Organisation* (ILO).[69]

General unemployment figures, however, do not tell us much about intergenerational shifts in social mobility. During the 1980s, the picture was gloomy: first-generation Turkish immigrants as well as their children only managed to marginally improve their position, and their segmentation on the labor market seemed to have become permanent.[70] As was the case with the Caribbean migrants in England, however, a few decades are too short to draw up the balance sheet. In that short a period, many young workers in the 1980s either were born in Turkey (first generation) or were at the very beginning of their careers (second generation). To obtain a better view of the position of the German-born second generation we have to look at the developments in the 1990s.

If we compare the skill level of the first-generation Turks who were active in 1972 and 1980 with that of those working at the end of the twentieth century, which includes many of their children, it is clear that the idea of a closed second segment for the Turkish immigrants cannot be upheld, certainly not for women (see table 17). Both men and women, by now predominantly of the second generation, are still overwhelmingly unskilled or semiskilled, but the size of this group is decreasing, whereas the number of those in the more promising white-collar occupations in the service sector (*Angestellten*) is slowly increasing. Gender differences are conspicuous in these shifts: women are doing considerably better than men, and they clearly adapt better.

At the same time, these figures do not provide a basis for too much optimism. Turks as a whole may not be locked in an underclass, but, for the time being, unemployment among them remains very high, while a significant portion of the second generation seems to have inherited the status of their parents.[71] The German apprenticeship system, a combination of vocational and job training, may have stimulated this process. Although this system has helped to reduce unemployment among second-generation Turks considerably, ethnically specific access to job training and employment has developed, with many children following in the footsteps of their parents, the guest-worker generation.[72] The only bright spots are that the period of unemployment for the second generation is much shorter, and there are few signs of ethnic segregation and wage discrimination in the labor market.[73] Finally, figure 6 suggests that Turks (and Italians, for that matter) profited more from the economic upturn at the end of the twentieth century than the average German and foreign worker.

*Table 17.* Job Levels of Turkish Men and Women, 1972–99

| | Men (%) | | | Women (%) | | |
|---|---|---|---|---|---|---|
| | Unskilled | Skilled | White collar | Unskilled | Skilled | White collar |
| 1972 | | | | | | |
| Germans | n/a | n/a | n/a | n/a | n/a | n/a |
| Turks | 84 | 16 | 0 | 97 | 3 | 0 |
| 1980 | | | | | | |
| Germans | 24 | 41 | 34 | 26 | 8 | 66 |
| Turks | 76 | 22 | 2 | 91 | 5 | 4 |
| 1999 | | | | | | |
| Germans | 25 | 31 | 44 | 20 | 4 | 76 |
| Turks | 71 | 23 | 6 | 70 | 5 | 25 |

Source: Bender et al., *Migration und Arbeitsmarkt,* 69; Cepni, *Türkische Arbeitnehmer,* 118.

## Education

It will come as no surprise that, initially, Turkish children in German schools performed poorly when compared with their German peers. Many of them were born in Turkey and left for Germany in the middle of their school careers. In fact, they were more "one-and-a-half generation" than second-generation migrants.[74] Moreover, as their parents still intended to return to Turkey, many thought a German education would be of little value. This attitude changed in the course of the 1980s and 1990s, when it became clear that their future lay in Germany, and when the share of children born in the host country outnumbered those born back home. Nevertheless, the situation improved only very slowly. When we look at those Turks who finished their education in 1997, it is clear that the children of "foreigners" were far behind their German peers, with (as usual) girls doing better than boys. In 1997, for example, two-thirds of the foreign pupils—as opposed to only one-third of the German students—left school without a diploma or with only a *Hauptschule* diploma, which is the least academic level of education.[75]

However, Turks are catching up, albeit slowly, with girls doing slightly better than boys.[76] Whereas in 1989 the large majority (62 percent) did not get beyond the *Hauptschule,* this share decreased considerably in the 1990s.[77] Furthermore, the number of Turkish students who enter universities is also rising.[78] There is, nevertheless, no reason to be very optimistic for the near future: in a study carried out in 2000, Turks were still clearly underrepresented in the higher levels of the German school system, even when compared with other immigrants.[79] Turkish youth are still not doing as well as Italians, Greeks, and Spaniards. This may signal the beginning of a split between those who have succeeded in obtaining higher education qualifications and those who are stuck at the bottom of the educational ladder—those with mainly elementary vocational education (*Hauptschule*) who, moreover, have the least chance of obtaining an apprenticeship (*Lehre*), which functions as an important gateway to obtaining a regular job.[80]

Furthermore, the dropout rates of second-generation migrants are almost three times as high as among Germans (similar to the situation of Caribbean boys in England).[81] We have to realize, though, that the statistics on Turks in the educational system refer only to young people under age 25 with a foreign passport. Turks with German citizenship, who are probably more integrated and are therefore likely to do better, have not been included. This "creaming effect" will only increase in the years to come and make the evaluation of social mobility among the second-generation migrants increasingly difficult.[82] Moreover, Turks with no German primary education (35 percent) are more numerous than Italians (30 percent) and Greeks (23 percent), and their performance is therefore partly explained by their less fortunate starting position.

Finally, it should be mentioned that within Germany there are important differences in school attainment levels for foreign students, depending on the state (*Länder*) they live in. Conservative southern states, such as Bavaria and Württemberg, for example, decided in the 1970s to instruct some foreign children in separate classes, in which their home language played an important role,[83] with the idea that this would facilitate a possible return to their homelands. Moreover, the educational policy of these largely conservative southern states tends to discourage immigrant children from reaching anything higher than the very lowest academic levels. The chances of foreign pupils in Bavaria, who appear in proportionally larger numbers in the least academic types of secondary schools, are even more hindered by the national policy to frustrate the circulation of students from lower to higher forms of education.[84]

These political and geographical differences, however, do not explain why Turkish pupils, compared with similar former guest-worker groups, are not doing as well, since Turks are more concentrated in the progressive states (like Rhine-Westphalia) than in the south, where Italians are the most populous foreign group. Apart from the (low) socioeconomic position of their parents, the relatively poor performance on the part of the Turks seems to result from the first generation's failure to identify with Germany, as well as from their lack of proficiency in speaking the German language (only one-third are proficient, as opposed to two-thirds for other groups). Around 1990, for example, scholars found a clear relationship between the parents' lack of fluency in the German language and the chance that their children would end up at the *Hauptschule*.[85] Given the increasing likelihood that Turks will remain in Germany, one would expect that this effect will become less important and the differences between Turks and similar guest-worker groups, such as the Greeks and Italians, will decrease further. Thus, two questions arise: To what extent do Turks in Germany identify with their new homeland, and how are their social networks constructed?

## Transnationalism and Identification with Germany

A familiar scene on Europe's highways during the summer months: packed minivans heading for Morocco or Turkey, crammed with children, luggage, and gifts for the family back home. This phenomenon, together with the forests of satellite-dish antennas in the residential areas of former guest workers, have led many people, including migration scholars, to assume that the immigrants do not really integrate, preferring rather to live in a sort of transnational social space in which the language, culture, and social contacts of the homeland are cherished. This assumption is both true and false, depending on the stage of the integration process one has in focus, and depending on the generation under observation. In the first stage of the immigration process, roughly from 1960 to 1990, the idea of returning home was very strong among Turks, and their life strategies reflected this goal. Their stay in Germany was, for many, a transitory phase in life: a good place to make money and live for a while, but not a place to set down roots. It was a perspective that the Turks share with many other migrants, past and present. Moreover, this temporary-residence mentality was supported by the German government, which made naturalization difficult and stimulated return migration, and compounded by the Turkish government, which was active in preserving the national character of its migrants abroad. In the course of the 1980s, however, more and more Turks began to linger and at least postpone any return in the immediate future. Prospects in the homeland were not very good, and in Germany they at least had a job, or the right to social security and child allowances. What may have been more important is that the longer they stayed, the more they got accustomed to German society. This awareness became especially apparent during their summer trips, often as long as six weeks, to Turkey, where they—and especially their children who had grown up in Germany—were labeled "Almancilar" ("German-like"). They also realized that many of aspects of Turkish society (corruption, family claims, inefficiency, lack of affluence) had begun to irritate them. Although the large majority still felt Turkish (and were regarded as such by most Germans), the repeated confrontations with the society they left behind made it clear that they were less Turkish than they had thought.[86]

As a result, a large majority of the Turks in Germany in the mid-1990s (83 percent) declared they were no longer considering remigration to Turkey, and three-quarters opted for German citizenship, on the condition that they could keep their Turkish passports as well.[87] This is especially the case in the more liberal states, like Berlin and North Rhine–Westphalia. It would be wrong, however, to interpret the increased number of naturalizations mainly as an instrumental response, as a way to obtain merely legal advantages. Recent research shows that, especially to better-educated Turks, German citizenship is a way to further their individual assimilation and upward mobility. For those who are already more assimilated, a German passport offers the prospect of a higher social status. This is in line with the outcome of another study, which stresses that those Turks who opted for naturalization are significantly better integrated than their co-migrants who did not.[88]

During this time, the Turkish media in Germany, both television and newspapers, became increasingly oriented toward Germany as well. Again, this does not imply that the Turkish identity is vanishing—far from it. But it does reveal that Turkish identity is slowly adapting to the receiving society (and vice versa), and as such it is fluid, flexible, and "processual."[89] Another sign of adaptation is apparent at the family level. In Turkey, especially in the villages, extended networks and solidarities were common; in Germany (and the same is true for other countries in western Europe as well),[90] networks are restricted more to just immediate kin.

On the other hand, some immigrant Turks tended to become much more religious than they had been back home, and identified increasingly with Muslim symbols and organizations, which can be interpreted as a defensive reaction to the categorization as the "essentialized ethnic other."[91] This reaction bears many striking similarities with that of the Poles in the Ruhr area a century earlier. It remains to be seen, however, to what extent the defensive aspect of ethno-religious organizations is mainly a superficial wrinkling caused by the events in the 1990s, both in Germany and worldwide, and to what extent it is fundamentally influencing the behavior of both Germans and Turks. One way to find out is to map out the development of personal contacts between the two groups. In the late 1980s, research showed that the friendships of Turks compared with those of Yugoslavs were much more restricted to their own group.[92]

During this time, ethnic homogeneity decreased with the second generation, albeit for Yugoslavs much faster than for Turks. Two explanations, not mutually exclusive, are feasible. On the one hand, this difference in homogeneity could be the result of cultural patterns; on the other hand, it may be related to the actual chance meeting of people from different ethnic groups. According to Hartmut Esser, who conducted this study, the latter seems to be the case. His first argument is that children, both Turks and Yugoslavs, who were born in Germany have more friends in other ethnic groups than those who came to Germany at an advanced age (six to twelve years old); if we look only at those who were born in Germany, the likelihood of exogamous contacts are similar for both ethnic groups. Esser therefore concluded that the opportunities of meeting and socializing with Germans are more important than one's cultural background.[93] Increasing opportunities are also reflected in the number of Germans who report having friendly contacts with "foreigners" in the workplace. Between 1980 and 1996 this rose from 15 to 51 percent.[94]

However, during the 1990s the intensity of contacts between Turks and Germans, influenced probably by the prevailing anti-foreigner feeling, seems to have stabilized. The percentage of Turks who claim to have no German friends, for example, has remained more or less the same between 1989 and 1995, and at a relatively high level: 67 percent, as opposed to 58 percent for "foreigners" in general.[95] Although these figures do not distinguish between men and women, nor between generations, the conclusion seems justified that in daily social interaction, Turks are, at least temporarily, withdrawing in their own ethnic group. If we consider that during the same period, the second generation's identification with Germany is increasing (from 15 to 24 percent between 1984 and 1993),[96] one can deduce that the first generation is mainly responsible for this withdrawal. As the xenophobic wave ebbed during the second half of the 1990s, the proportion of Turks without close contacts with Germans decreased further to 45 percent in general, and to less than 20 percent for youngsters.[97]

## Mixed Marriages

It is a well-known fact that Turkish migrants in western Europe have a strong preference for marrying within their own group, either with second-generation peers or with partners from Turkey.[98] A mix of nationalistic, cultural, and religious reasons accounts for this strong national preference, and it is also related to the anti-Turkish feeling among part of the population in the countries where they have settled. But despite the violent attacks on Turks in the first half of the 1990s, the percentage of young Turks who nevertheless choose a German partner is rising, as table 18 shows. Moreover, these increases reflect only part of reality, as since 1995 the numbers of naturalized Turks, who are more inclined to marry outside their group, are growing.[99]

Equally telling is the shift in opinion among the unmarried Turks about mixed marriages. Whereas in 1980 about 28 percent could imagine marry-

Table 18. Intermarriage Rates among Italians, Greeks, and Turks, 1980–2001

| | Italians | | | Greeks | | | Turks | | |
|---|---|---|---|---|---|---|---|---|---|
| | 1980 | 1995 | 2001 | 1980 | 1995 | 2001 | 1980 | 1995 | 2001 |
| With German women | 11 | 20 | 22 | 7 | 9 | 15 | 3 | 6 | 11 |
| With German men | 4 | 8 | 17 | 2 | 4 | 16 | 2 | 9 | 13 |

Source: Venema and Grimm, *Arbeitnehmer,* table 5.2.

ing a German, within two decades this had doubled, with men slightly more positive toward intermarriage than women. Negative opinions concurrently decreased from 45 to 28 percent.[100] Turks may still display the greatest hesitation compared to other guest-worker groups, but their statistical rise is much more pronounced. Given the relatively short period that Turks have lived in Germany and their strong ethnic and religious bonds, the growing openness in the domain of marriage is a remarkable indicator of progressive integration.

## Conclusion

The widespread idea in Germany, as well as in other western European countries, that Turks are developing their own ethnic enclave and barely integrating at all has not been confirmed. Overall, we see that, over time, integration has taken place in most domains, particularly if we focus on the second generation. At the same time, however, it is clear that this process, as witnessed in the labor market, at school, and through intermarriage, is developing very slowly, and in various other fields integration seemed to have ground to a halt at the end of the twentieth century. This is particularly true for the level of segregation, which has stabilized since 1990, in accordance with the increasing number of Turks who declare a preference for living among their fellow countrymen. This conclusion should be qualified and modified, however. First, the phenomenon that women perform better in school and in the labor market is very similar to what we have seen among Caribbean migrants, which once again stresses the importance of gender as an analytical category when it comes to integration. Second, a fully-fledged second generation has only recently become active on the labor market, and many children of Turkish guest workers were, in fact, "one-and-a-half-generation" migrants, who started their school careers in Turkey. Finally, we have to be aware of what Dietrich Thränhardt has called the "creaming effect." Data on Turks in Germany refer only to those with Turkish nationality and do not include those who have opted for German citizenship, a group that has grown rapidly since 1995 and by 2003 already accounted for about one-fifth of the total Turkish population. Since they probably are better integrated, the data used to measure integration is negatively biased.

It is misleading to explain the slow integration of the Turks by one-sidedly stressing the exclusionary ethno-cultural German tradition when it comes to citizenship. One might as easily argue that Germany is a special case, in the sense that it was very much aware of its "brown" (national socialist) past, and that the authorities therefore did their utmost to avoid the impression that they were discriminating against guest workers, which has clearly stimulated their structural integration in the welfare state. Moreover, the generous asylum legislation (at least until 1993) and the welcoming reception of Jews from eastern Europe would seem to indicate the opposite. This does not imply that the German ethno-cultural hangover was of no consequence. The idea that Turks could never become real Germans has had implications for the integration process, especially at the level of identification. Although citizenship laws have become much more open, it will take some time before the offspring of Turkish guest workers are accepted as Germans. Finally, the cultural distance between the Turkish Germans and the rest of the population can be explained by the identity of the migrants themselves. Nationalistic and religious factors, especially, have heavily influenced the self-image of the first generation, a relationship that is partly an inheritance of the specific Turkish state formation and partly derives from Islam; but above all else, it is the result of the dynamic interaction between the migrants, their offspring, and German society.

# 7

# Islam and the Colonial Legacy:
# Algerians in France
# (1945–2002)

Few events in the modern migration history of western Europe have generated so much national and international public attention and scholarly analysis as the "headscarf affair" in the French town of Creil, fifty kilometers north of Paris. In October 1989 three teenage girls, two of Moroccan and one of Tunisian descent, were suspended from school because they refused to take off their headscarves. The headmaster justified his decision, which soon became headline news in French and foreign newspapers, by referring to the 1906 French *code de laïcité* (code of secularity), which laid out the formal separation between church and state. He and many others regarded wearing a headscarf in the classroom and inside the school building as a deliberate act aimed at launching religion into the public arena where it had no place. Alec Hargreaves notes that the headmaster based his decision on the wrong assumption—namely, that these girls were attempting to persuade others to become Muslims, which is an act of proselytism.[1] The dominant opinion in the press was that he was right, and that the very principles on which the French state had been built were under severe attack. In the eyes of many (the general public, politicians, and scholars alike), the affair symbolized the non-assimilation of immigrants from developing countries, especially North Africa. Fundamentalist thinking and its huge influence on millions of new immigrants posed the most significant threat, according to commentators from the right and the left of the political spectrum. By not acknowledging the fundamental separation between church and state, Muslims were felt to be an unprecedented threat, reaching much deeper than any of the conflicts French society may have experienced with immigrants in the past. In the years following the Creil incident, discussions about the *foulard* (headscarf) continued to dominate the public debate in France and eventually led to a March 2004 law forbidding the wearing in schools—the secular space *par excellence*—of all signs or clothes that symbolize a particular religious adherence.[2] Although this law aims deliberately at all religious symbols, it is clear that its prime target is the Islamic headscarf.

The problematization of Muslim immigration in France, however, cannot be explained solely by referring to Islamic fundamentalism. The public debate on immigration was already well underway in the late 1970s and focused primarily on North Africans, usually Algerians, and much less on the Muslim migrants from Turkey, sub-Saharan Africa, or Pakistan. Although the latter groups were more devout Muslims than the *Maghrébins* (Algerians, Tunisians, and Moroccans), they did not play a prominent role in the public debate. This one-sided focus on migrants from North Africa is partly the result of the considerable social problems experienced by the second generation, which became visible when the children of immigrants from the Maghreb came of age. The deeply rooted negative stereotyping of this group as "Arabs" compounded the problem. The final blow to their image was stimulated by the political mobilization process among the second generation, known as the *beurs*, who became highly visible players on the political stage in the course of the 1980s.[3] Using the term *beur* (a complicated inversion of the word "Arabe") as a collective denominator, they established numerous sociopolitical organizations, demanded to be treated as first-class citizens with equal rights, and protested against all forms of racism. Aiming at equal treatment but unwilling to play the ethnic card, so to speak, the mainstream nevertheless soon saw the *beurs* as being primarily interested in their own ethnic networks and, moreover, were thought to sympathize with growing worldwide fundamentalism. This idea was nourished by a small minority's vociferous support of the Palestinian movement and of the Iraqi government during the Gulf War in 1991.[4]

It was easy to make the transition from this image to an ethno-cultural explanation of the *beurs'* socially isolated position in French society. Scholars like Emmanuel Todd, for example, argued that the failing assimilation of the *Maghrébins* could be seen as a direct result of their tribal family structure.[5] Stressing, as did many others,[6] the importance of the French secular Republican tradition, he predicted that the assimilation of North Africans was bound to take place at a much slower rate than that of European migrants—if it were to occur at all. The reason he gave was the difference between the two anthropological systems: the North African code stimulated endogamous relationships and solidarity between family members, resulting in the suppression of western values like individualism and women's rights. He even went so far as to interpret the colonial conflict between France and Algeria as being a clash of cultures rather than a fight for power and domination.[7]

To address and test this assumption, it is important to look into the legacy of colonialism, which so deeply influenced the relationship between France and Algeria. First, however, the basics: who came to France, when did they come, and under what circumstances?

## From Algeria to the Hexagon

Unlike other "guest-worker" migrations from North Africa and Asia, the presence of Algerians, and to a lesser extent Moroccans, in France can be traced back to as early as 1912, when there were some four to five thousand predominantly Berber-speaking Algerians from the Kabylia region employed in France. Some two thousand worked in the Marseilles region as dockworkers and laborers in the chemical industries, with another fifteen hundred in the mines and metal industry in the North, and a few hundred in Paris. During World War I, their numbers increased dramatically to more than one hundred thirty-two thousand, consisting of some eighty thousand Algerians, thirty-five thousand Moroccans and eighteen thousand Tunisians. They, as well as Chinese and southeast Asian colonial migrants, were filling the gaps left by the Frenchmen fighting in the trenches, but they were also active in clearing minefields and similar dangerous missions behind enemy lines. In addition, some one hundred seventy-three thousand Algerians were drafted into the army, twenty-five thousand of whom lost their lives during the war.[8]

It is not difficult to understand why Algerians were by far the largest and most visible colonial group in France. Unlike Tunisia and Morocco, which became protectorates in 1881 and 1912, respectively, Algeria was captured from the Ottoman Empire in 1830, and from 1848 onward it was officially a French *département*.[9] Algeria also differed from the other two *Maghreb* countries in that, straight from the beginning, France devised a policy of populating Algeria with French settlers (*colons*) who, backed by the French state, soon took possession of much of Algeria's fertile land and employed the former indigenous peasants and tenants as wage laborers. Although the French firmly established their system of government in Algeria, complete with *arrondissements, communes, prefects,* and *maires,* and placed the Algerian population immediately under French rule, they made a clear distinction, just as they had in most other colonies, between French *citizens,* with political rights and freedom of movement, and French *subjects.*[10] As subjects, Algerians could not vote, had to pay special "Arab" taxes, were subjected to a special, much more repressive, judicial system, and were not allowed to move freely throughout their *département,* let alone travel to the mainland. In order to bring this discriminatory treatment in line with the famous creed "equality, liberty, and brotherhood," the French offered the colonial subjects the prospect of full "assimilation" in the near future, much to the dismay of the settlers, who were opposed to any concessions.

These restrictions on mobility, devised for security reasons and labor-market considerations, explain why migration to France in the nineteenth century was virtually nonexistent. Just before the turn of the century, however, the proto-nationalist "young Algerians" put increasing pressure on the French government to grant citizenship to the Algerian population, or at least to abolish the most blatant discriminatory provisos. Very gradually, the French gave in, and one of their concessions was the Law of 15 July 1914, enacted only six weeks before the outbreak of World War I, granting the Algerians freedom of emigration to the *métropole.* From that moment on, French industry and agriculture could mobilize labor from Algeria as if it were an ordinary French province.[11] The *colons* strongly resented this freedom of movement, afraid as they were of losing their cheap labor force. Furthermore they assumed—not unjustly—that the social and political freedom Algerians would encounter in France would give new impetus to their nationalist movement. The *colons* therefore tried to frustrate migration by administrative measures; in the long run, however, these attempts to hamper the 1914 law failed, and after World War I migration to France became an irrevocable aspect of French-Algerian relations.

British historian Neil MacMaster has shown that Algerian emigration was a very selective process. In contrast to what many migration scholars have long assumed, Algerians who left for France were not those living in the fertile areas where the French settlers dominated; they were primarily men from the mountainous region of Kabylia, east of Algiers (see figure 7). Kabyle were Berber-speakers who had successfully resisted Arabification under Ottoman rule and hence had developed a separate identity, one quite similar to that of the Berbers in neighboring Tunisia and Morocco. The French had also made few inroads in these inaccessible mountains, which they deemed not very attractive from an economic point of view. The economic and social fabric of this region, dotted with small farms, changed only marginally under French colonial rule. The Kabyle peasants, however, did not remain in these

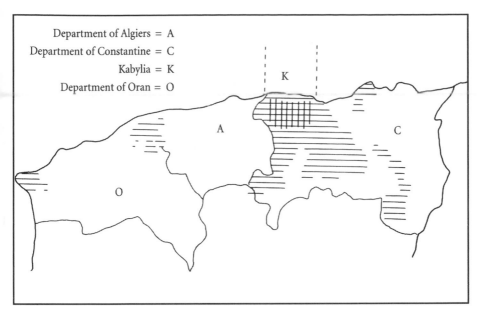

Figure 7. Regions of Emigration in Algeria
Source: MacMaster, *Colonial Migrants*, 35.

mountains for the entire year. As in most mountainous areas throughout the world, the plots were too small to make a living, and a system of seasonal labor had already developed under Ottoman rule, very similar to seasonal migration systems in Europe.[12] This tradition of seasonal migration to the Algerian lowlands explains why, when France became a possible destination from 1914 onward, it was especially attractive to men from Kabylia.

The existing migration system, in which men worked in the fields during the summer and returned home afterward to take care of their own farms, explains why male sojourners initially dominated migration to France.[13] Most Kabyle men, attracted by the relative high wages in French industry, never intended to settle down in France and remained an integral part of their extended families, who expected them to save as much money as possible and thus contribute to the family finances. So despite the long tradition of Algerian migration to metropolitan France, in the first decades of the twentieth century the integration of these migrants into French society was extremely slow. The few Algerians who eventually opted to live in France in the 1920s and 1930s were extremely isolated and came up against widespread racism directed against "Arabs." During the interwar years this discrimination is illustrated in opinion polls that show that North Africans ranked very low compared to other foreigners.[14]

Algerians, like some of the Italian migrants before them, were recruited for the most dangerous and low-wage jobs, a fact that further hampered their integration. Unlike the Italians, however, the Algerians had no middle class to fall back on. As the number of Algerians steadily increased after World War I, with a slight fall during the crisis in the first half of the 1930s (see figure 8), their pattern of work retained its seasonal character, as can be seen in the huge volume of return migration and the extremely uneven sex ratio (3 women to 100 men in 1926).[15]

After 1918, when French employers involved in agriculture and industry set up an organized recruitment scheme for foreign labor,[16] Algerians became possible candidates to replace the dwindling numbers of erstwhile *frontaliers,* seasonal workers from Belgium and Italy. However, their aversion to agricultural labor[17] meant that Algerians could only partly fill the vacancies left by the Belgians. Instead, they set their sights on the metal industry (including the automobile industry in Paris), chemical plants, and the mines.[18] Working and living conditions were often appalling, but as long as they could save enough money and retained their "inner landscape of the native village,"[19] the Algerians came to France undeterred. Just like the labor migrants from Italy

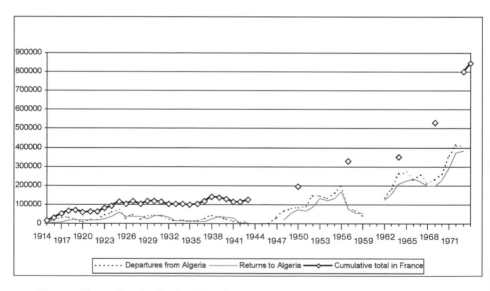

Figure 8. Fluctuations in Algerian Migration, 1914–75
Source: Gillette and Sayad, *L'immigration algérienne en France,* 257–59.

and Poland, the Algerians were conspicuously concentrated in the northeast, in Paris, and in the area around Marseille (see figure 9).

As MacMaster shows, although the Kabylia region may have successfully withstood the disruptive influence of French settlers, in the long run the dynamics of seasonal migration to France changed (and eventually transformed) family finances back home. Until the 1950s, the rotation system of single males prevailed, but very gradually the patterns of chain migration gave way to a form of permanent settlement in France. An important reason was the polarization in the Kabyle villages, where the differences between rich and poor became more apparent. First, there was the inflow of capital through remittances, which increased enormously in the interwar years and which resulted in the accumulation of wealth (invested in houses and land)

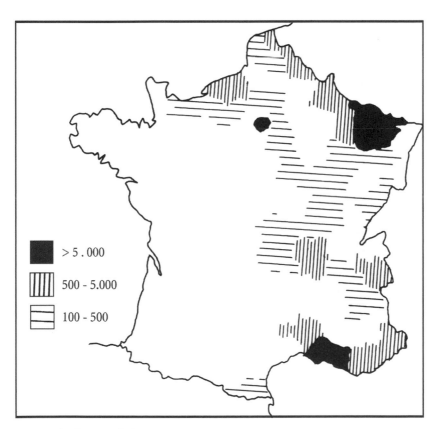

Figure 9. Distribution of Algerians in France, 1937
Source: MacMaster, *Colonial Migrants*, 76.

among a minority of successful migrant families. Consequently, the price of land and property skyrocketed, leaving the few opportunities for the less fortunate to invest in their home region and making family reunion in France an attractive option.[20]

The switch from temporary to a prolonged, sometimes permanent, stay became visible after World War II, when the number of female as well as male migrants swelled. In 1954 Alain Girard, one of the leading demographers who was carrying out research among immigrants at that time, remarked that from 1948 onward, a growing number of Algerian women and children were coming to France. In addition to seven thousand mixed Algerian-European marriages, there were some one thousand Algerian families, half of them in Paris and about 350 in Marseilles. Girard warned people about the social problems that could arise from immigration on this scale.[21] Women still formed a small minority among three hundred thousand Algerians at the time, but it is clear now that Girard predicted the beginning of an irreversible trend and a fundamental shift in the pattern of Algerian emigration.

The most important change was the dwindling rotation system and the growing number of Algerians who decided to settle in France, at least for a number of years, and who were bringing their families with them. This pattern would become common in western Europe among almost all labor migrants from the periphery two decades later. These Algerian emigrants no longer came chiefly from the Berber-speaking region of Kabylia but arrived increasingly from Arab parts of the country as well (Oran, Constantine, and some southern parts of Algeria), regions that, by the 1950s, eventually superseded Kabylia as sending areas.[22] For these migrants, leaving their village and country was not only a means of making and saving money, it was also a way of escaping from a colony where there were no prospects for them and where they were treated like second-class citizens, their lives regulated by the much-criticized *code de l'indigénat.* By going to France they plunged into an egalitarian society, at least in principle. Rotation was still very much alive, but the difference between the numbers of immigrants arriving and departing increased each year, augmenting the numbers of Algerians in France.

Although Algerian migrants and their families were unwanted by the French state and its regulatory institutions (such as the National Immigration Office, or ONI, established in 1945 to further and monitor labor migration), the migration of these colonial subjects could not be stopped. As with the West Indies in Great Britain, Algerians were not foreigners but internal migrants, moving from one *département* to another, as the Bretons and other French internal migrants had done in the past. The changing character of Algerian migration is shown not only in the rise in numbers and length of stay, but it is also apparent in the changing sex ratio. Whereas immediately after the Second World War only 2 in 100 Algerians were women, since 1962 this proportion rose steeply (32 in 100 by 1975) and reached 41 in 100 by 1990.[23]

The steepest rise in Algerian immigration occurred after the war of independence with France (1954 62). Notwithstanding the bitter resentment this war caused among Algerians, both in Africa and in France, the situation in the former colony was so desperate that hundreds of thousands decided to leave. This was made possible by a provision in the Evian accords, a settlement made between the independent state of Algeria and France when the war came to an end in 1962. One of the sections stipulated that all Algerians with valid identity cards were free to move between Algeria and France. The liberal French policy was motivated by the demand for labor—and by French oil interests in the Saharan region.

This era of relatively free migration came to an end in 1973, when the Algerian state put a stop to emigration after an outburst of racial violence against Algerians. France did not really mind, because two years earlier, the Algerian president Houari Boumédienne had nationalized the oil industry, and the western European economy suddenly plunged into a recession.[24] The influx had already slowed down as a result of the French-Algerian agreement ratified in December 1968 which stipulated that "only" thirty-five thousand Algerians per year could enter France, but the real blow to immigration came in 1974, when new migration from North Africa, including that of family members, was severely curtailed. The growth of the Algerian population in France during the last quarter of the twentieth century was therefore due more to fertility than to immigration.[25] Together with the labor migrants from other Maghreb countries like Morocco and Tunisia, the share of migrants from the Maghreb as a percentage of the total immigrant population in France rose spectacularly, from 2.3 percent in 1946 to 38.7 percent in 1990.[26] Thus, at the end of the twentieth century the total population of Algerians, including their offspring in France, amounted to about 1.5 million people; together with Moroccans and Tunisians, almost 2.5 million people from the Maghreb lived in France, constituting 4 percent of the total French population.

## Harkis and Pieds Noir

These population numbers do not include all migrants from Algeria to France. Some eighty thousand Algerians who had collaborated with the

French as soldiers (*harkis*) or civilians (*moghaznis*) were forced to leave the former colony in 1962.[27] This group, whose history bears a striking resemblance to that of the Moluccans in the Netherlands,[28] lived isolated in special camps in the south of France for many years. Their children suffered badly from social isolation, as is illustrated by the 80 percent unemployment rate among *harkis*. Many of these youngsters joined forces with the *beur* movement started by second-generation Algerians. Whereas the parents of the *beurs* bitterly resented, and still do resent, the *harkis* because of their pact with the enemy, their children have obviously found common ground in their political battle against racism and discrimination. Also, almost one million French colonizers and officials, known as *pieds noir* (black feet), left Algeria and settled in the mother country, mainly in southern France.[29] Within this group, the disappointment was immense when French president Charles De Gaulle decided to end the war and give in to the demand for independence. As we will see, a number of *pieds noir* have played a major role in keeping the Algerian trauma alive and in nurturing anti-Arab sentiments.

## The Heart of Darkness

In September 1983 Jean Marie Le Pen's xenophobic nationalist party got 17 percent of the votes in municipal elections in the small town of Dreux, west of Paris, and also won votes in other cities like Toulon, Roubaix, and Grenoble.[30] From that time on, the *Front National* became a forceful new player in the French political landscape, attracting between nine and eleven percent of the voters in various nationwide elections.[31] This electoral victory may have been unprecedented, but the ideas of Le Pen and his *Front National* were not. By associating "immigration" with North Africans, Muslims, and social problems, and at the same time appealing to deep-rooted colonial stereotypes, Le Pen revealed the dark side of the French discourse on immigration. Although the Republican creed stated that, in principle, all immigrants were welcome as long as they subscribed to the secular Republican ideal, there was also a parallel tradition, a France in which racist notions about non-Europeans thrived. Scholars who juxtapose the Republican French and the ethno-nationalist tradition in Germany, however, have largely ignored this tradition.[32]

Recently, a number of studies have stressed that the anti-Algerian attitudes among the French population can only be understood by looking at the colonial past. One of the most explicit advocates of this view is Neil

MacMaster, who convincingly argues that it is not enough to focus on the Algerian war of independence; in addition, we need to unearth the roots of the colonial experience. That is where we find the real heart of darkness. Once they had expelled the Ottoman rulers in 1830, the French implemented a comprehensive colonization program in which French farmers (*colons*) and administrators played a key role. When, in 1848, Algeria became a French *département,* French colonizers took the opportunity to buy or confiscate large stretches of land, especially in the low-lying areas, reducing the Algerian peasants to wage-laborers.[33] Although they were French subjects, Algerians were second-rate citizens and subjected to severe controls over their mobility. This made traveling or migrating virtually impossible and guaranteed French farmers an abundance of cheap labor. As in all colonies, the French could only maintain and justify this discriminatory regime by resorting to racist tactics. Algerians, or *Arabes,* were deemed less civilized (or downright uncivilized) and racially inferior and could therefore not be granted the same rights as French citizens.[34]

Not everyone in France shared these deterministic ideas, and from the end of the nineteenth century progressive voices pleaded for more autonomy and the granting of French citizenship to Algerians. When in 1914 the Algerians received the freedom to migrate to France—much against the will of the *colons*—these racist ideas about Algerians also crossed the Mediterranean and were activated in metropolitan France. Unlike the Italians or Poles, who arrived during the same period, people were not open-minded about the Algerians. From the very beginning, they were stereotyped as dirty and uncivilized *Arabes* who constituted a threat to the French population. They may have been useful for dirty, heavy work, but as soon as they left their isolated barracks and sheds and mingled with the mainstream French population, people's reactions became overtly hostile. This stigma can be traced back to two ideas rooted in the colonial context: apart from being portrayed as dirty, stupid, and uncivilized, Algerians were above all else seen as violent, criminal, and molesters of women and children.[35] These allegations were backed up by an incident in November 1923, when a mentally ill Algerian migrant murdered two Frenchmen in Paris, setting off large-scale riots in the 15th *arrondissement* (where four thousand Algerians who worked in the nearby Citroën automobile factory lived) and led to the lynching of one Algerian worker. More important, however, was the role of the press, which massively reproduced the anti-Algerian stereotype. As one of the leading Parisian newspapers wrote: "The crimes and offences committed by Arabs are increasing . . . almost all the rabble which infests us is foreign."[36]

According to MacMaster, the events in the first half of the 1920s were crucial in firmly rooting the anti-Arab stereotype in France. He stresses the important role of colonial pressure groups who opposed the freedom of migration and who convinced the French government in 1925 to establish a special police force to control and monitor the Algerians in France.[37] Georges Mauco's study on foreign labor, published in 1932, traces this anti-Algerian sentiment. Although the author remains rather benign about immigrants in general (especially those from Belgium, Italy, and Poland), his tone changes markedly when he discusses the "Arabs," who numbered about seventy thousand in the mid-1920s. According to Mauco, they were lazy, feeble workers, likely to commit crimes, and their values and traditions were diametrically opposed to those of French civilization.[38]

These malevolent ideas about North Africans were confirmed by opinion polls and reflected in the work-suitability rankings of their industrial supervisors, who consistently relegated the "Arabs" to the bottom of the list. Their ratings showed little improvement in the following decades. In 1951 the National Demographic Institute (INED) carried out an opinion poll to measure the extent of sympathy shown by the French population toward ten nationalities: Algerians ended in the ninth position.[39] In a similar poll in 1985, "Arabs" had moved down one rung to the lowest position, falling behind (using the labels from the poll) Muslims, Asians, and Jews, and far behind Antilleans and South African Blacks.[40]

To highlight the specific nature of the French case, it is instructive to draw a brief comparison between other European countries and their colonial migrants. What makes the Algerians special is a combination of three factors: Algerians came to France in large numbers *before* the Second World War; the negative stereotype of Algerians among colonial pressure groups influenced politicians and policymakers; and a racist stigma surrounding Algerians developed in the mother country before 1940. Other colonial powers, or former colonial powers, faced a different reality. After the war and the horrors of the Holocaust, official racism in western Europe was strictly taboo, thus making the reproduction of colonial stereotypes in the "mother countries" much more difficult. As a result, Eurasians in the Netherlands and West Indians in Great Britain encountered far less prejudice, at least where official reactions were concerned, after the Second World War than the Algerians had experienced twenty-five years earlier. Although anti-Caribbean racism also flourished across the Channel, policymakers did not openly support it and established no special services to control the ex-colonials. Finally, ex-colonial officials and others did not lead a lobby to try to extend colonial controls on the migrants—quite the opposite, as the British Colonial Office's position in the 1950s shows.[41] This negative attitude towards Algerians after the Second World War persisted: anti-Algerian sentiments among broad segments of the French population, including policymakers and politicians, had not changed, and "crimes committed by Algerians" were still widely publicized. A telling example can be found in the prestigious newspaper *Le Monde,* which in 1949 labeled the Algerian presence as a "national problem," and thus reinforced the image of Algerian migrants as child molesters and perpetrators of violent crime. Another sign that nothing had changed was the establishment in 1945 of a new police branch (the *Brigade des agressions et violences*), established to control Algerians in France and gather intelligence on political activities.

In this hostile atmosphere, Algerians in Africa and in France were not passive victims. During the interwar period, national consciousness among Algerians had already started to grow. Supported by the French communist party *Étoile nord-africaine* (ENA), the "North African star" saw the light of day in 1926, lead by Messali Hadj and Hadj Ali Abdelkader. This movement, which the French soon outlawed, strove for an independent Algeria, Tunisia, and Morocco. After the Second World War, the call for independence grew stronger by the day, although the nationalists themselves were split into two factions and were engaged in a bloody feud. The strongest party was the *Front de la Libération Nationale* (FLN), which started the war for independence on November 1, 1954. The FLN soon extended its sphere of influence to include migrants in France; in its struggle for hegemony, the FLN not only fought the French (both in Algeria and in France), but also the competing nationalist *Mouvement National Algérien* (MNA). Between 1956 and 1961, almost four thousand people were killed and some eight thousand wounded in this internecine struggle, which was fought mainly in the streets of Paris, Lyon, and Marseilles.[42] The FLN was very successful in gaining total control over the Algerian migrants, whom the FLN pressured into paying for the revolutionary cause. The FLN was also successful in their attempts to isolate the migrants from French society. Just like the Irish nationalists in the nineteenth century, the FLN was vehemently opposed to integration and hoped that, in the end, most Algerian migrants would return home. Furthermore, the FLN was responsible for terrorist attacks in France (their second front), which led to the deaths of 150 policemen and dozens of soldiers, contributing to the decline of their already negative image.

During this time, the FLN encouraged the migrants to take an anti-French stance, which virtually halted the integration process. In reaction, the French state used an extremely repressive form of retaliation. During the Algerian war, thousands of migrants were arrested on suspicion of supporting the FLN, and while the war continued to escalate in Algeria, with horrendous acts of atrocity on both sides, the French police acted ruthlessly. The lowest point was reached in October 1961, when the Paris police and French special forces crushed a peaceful demonstration of tens of thousands of Algerians marching in favor of independence. Without provocation, the police killed at least two hundred Algerians, a number of them being knocked unconscious and then thrown into the Seine. In the weeks following this demonstration, the state more or less gave the police carte blanche to kill and batter Algerians.[43]

## The Algerian Syndrome

When the war ended in 1962 and Algeria became independent, the battle scars were deep and lasting on both sides. On the one hand, the migrants, deeply influenced by the anti-integration policy of the FLN and traumatized by French repression, found themselves in an extremely isolated position and facing discrimination (most of them were already forced to live in shanty towns, or *bidonvilles,* on the outskirts of the big cities). On the other hand, a million French colonizers (the *pieds noir*) had lost their property and were forced to return to France. Together with almost half a million French soldiers who had fought in Algeria and who had been exposed to extreme anti-Algerian propaganda, they constituted a large and influential part of French society. Many of them were frustrated by the loss of Algeria and held a deep grudge against the French politicians and the Algerians themselves, whom they held responsible. It was therefore no coincidence that the movement opposing the presence of Algerians in France, whose numbers had almost doubled during the war, should mainly attract ex-servicemen and *pieds noir.* Both Le Pen, a former paratrooper who fought in Algeria, and the populist politician Pierre Poujade had "Algerian roots" and played a key role in the problematization of Algerians (or "Arabs") from the 1960s onward. In 1969 Poujade, for example, warned against an "Arab invasion" and supported the secret, extremist *Organisation Armée Secrète* (OAS), which was responsible for a number of murderous terrorist attacks against Algerians in France during the early 1970s.[44] Frustrated by the loss of Algeria, the OAS and many *pieds noir* considered the presence of Algerians on French soil as the "ultimate insult," which justified getting rid of them in any way they could. Apart from political arguments, the anti-Algerian rhetoric was based mainly on the conviction that these Muslim "Arabs" were alien to French civilization and could never assimilate.

The anti-Algerian campaign initiated by *pieds noir* followers was taken over by parts of the French population from the end of the 1960s on. Influenced by anti-Arab sentiments, many French people saw North African migrants (Algerians as well as Tunisians and Moroccans) as intruders. Just like guest workers in other western European countries, they lived in isolated, squalid conditions, and when unemployment rose after 1973, they became an easy target. The anti-immigrant feelings in France were much more aggressive than in the Netherlands, Belgium, and Great Britain and are largely explained by the "Algerian syndrome." Small incidents, such as a demonstration of two hundred illegal workers in the southern town of Grasse, easily escalated into large-scale riots and attacks on North African migrants. Between 1971 and 1977, at least seventy Algerians were killed in such incidents, especially in the south of France, where many Algerians, as well as *pieds noir,* were concentrated.[45]

In the 1980s, when Le Pen's *Front National* had taken over the role of the OAS and other extremist organizations, the aggression against "Arabs," or *Maghrebi,* increased even further, with some two hundred North Africans killed in various attacks and incidents.[46] It was in that same period that the *beurs,* young Algerians and other second-generation North Africans, organized numerous marches against racism and discrimination and became involved in initiatives such as *SOS-Racisme* (1984) and *France Plus* (1985). Simultaneously, other second-generation youths, especially boys, engaged in riots against police harassment in the *banlieues* of major towns.

It would be misleading, however, to attribute the problematization of North Africans in France wholly to the extreme right. As Maxim Silverman and others show, politicians from the left to the right have played an important role in associating people from the Maghreb with social problems, thus narrowing the problems linked with immigration to this specific category of migrants. The dominant theme in political discourse is that these newcomers are much more difficult to incorporate than other nationalities and more difficult than migrants in the past.[47] Even the communists, who traditionally defended the interests of migrants—including those of North African descent—have chosen the side of the native French working class and contributed to the dichotomy between "them" and "us."[48]

Although a number of scholars have rightly criticized the social construction of North Africans as problematic migrants, it is undeniable that many of these migrants and their children are in a very difficult position, as they suffer extremely high levels of unemployment, delinquency, discrimination, and isolation from mainstream French society. It is too easy, therefore, to dismiss the attention given to these problems by politicians and scholars as a racist or prejudiced reflex. Nevertheless, to understand the specific path of integration taken by Algerians in France, we have to look beyond the homogeneous gloomy picture of the North African presence and focus on developments made over the years in the various domains of integration. Only then will we be able to assess the extent to which this picture is correct and how the Algerians in France are doing in comparison with other "problematic" second-generation migrants like the West Indians in Great Britain and the Turks in Germany.

Although it is clear to most French politicians and policymakers that the second generation of migrants from the Maghreb face huge problems, it is very difficult to obtain representative data on their situation. This is the result of the schizophrenic French attitude toward ethnic diversity: everyone is aware of the fact that the integration of North Africans is moving very slowly, and in everyday life the "Arabs" constitute a very real social category, but it is nevertheless deemed wrong to make them visible statistically or as a policy category.[49] The dominant French Republican tradition of integration through national institutions like schools, the army, churches, unions, and political parties has created an ideological revulsion toward ethnic categorizations —even toward groups that are considered to be unfit for assimilation.

The five-yearly census only differentiates between French by birth, French by acquisition (naturalization), and foreigners. Because most children of foreigners born in France almost automatically become French, they do not show up in any form of statistics. Furthermore, in surveys based on the country of birth for the parent, it is often impossible to distinguish between first-generation Algerians migrants and *pieds noir*, because members of these groups were all born in Algeria.[50] Thanks to the efforts of demographers like Michèle Tribalat, who, after much opposition and debate,[51] was given permission to create a representative sample of the 1992 census and break it down for ethnicity, there are now data available on the second generation in most of the domains that interest us here. For the period before and after 1992, however, we have to rely on scattered and impressionistic evidence.[52]

## Settlement and Segregation

The housing history of postwar labor migrants in western Europe is characterized by a more or less similar pattern. As the "guest workers" were initially predominantly men who intended to return home and who tried to maximize their profits by spending as little as possible, many were content with cheap, substandard lodgings. It was only when it became clear that they would stay much longer and have their families join them that camps and boarding houses made way for cheap housing, often in the less attractive parts of towns. France is no exception to this general rule, but compared to Germany and the Netherlands, the extent of segregation in France seems to be much more pronounced, evidenced by the high concentrations of North Africans in the rundown suburbs of French cities.[53]

This deplorable situation, especially for North Africans, is not a recent development, but it has become a structural aspect of the Algerian settlement process in France since the 1950s. Most Algerians found their way to Paris, Lyon, or Marseilles, with a few making their way to industrial cities in the north, such as Roubaix and Lille. Arriving earlier and in much greater numbers than the Turkish and North African guest workers in neighboring countries, the Algerians faced a huge housing shortage and a largely hostile population, especially during the Algerian war (1954–62). As a result, most of them had no alternative but to squat in large-scale shantytowns (*bidonvilles*) on the edge of Paris and other cities. Others rented rooms for high prices in specific neighborhoods, such as the 18th *arrondissement* in Paris, Belsunce in Marseilles, and La Place du Pont in Lyon. These appalling *bidonvilles* lacked such basic provisions as sewers and water pipes, and resembled the shantytowns of present-day cities in developing countries. The 1966 census listed 119 of these *bidonvilles* around Paris, with 46,827 inhabitants, the majority of whom were from North Africa and whose segregation index at that time was three times higher than that of the Portuguese.[54] The isolated character of these residential areas is aptly summarized by the geographer Paul White: "The almost absence of French made these areas of exclusively immigrant residence at a scale and level of concentration that have occurred nowhere else in Western European cities in the postwar years."[55]

Programs for slum clearance, such as SONACOTRA,[56] launched in 1956, were largely ineffective, and it was not until the *Debré* law eight years later that the *bidonvilles* slowly disappeared and council housing in the suburbs took their place. These *Habitation à Loyer Modérée* (HLM), or low-rent housing, consisted of large-scale, high-rise developments in the suburban districts of Paris, Lyon, and Marseilles. Soon these estates became virtually synonymous with immigrant quarters and although, strictly speaking, they do not constitute ghettos, as they do not consist of migrants from the same country, the North African (Algerian) presence often amounted to more than 50 percent and in some buildings could reach 80 or 90 percent.[57] This development has transformed these suburbs so much that the French word for suburb (*banlieue*) is nowadays immediately associated with ghetto-like residential areas peopled by North African immigrants and their descendants.[58] Although Algerian networks, often determined by local and regional loyalties, were close knit and may have encouraged high concentrations of their fellow countrymen, it is important to realize that the specific *banlieue* problem was largely stimulated by national policies. In the beginning of the 1970s, foreigners were assigned explicitly to the HLM areas, also called "Grands Ensembles," preferably in boroughs governed by communists, without any form of extra subsidy given to the local authorities to deal with the influx.[59] The effect was that white residents moved out, and the Communist Party increasingly distanced itself from these migrants. It was the Algerians in particular who came to depend on these HLM areas, much more than any other migrant group. Even the Portuguese, similar in class and background and with the added difficulty of arriving later, stood a better chance of finding housing outside these isolated quarters than the Algerians did. Instead of explaining this ghetto formation in terms of an ingrained preference among Algerians to live together, it would be more convincing to interpret it in terms of racism and discrimination.[60] This concentration in the HLM estates added to the growing dichotomy between the native French (*Français de souche*) and the *Maghrébin* immigrants.

Large-scale riots between second generation youths and the police in the *banlieues* of Paris, Lyon, and Marseilles in the 1980s, and the ensuing discussion about ghetto formation in France,[61] finally prompted initiatives to redevelop these suburbs,[62] which at that time had changed to virtually no-go areas with exceptionally high unemployment rates, drug addiction, and widespread crime, especially among Algerian boys. It remains to be seen to how quickly and successfully the French authorities will succeed in redressing this situation.

## Schooling and the Labor Market

One of the most famous Republican institutions responsible for the integration process of newcomers to France is the school.[63] The children of immigrants may come from very different cultural backgrounds, but at school they all learn French and the fundamental values of *liberté, fraternité,* and *égalité.* Thus, schools played a central role in the assimilation of large and various groups of immigrants in France's past, such as the Italians, Poles, Belgians, and Spanish. Considering the unskilled and illiterate background of their parents,[64] their extreme residential segregation, and the discrimination they encounter in everyday life, Algerian youth might be expected to do much worse than their French peers and other immigrants such as the Portuguese and Italians. In the mid-1980s, studies on the school performance of second-generation Algerians were indeed rather pessimistic, blaming pervasive racism and the cultural clash between the home and the (French) school culture.[65]

Surprisingly, these gloomy predictions, often based on in-depth interviews with Algerian youth in specific local settings, are only partly confirmed in the research by Michèle Tribalat.[66] The outcomes in her book *Faire France* ("making France"), which summarizes the main results of her 1992 survey on the social and economic situations of various immigrant groups and their children, are revealing. She points out that the starting position of the first-generation Algerians in France (even if one ignores the bad feelings caused by the Algerian war) was very bad, illustrated by the high proportion of illiterates, both men and women (41 and 44 percent, respectively) among them—rates which were much higher than for Turks (8 and 31 percent) or Portuguese (8 and 7 percent).[67] Algerian migrants had the lowest level of human capital, immediately followed by Moroccans, whereas in educational terms the other "usual suspects" (the Turks and Africans) are far ahead of them. When we then look at the language spoken before migration, it appears that (notwithstanding the fact that Algeria was a French province) at least one in five migrants spoke only their own language (Arabic or Berber) and that only one-third spoke French as their mother tongue— even fewer than the Spanish and many fewer than Sub-Saharan Africans (54 percent).[68] Of the migrants who arrived before their sixteenth year, however, 92 percent have learned to read and write in French. The most spectacular shift took place within the second generation, whose members have refused to learn any Arabic or Berber and speak French almost exclusively; the same can be said of Spanish and Portuguese youths as well.[69]

This shift to French is partly reflected in the school results of Algerians and Moroccans, who perform at about the same level as Portuguese and Spanish youngsters but much worse than that of their French peers (see tables 19 and 20). It is striking that, in contrast to the West Indians in Great Britain and Turks in Germany (and the Netherlands as well), Algerian girls are doing only slightly better than boys.[70]

When we control for class background, however, the differences between Algerian immigrants and their French peers decrease considerably, although less so for girls than for boys. A similar picture arises when we focus on graduation figures. Drop out rates are high among Algerians (23 percent for men

*Table 19.* School Levels of the Male Second Generation, 1992 (Born 1961–67)

| Level | Algerians (%) | Portuguese (%) | Spanish (%) | French (%) |
|---|---|---|---|---|
| Primary | 1 | 0 | 0 | 6 |
| Advanced | 3 | 2 | 1 | 2 |
| Vocational (lower) | 11 | 13 | 11 | 13 |
| Vocational (higher) | 54 | 62 | 56 | 40 |
| Professional | 14 | 4 | 12 | 19 |
| University | 17 | 19 | 20 | 26 |

Source: Tribalat, *Faire France,* 147.

*Table 20.* School Levels of the Female Second Generation, 1992 (Born 1961–67)

| Level | Algerians (%) | Portuguese (%) | Spanish (%) | French (%) |
|---|---|---|---|---|
| Primary | 1 | 0 | 0 | 1 |
| Advanced | 8 | 7 | 2 | 4 |
| Vocational (lower) | 11 | 7 | 8 | 7 |
| Vocational (higher) | 50 | 61 | 37 | 28 |
| Professional | 19 | 9 | 18 | 25 |
| University | 21 | 16 | 35 | 35 |

Source: Tribalat, *Faire France,* 147

and 16 percent for women), but not higher than for the Portuguese, and the gap with the French (16 percent for men and 10 percent for women) is not dramatic. However, the proportion of Algerian students with diplomas that open the road to higher education is about two-thirds that of their French peers. The conclusion from these data is that Algerians are doing less well —but better than one would expect if one takes into account their parents' humble background and their marginal position in French society. So far, the reputation of the French school as a key instrument in the integration process has not been tarnished.

## The Missing Link: From School to Work

Many Algerians and other North Africans may have the right education, but it is no guarantee for finding a job in the French labor market; this becomes clear if we look at the vast differences in unemployment rates. Also, when we look at men who, in 1992, were unemployed for at least a year after leaving school, the figures for Algerians are twice as high as for the Portuguese (50 percent compared to 25 percent).[71] Neither the human capital of the first-generation migrants nor the school results clearly explain the large differences in unemployment between the two groups. If these variables were decisive, the Portuguese and the Algerians would be in roughly the same league. This, however, is not the case: unemployment rates among young Algerians (40 percent) are twice as high as for Spanish and Portuguese men and women. It is striking that second-generation Algerian women—in contrast to their Portuguese counterparts—are not doing better than the men.[72]

Algerian migrants and their children face much greater obstacles in the labor market, just as other North Africans, especially the Moroccans, do.[73] Also, compared with migrants from Turkey and sub-Saharan Africa who arrived before age sixteen, the prospects of North Africans are significantly bleaker. This incongruity between human capital, in terms of rising education levels and opportunity in the labor market, also applies to people from the second generation who, at the time of the research in 1992, were in their twenties and had worked for at least a few years.[74] Although Algerians, especially men, have on average managed to move into the higher segments of the labor market (and even more so than the native French from working-class families and second-generation Portuguese men), their unemployment rates in 1992 were again much higher: 16 percent, compared to 4 percent for the Portuguese and 8 percent for the working-class French.[75] In other words, many sons of Algerian migrants have left the working class but have found it far more difficult to achieve upward social mobility. The picture in 1992 was that many who were then in their twenties failed to obtain jobs at all, while others ran a far greater risk of losing their jobs again.

Finally, it is important to note that although Algerian women were educated to a modest level, their chances of finding jobs were significantly greater. The exceptional position of the Algerian second generation, largely explained by the specific relationship between the Algerians and the French, is therefore highly gender specific. If discrimination by French employers is the main cause of the disproportionately high unemployment rates for Algerians as a whole, it is clear that men are seen as being even less desirable than women. This phenomenon is not exceptional, since we have seen similar developments in the case of the Irish and the West Indians in Great Britain. Before reaching a general conclusion about why Algerians are much less desirable than the average migrant (even Turks and black Africans), we have to take a short look at two other important dimensions on the integration spectrum.

## Social Contacts and Mixed Marriages

In light of the exclusion of many young *Maghrébins* from the labor market at the beginning of the 1990s, and taking into account their extremely high residential segregation, one would expect North Africans of the second generation to have retreated massively into their own ethnic group. The social contacts of youngsters from various immigrant groups in France, however, show a much more differentiated picture. The most open attitude toward native French peers is found among the Spanish, followed at some distance by the Portuguese. At the other end of the spectrum, however, we do not find Algerians and Moroccans, but rather Turks and Asians, who stick together much more.[76] Evidently *Maghrébins,* notwithstanding the fact that they experience significantly greater discrimination, feel more attracted to French mainstream society, which is reflected in their eagerness to socialize with the native French population.

The marriage market is quite similar. If we limit ourselves to migrants from Muslim countries, the percentage of arranged marriages among the second generation has decreased in all groups,[77] but the decrease is much faster among Moroccans and Algerians than among Turks or Pakistanis. The latter groups also have a stronger preference for marrying co-ethnics, whereas men and women of Spanish and Portuguese parents usually choose French partners; the Algerians are somewhere in between.[78]

The willingness to find partners outside their own ethnic and religious group is especially manifest among male second-generation *Maghrébins,* although for many in the early 1990s an official marriage was still a bridge

*Table 21.* Percentage of Mixed First Marriages in France among Spanish, Portuguese, and Algerian Migrants, 1992

|  | Men | | | Women | | |
|---|---|---|---|---|---|---|
|  | 1 | 2 | 3 | 1 | 2 | 3 |
| Spanish | 18 | 58 | 66 | 25 | 65 | 65 |
| Portuguese | 15 | 40 | 59 | 6 | 31 | 47 |
| Algerians | 15 | 17 | — | 9 | 9 | 15 |
| Algerians (cohabitating unmarried couples) | 20 | 25 | 50 | 10 | 14 | 24 |

Note: 1 = arrived in France older than age 15; 2 = arrived in France younger than age 16; 3 = born in France from two immigrant parents.
Source: Tribalat, *Faire France,* 69 and 77.

too far. The growing tendency of Algerians, especially men, to choose French partners to cohabit with, however, may prove to be a major gateway to a more exogamous marriage pattern in the near future. This is especially likely when they manage to overcome the barriers in the labor market, because research targeting Algerians married to native French partners shows that the more highly educated and successful Algerians have greater chances of marrying outside their own group. It is interesting to note that more than 50 percent of the marriages between second-generation Algerians and partners born in Algeria end in divorce, perhaps because the French-born partners are much more acculturated.[79] Table 21 shows a significant gender gap, with Algerian men being more inclined to marry outside their group—a difference noticed among the children of North African migrants throughout western Europe.

## Islam and Social Mobilization

In the beginning of the 1980s, the children of North African migrants—the vast majority of whom were living in isolated, rundown estates in the *banlieues* (suburbs) of Paris, Lyon, and Marseilles—took to the streets to vent their fury at the police, who, in their eyes, treated North Africans as criminals and second-class citizens. The immediate cause was often an arrest or some other injustice carried out against one of their number, action seen as yet another example of racial harassment. The riots nearly always ended in the large-scale pillaging of stores and violence against the police. In this respect the situation of the North Africans, or "Arabs," as they were often called, is akin to the West Indians in the United Kingdom. There was one important difference, however: North Africans, and especially the Algerians (the largest national group among them), were not only former colonials, but they also differed from the French population in religion, being almost exclusively Muslim. This meant they posed a double-edged "threat," making them the ultimate outsiders whose assimilation was deemed extremely difficult, if not impossible.

This image of Algerians as an alien element in French society, so successfully exploited by the *Front National,* was strengthened by the first generation's refusal to adopt French nationality. In 1990 less than 13 percent of the first generation had acquired French citizenship, whereas more than half of the Spaniards and Italians had been naturalized. Only Moroccans (11 percent) and Turks (less than 8 percent) had lower rates.[80] Holding on to their Algerian nationality was one of the legacies of the Algerian War. In the course of the 1990s, however, the first generation increasingly gave up Algerian citizenship,[81] which might be a sign that after half a century, the sharp edges of a very traumatic past have gradually softened.

For the second generation, French citizenship was not an issue, as most of them automatically became French by birth. Here the hotly debated issue is the Algerian adherence to Islam. Xenophobic movements, such as the *Front National,* in addition to more mainstream political parties, have become very concerned about the rise of Islam in France, especially among young North Africans. Around 1990, at the time of the Rushdie affair, the first Gulf War, and the radicalization of the Algerian Islamic movement *Front Islamique du Salut* (FIS), France officially housed some three million Muslims, more than a thousand mosques, and some six hundred religious associations, making Islam the second-largest religion in France.[82] At the time, many feared that the second-generation Algerians and other *beurs* would convert massively to extremist Islam und thus become a kind of fifth column.[83] So far, however, this fear does not seem to have been realized. In 1992 more than two-thirds of Algerians were either not religious at all (30 percent) or not practicing (38 percent), and support for the fundamentalist Algerian FIS movement did not exceed 10 percent.[84] The lack of interest in religion among young Algerians is remarkably high compared to other groups (see table 22).

Among Algerian migrants from Kabylia, about one-quarter of the total Algerian population in France, adherence to Islam is even lower. Although many still hold on to some aspects of Islam, such as the annual period of fasting, Ramadan, and certain prescribed dietary restrictions, very few Algerians go to mosques to worship. Of the Algerian boys born in France, only

*Table 22.* Percentage of Second-generation Migrants Who Report Being Nonreligious or Nonpracticing, 1992

|  | Children from endogamous marriages | Children from mixed marriages |
| --- | --- | --- |
| Southeast Asians | 48 | 66 |
| Algerians | 44 | 75 |
| Spanish | 41 | 57 |
| Moroccans | 31 | 62 |
| Turks | 27 | 67 |
| Portuguese | 27 | 60 |
| Black Africans | 20 | 39 |

Source: Tribalat, *Faire France,* 90.

1 in 10 prays on a regular basis, and another 2 in 10 pray occasionally; girls are slightly more religious.[85] In fact, the *beurs* show few signs of developing an Arab or Muslim subculture, whatever that may be. Instead, by their oppositional stance, they show how deeply they have been influenced by French culture, or in the words of the French scholar Olivier Roy: "... by the very violence of their attitudes, they show a fascination for the society that appears to exclude them. The culture of the urban-zone *beurs* has virtually no Islamic constituent. It is a subculture that functions along the lines of popular culture by pirating the dominant culture."[86]

The fear of Muslim fundamentalism arising among Algerians, or North Africans in general, is therefore unfounded. And if fundamentalism should get a greater hold on the offspring of Algerian migrants in the future, these data make it clear that such a development cannot be explained by an ingrained cultural tendency, but would rather be the result of frustration resulting from the experiences of exclusion and discrimination they encounter in French society.

## Conclusion

It is easy and tempting to interpret the unenviable social position of the Algerians and their descendants in France as the outcome of a failing integration process. After half a century, the French still view them primarily as an alien group, and many still live in segregated and rundown parts of major cities. Moreover, their children encounter widespread discrimination, often drop out of school, are disproportionately unemployed, and are involved in a violent, oppositional street culture. Indeed, theirs is not exactly a happy ending. It is tempting to explain this situation by referring to the cultural factors of Islam, tribal family structures, or a mix of these two.

Both interpretations are unjustified. To say that the slow assimilation process is due to the specific North African family structure, which is diametrically opposed to Western liberal values, has not been confirmed. Where the first generation is concerned, it seems that adherence to Islam, predilection for endogamous marriages, and restrictions on the role of women are indeed rooted in North African culture in the broadest sense of the term. This does not imply, however, that this culture is so static or so strong that it will produce a closed, inward-looking ethnic group. This becomes clear when we look at the second generation, which shows numerous signs of embracing the key aspects of French culture, even in the face of widespread racism and discrimination. Furthermore, it is remarkable how radically the *Maghrébin* youth have rejected the core elements of their parent's culture: their language, demographic behavior, and religion.

Instead of an essentialist anthropological explanation, the arguments put forward by MacMaster and Hargreaves, who both focus on the traumatic colonial relationship between France and Algeria, are more convincing. They give a plausible explanation of how and why the racist anti-"Arab" stereotype came to be firmly rooted in French culture even before the majority of the migrants settled. They also explain the reluctant attitude of many Algerian migrants toward integration, who were seen as betraying their own country after the bloody war of Independence. Combined with generally unfavorable developments in the housing and labor markets, which apply to other former guest workers throughout western Europe as well, the political factor seems forceful enough to explain the peculiar path of integration followed by Algerians in France.[87]

This brings us, finally, to the unfounded assumption that Algerian integration has largely failed. Michèle Tribalat's important and pioneering research in the early 1990s shows that, notwithstanding severe handicaps that resulted from discrimination and mutual distrust, integration has moved forward in all domains. Although it is regrettable that in the period 1970–90, we have only one measuring point (1992), Tribalat's meticulous research maps a number of fundamental differences between the first- and the second-generation Algerians and convincingly demonstrates that Algerians increasingly resemble the French, especially where cultural norms are concerned. Not only do the children distance themselves from their parent's culture, but they also manage to attain relatively good school results, given the largely illiterate background of the first generation. In fact, Algerians do not perform much worse at school than their French peers from similar backgrounds.[88] The only major problems that arise are the high levels of unemployment among young Algerians (men more than women), partly caused by discrimination, and the oppositional, violent, and criminal subculture among part of the French-born male youths. Due to the lack of data later than 1992, it remains unclear whether this will lead to some of the second-generation Algerians forming an ethnically colored underclass. What *is* clear, however, is that the culture and religion of second-generation Algerians do not constitute a stumbling block, and that the old notion of unassimilable "Arabs" can definitively discarded.

# Conclusion

This book was born out of a mixture of irritation and inspiration: *irritation* caused by current public discussion on the allegedly failing integration of non-Western migrants in western Europe, a debate characterized by a one-sided and ahistorical view of the long-term settlement process of migrants past and present; *inspiration* gained from the interesting exchange of ideas on the similarities and differences between old and new migrants in the United States, a discussion which has produced a number of important new insights into the integration process of migrants in liberal democracies on both sides of the Atlantic. By shifting the focus of this debate to western Europe and using it as a starting point for comparing "large and problematic" groups of immigrants then and now, I had three aims in mind. First, I wanted to map out the key aspects of the long-term integration process, both past and present, and thereby reach a better understanding of the integration of immigrants and the specific way in which integration has developed in the western European context in contrast to the United States. Second, I have tried to bridge the gap between historians and social scientists who specialize in migration and ethnic studies. It is a gulf that has been repeatedly lamented[1] but shows few signs of narrowing. Finally, I have attempted to offer a balanced contribution to the public debate on new migrants, by stressing the (semi-autonomous) dynamics of the settlement process, the highly differentiated outcomes, and the danger of making easy generalizations. Thus, this book not only questions assumptions shared by those who feel threatened by the "new Barbarians," it also criticizes claims made by multiculturalists who believe that integration will follow different paths from those taken in the past, and that assimilation is an unlikely outcome.

In a recent publication, American historian Joel Perlmann and sociologist Roger Waldinger summarized the American debate on differences and similarities between immigrants then and now with the comment that we tend to be too optimistic about the past and too pessimistic about the present.[2] If we consider the last one-and-a-half centuries, I believe that this conclusion is also relevant for western European immigration.[3] Inasmuch as people were aware of the existence of the "big three" in the past (Irish, Poles, and Italians), they often had the impression that their integration had taken place far more smoothly than that of comparable groups in the present. However, in Western Europe, unlike in the United States, any awareness of first wave of immigration is often lacking. It is true that, especially when we compare Poles and Turks in Germany, some scholars display an awareness of similarities and point out that the road to integration for old migrants was slow. But on the whole, there seems to be no overall notion that western Europe's past provides a fruitful ground for comparisons with "large and problematic" groups in the present.

Following Gérard Noiriel, Dirk Hoerder, Leslie Page Moch, and others,[4] I have argued that this lack of historical consciousness is caused by the specific construction of national histories in which immigration just does not fit. The self-image of the United States is dominated by the heroic immigrant heritage, whereas in western Europe the idea of stable and static national populations, disturbed only by occasional refugee movements, still has the upper hand. This also explains why there is a stronger conviction in Europe than in America that the mass immigration witnessed after World War II is unprecedented and will lead to different integration processes. What, then has the discussion in this book yielded, in terms of similarities and differences? What does this book have to offer to the American debate from which it has profited so much, and to what extent does it help to make sense of the contemporary integration debate in Europe?

## Similarities

### THE THREAT

The comparison in this book between the "big three" immigrant populations of the past with the groups (just as large and perceived to be just as problematic) in the second half of the twentieth century has produced primarily a "feast of recognition," both in terms of the nature of the threat and the process of structural integration. The examples of the Irish, Polish, and Italian immigrants from the mid-1800s through the early 1900s have brought to the surface an understanding that the various threats these groups posed in the eyes of the native population are not so different from those we see today.

This is especially true for the religious threat that emanated from Irish migration to Great Britain. It was not only due to their adherence to Roman Catholicism that these poverty-stricken migrants were feared and detested. Once they set foot on English soil, from the 1840s onward, their religion played a crucial role in activating the already prevalent negative stereotyping of the Irish as being backward, racially inferior, and violent. The deeply felt revulsion among Protestants toward Catholics, which is rooted in the Reformation and the religious wars of the sixteenth and seventeenth centuries, is perhaps difficult to imagine in the now largely secular western European societies (except for specific regions like Northern Ireland). Nevertheless, the example of the Irish in Great Britain shows how important and pervasive religion was as a fundamental organizing principle not so very long ago.

Instead of being a culturally and ideologically homogeneous territory characterized by common values and ideas, as many people now tend to assume, western Europe was deeply divided nationally, socially, and (above all) religiously. Catholics, Protestants, and Jews managed to live together but were largely locked in their own worlds and integrated with only the greatest reluctance. Protestants not only distrusted Catholics because of their allegedly backward and superstitious faith, they thought Catholics also lacked proper feelings of national loyalty. In the anti-Catholic stereotype the supranational character of Catholicism, which is epitomized by the prefix "Roman," made them members of an international association whose allegiance was first and foremost to the Pope in Rome. This idea of a "Roman conspiracy" or "Popery" was strongly stimulated by the restoration of the Episcopal Catholic hierarchy in 1851, which caused an anti-Catholic backlash throughout western Europe.[5] Only with this historical context in mind is it possible to understand the mass appeal of the religious, anti-Irish discourse by priests and agitators like William Murphy, whose lectures against "Papal aggression" in general and against the Irish migrants in particular mobilized tens of thousands of people. His inflammatory and radical anti-Catholic propaganda provoked a number of serious anti-Irish riots in places like Stockport, Wolverhampton, and Birmingham in the 1860s. The portrayal of Catholicism as a fundamentally different worldview and part of an international network aimed at world hegemony coordinated by the Pope in Rome bears a striking resemblance to current ideas about Islam and the international Jihad. In the case of the Irish, this fear was even more deeply rooted because of the historical animosity between Protestant England and Catholic France, which, as Linda Colley has demonstrated, gave English nationalism a religious, anti-Catholic flavor from the eighteenth century onward.[6]

A second similarity with regard to the threat of immigration relates to national allegiances. Nowadays many people think that migrants do not want to integrate because they would rather remain faithful to their ethnic community and their home country. The fact that many states support their citizens abroad and actively encourage them to remain loyal to their original nationality (to the point, sometimes, of forbidding dual citizenship) only serves to strengthen the conviction that migrants today refuse to assimilate and identify with their new homeland. This situation is often contrasted to assimilation in the United States, where new citizens are officially and symbolically inserted into the nation.

The emphasis on the influence of the institutions in the country of origin (state or ecclesiastical) or on nationalistic movements of the migrants abroad (who are considered as part of the "imagined community" ) is not new. Also not new is the threat of these forms of "organized nationalism," as the German historian Otto Dann called them,[7] to the national cohesion and integrity of western European states, at least in the eyes of the native population and the authorities. Such political and ideological forces have influenced migrants past and present, and the migrants have (at least in part) shared and supported their claims. The history of Irish and Polish nationalism and its influence on immigrants in Lancashire and the Ruhr area, respectively, bears witness to a rich and widespread associational life. More recently, Algerians and Turks have displayed a similar allegiance to their state of origin, and this has inspired them to fight assimilation in a way that resembles the behavior of many first generation Irish and Polish migrants a century earlier. As in the past, it is not likely that this national loyalty will survive into the next generations. Children of Algerian immigrants born in France prove to be largely immune to the nationalist passions of their parents, and they take a great interest in French culture, notwithstanding the widespread exclusion they experience in French society. With Turks, who do not have a background of colonial socialization and who were raised in an ultranationalistic state, such a shift did not occur, but in their case, too, the second generation shows signs of a preference for Germany or for western Europe in general.

The social threat, finally, as illustrated by the largely male group of Italian immigrants in France after 1870, but also by the Irish in Great Britain, has proved to be the least enduring. As soon as it became clear that these workers were not about to undermine the labor market and were prepared to adjust to the existing labor relations—either by joining unions or establishing their own (as in the case of the Polish ZZP)—the initially bloody clashes (especially between French and Italian workers in the later decades of the nineteenth century) died out.

## THE INTEGRATION PROCESS

Unfounded optimism about the pace at which immigrant groups integrated in the past is a recurrent phenomenon. Looking at issues with hindsight leads easily to distortions. Knowing the result of certain processes makes it tempting to interpret the developments that preceded them mainly in the light of the outcome and obscures the often arduous and winding road that led up to the dénouement. This teleological fallacy applies especially to the process of integration. Moreover, its credibility is strengthened by the fact that the historical sources consulted are largely incomplete, particularly where information on the second and third generations is concerned. The important point made by Perlmann and Waldinger, that the social mobility of the offspring of Italian migrants in the United States progressed at a slower pace than is often assumed, is also applicable to the "big three" in western Europe's past. The descendants of the Poles and Irish, especially, freed themselves only very gradually from the occupational and social isolation that characterized the life of their parents. Their history was far from a success story: sons of Polish and Irish migrants often remained in the same social position as their fathers and were reluctant to marry outside their own ethnic group.

There is even evidence that the present-day "problematic migrants"— Turks, Algerians, and West Indians—are making faster progress either in the *identificational* (as with the Algerians) or the *structural,* socioeconomic domain (as with the Turks). In the case of the West Indians, especially the women among them, integration is occurring in both domains at the same time. Notwithstanding the strength of anti-immigrant stereotyping, western European societies offer greater opportunities to the offspring of immigrants, mainly through a more open educational system, and at the same time—through the process of globalization—they represent an attractive cultural model, be it in the sense of popular culture, consumer freedom, human rights, or emancipation of women.

In light of the warning by Nancy Green that historians, by training, tend to be more interested in continuities,[8] we would expect to find similarities. Being trained to look for sameness should not close the historian's eye to changes and discontinuities. Migrants, as well as western Europe, have changed enormously and, in the context of the reception of migrants, it would be surprising if these differences were to have no repercussions on the nature of the immigrant threat and the integration process.

## Differences

### THE THREAT

An important difference between the stigmatization of immigrants then and now is that, at present, Europeans tend to worry more about the second generation, whereas in the past it was the migrants themselves who were the object of hatred and derision. This marked difference explains why today's anti-immigrant movements, emanating both from the extreme right and from those with a more liberal background, emerged in the wake of the permanent settlement and family reunification process in the late 1970s and 1980s. When it became clear that the migrants were not going to be temporary residents but would stay permanently, anti-immigrant propaganda became stronger. Once the children of migrants became adults, anti-immigrant discourse was no longer restricted to the extreme right but also, from the 1980s onwards, graduated to mainstream politics, especially in Germany and Great Britain, where conservative governments set the agenda.

This had been quite different in the past. In the second half of the nineteenth century, the migrants themselves (especially mainly men during the first phase of their stay) had almost invariably been the targets of native anti-immigrant movements. These differences in gender and generation are important in understanding present-day integration processes. If we look at the anti-immigrant rhetoric towards the Irish, Poles, and Italians, it is clear that the vitriol was aimed predominantly at the men. In contrast to the guest workers in western Europe in the 1960s, who were also largely male, the Poles and Italians were dreaded and mistrusted. But in the case of the Irish, who came in family groups, it was also the men who were targeted.

The explanation for this gendered stereotype of men as criminals and strike breakers is found foremost in the role played by the state in social relations. In the case of the guest workers, the welfare state (in cooperation with the unions) had agreed upon equal wages and negotiated the specific sectors of the labor market in which the guest workers would be employed.[9]

This was not the case before the First World War, when the state remained largely absent from the social and economic domains, even though many migrants competed directly with the local population, particularly at the bottom end of the labor market. Strikebreaking and undercutting by immigrants did occur (albeit to a lesser extent than people assumed at the time) and added to the already strained relationship between established citizens and outsiders. Women, both of the first and the second generations, were much less problematized and are largely missing from the picture. In contrast to the present, the immigration of women and children, often ten to twenty years after their husbands, was perceived as a positive development because it showed that the men had finally chosen to settle down and integrate. As long as migrant men wandered in groups and displayed a highly mobile, "nomadic" lifestyle, as was the case with Italian workers in France, they remained a threat, both economically and socially. Receiving societies therefore welcomed family reunification.

The settlement process of former guest workers and colonial migrants in western Europe is much more differentiated and tells a somewhat different story. Guest workers from Turkey and North Africa were initially welcomed, as they would "help out" and keep the economic engine roaring. Employers, politicians, and the media were positive about these migrants, and there is evidence that the population at large was also much less against these newcomers than it would be later on.[10] However, when it became clear that the Turks and Moroccans were there to stay, and they started bringing over their families during the 1970s and 1980s, the climate changed. While the Italians in France were praised for settling down with their families after 1890, the situation of the labor migrants some eighty years later was quite different. Permanent settlement, literally embodied by the presence of their spouses and children, was for many natives an unwanted development.

This brings us to the issue of the second generation. In the past, adverse attention had almost invariably focused on the migrants themselves. As soon as the first phase of the settlement process was over and migrants' children grew up, the attention shifted to the next migrant group. This mechanism still functions at present, but at the same time public attention has also shifted to the offspring of migrants, at least to those who are having trouble finding their place in the educational system and in the labor market. Often the focus is on the "problem groups," although this is not necessarily the case, as the situation of the second-generation Italians in Germany shows. Although the overall image of Italians is quite positive, many youngsters are doing poorly in school and in the job market. The question is whether the disadvantaged social position of the second generation generates interest in their problems, or whether the interest is linked to the emergence of the interventionist state and belief in social engineering. Despite the lack of research and sources necessary to map the second generation in the past, there are indications that their integration progressed rather slowly, too, with the possible exception of the Italians in France.

This does not mean that the attention to the problematic social situation of second generation Algerians, Turks, and West Indians is only the product of a change in the role of the state. Yes, it is undeniable that the rise of the welfare state and the role of bureaucrats and policymakers at all levels, with the media in their wake, have contributed to the problematization of immigration and integration. Whereas in the past the state was largely disinterested in integration, except where national loyalty was concerned, integration is now constantly measured, discussed, and put under the magnifying glass. In the case of the Netherlands, integration was even the topic of a parliamentary inquiry in 2003.[11]

The difficulties the second generation faced in the past seem to be less grave than at present, at least where the large and problematic groups of immigrants are concerned. The offspring of the Irish, Italian, and Polish immigrants may not have been socially mobile or may only have managed to climb up a rung or two on the social ladder, but at least most of them had a working career, a situation that did not differ fundamentally from that of the native working class. Nowadays, in the increasingly postindustrial economies of western Europe, descendants of Algerians, Moroccans, Turks, and West Indians have found it very difficult to find jobs and often have parents who are poor role models, as many of them were laid off in the 1980s and have been unemployed for a good deal of their working lives. As a result of real and perceived exclusion, combined with widespread police harassment, many youngsters have openly rebelled against the police and authorities in general, as witnessed in a number of serious riots in Great Britain and France. Together with the articulation of a separate ethnic and political identity, most obvious in the case of the *beur* movement in France, this development clearly diverges from the patterns of the past.

There are important gender differences as well. Although second generation women, especially from a Muslim background, are often restricted in their ambitions, they generally do better than their male peers. Especially among the second generation West Indians in Great Britain, and to a lesser extent among Turks and Algerians, women perform much better at school and in the labor market than men. Ironically, this is explained by the existing discriminatory gender regime, which restricts women much more than men. As a result, adolescent girls have less access to the public domain and are more socialized to obey rules. They stay at home more, do their homework, finish school, and often gain higher qualifications than the men and thus have a much better starting position on the job market. Additionally, they are less involved in the displays of bad behavior typical of the second generation, such as criminality and oppositional behavior, which takes place primarily in the male domain. Women, therefore, seem to find jobs more easily than men, presumably because they are perceived as being less of a threat.

## THE INTEGRATION PROCESS

If we want to understand the integration processes of old and new migrants in western Europe, we first have to realize that their starting positions, irrespective of a number of similarities, differ in one important respect: the process by which they were selected. The Irish, the Poles, and the Italians, notwithstanding the push factors in their regions of origin, responded to the demand for labor in the target areas. Once networks were established, the selection of those who stayed was very much shaped by the human capital of the migrants and the changing opportunities at their destination. Instead of a massive, one-way migration and subsequent settlement process, there was a great deal of mobility and repeated return migration. The result was a highly selective group that settled down for good. Although I do not want to take the classic liberal argument too far, and while I realize that social and cultural factors influenced the selection process, too, it seems plausible that migrants in the past were more favorably self-selected and therefore fit better into the receiving society.[12]

The selection process of the new migrants in western Europe at first sight seems to be very similar to that of the past. Labor migrants came because there was work, and (in the first stage of the process) return migration occurred frequently. For people already in this phase, however, self-selection was highly restricted. Initially, guest workers did not arrive on their own; rather, employers and government officials selected them. Even the fact that, later on, many guest workers emigrated on their own, their socioeconomic composition was largely determined by the initial selection, which was aimed at the unskilled who had to fill vacancies in the second segment of the labor market—jobs that most western European workers no longer wanted to do. When the western European economy experienced a deep recession in the mid-1970s and these jobs increasingly disappeared through a process of economic restructuring, a new situation arose. Instead of leaving, as migrants in the past would have done, these migrant workers stayed and decided to bring their families over, too. Whereas in the past economic downturns led to return migration, in the later decades of the twentieth century, the opposite was true. To understand this momentous change in the dynamics of labor migration, two factors are essential. First, the shift can be seen as an unintended, boomerang effect caused by restrictive government policies toward aliens introduced at the time.[13] Guest workers realized that if they left, the chances of their being allowed back in (at least as legal migrants) would be slim, so many preferred to stay on. Moreover, the shift from a temporary stay to permanent settlement has been explained by scholars like James Hollifield as the result of the "liberal paradox." With the creation of nationality-blind welfare states, immigrants automatically—unintentionally and unknowingly—built up rights alongside the indigenous population. The longer they stayed and contributed to that welfare state, the more difficult it became for nation states to refuse them permanent residence and deny them the right to reunify their families.[14] As a result the number of Turks and Moroccans was bound to multiply in a period of mass unemployment, which made their integration process much more difficult.

The selection of colonial migrants, represented in this work by Algerians in France and West Indians in Great Britain, differed from that of the guest workers, but here, too, the welfare state played a similar trick. West Indians and Algerians were not selected by the receiving society but could enter and leave freely as British and French subjects, respectively. Initially, as with the guest workers, the demand for labor and the difference in wage levels stimulated migration, but soon immigration law distorted this economic mechanism. As a result of independence in Algeria and a change in immigration legislation in Great Britain, both in 1962, migration increased very rapidly before the door could close. With the prospect of entering the colonial "motherland" becoming more difficult in the near future, many decided to migrate without considering the opportunities for work or decent housing available in the host country. Once there, few left, since leaving would make reentry impossible (or at least very difficult).

In the long run, the difference between the way old and new migrants were selected was bound to have repercussions on their integration process. Through economic restructuring, and the physical toll many of the unskilled jobs exacted, many migrants lost their jobs and became permanently unemployed. Return migration was severely discouraged by the availability of welfare arrangements (provisions like unemployment, disability, and child benefits) and the lack of prospects in the countries of origin, which were often affected even more severely by the economic downturn in the 1970s and 1980s.[15] Looking at the social and economic position of the second generation, a differentiated outcome presents itself: on the one hand, there is a segment of the second generation, men more than women, who have great trouble catching up and whose position is characterized by poor education, low status jobs, unemployment, and criminality. This situation is the result of low human capital of their parents and their experience of exclusion and discrimination from the receiving society. On the other hand, there is a sizable minority of immigrant children, females more than males, who are doing well in school and who increasingly manage to obtain mainstream jobs.

Where the *identificational* part of the integration process is concerned, the outcomes are diverse as well. It is clear that colonial migrants in general (not just the Algerians and West Indians discussed in this book) tend to identify much faster with the culture of the receiving society, even when they are confronted with discrimination and exclusion. Within this category there is a difference between those with and without a Christian background. Most second-generation Algerians have renounced the Berber or Arabic language of their parents and are not interested in Islam as a belief, but they still marry largely inside their own group, although they increasingly resist arranged marriages. Caribbean migrants in Great Britain, on the other hand, not only embrace British culture, but they also intermarry much more than migrants with a non-Christian background (immigrants from India, Pakistan, and Bangladesh). The Surinamese immigrants in the Netherlands nicely demonstrate the salience of religion within colonial groups. Those of African ancestry have more friends among the native Dutch and intermarry much more than those with an Indian Hindu background.[16]

The delaying effect of non-Christian religions on the integration process, especially in the realm of national and cultural identification, is also evident for former guest workers from Muslim countries in western Europe, Turkey, Morocco, and Tunisia. Their second generation is making progress in the structural domain, but the great majority still prefers to marry within their own group. This does not automatically imply that there are no developments in the direction of integration. As with the Algerians in France, arranged marriages are decreasing, and women often choose emancipated men from the countries of origin.[17] Where religion is concerned, it is clear that when the second generation takes over in religious associations and institutions, they generally strive for a much more liberal version of Islam than their parents practiced and adapt to the local and national opportunity structures.[18]

Due to differences in selection and in the background of migrants, especially their religious backgrounds, the integration process, both *structurally* and *identificationally,* is taking a slower route than in the past, although we should not forget the resistance to integration among second-generation Poles and Irish, both among themselves and within the receiving society. This conclusion, however, is based on what we know now about the recent second generation, which in large part is still at the beginning of its adult life.[19] Sociological, demographic, and anthropological studies show, moreover, that the integration process of the second generation is dynamic and that changes can be very sudden, as the spectacular increase in intermarriage rates for West Indians in the 1990s illustrates. Finally, it is conceivable that some of the descendants of the new migrants in Europe, especially those from a Muslim background, will follow a differentiated integration path, combining integration in the socioeconomic realm with the retention and development of their cultural (and religious) singularity. They will thereby repeat, to a certain extent, the process of minorization that the Jews in western Europe once experienced. A final analysis, however, can only be made after the third generation lives another twenty to thirty years.

## Back to the States

What does this book on Europe, then, add to the largely American discussion on old and new migrants that inspired it? The situation in western Europe reveals that the American debate is to some extent parochial and only partly applicable to other contexts. In other words, the western European case demonstrates the limits of theorizing on the basis of the American experience, which can be illustrated by briefly looking at three differences.

## National Self-Definition

One obvious divergence from the European situation is the perception of the nation and the place of immigration in the collective memory. The image of the United States as an immigrant nation makes Americans much more self-assured and less nervous about integration. Americans seem to find it normal and natural that immigrants choose their "great" country and cannot imagine that they could have trouble identifying with America, although the events of September 2001 may have shattered this self-confidence somewhat, as illustrated in Samuel P. Huntington's latest book *Who Are We?*[20] Moreover, the American *E pluribus unum* philosophy makes it easier to accept ethnic and religious differences as long as they do not interfere with the national identity. This, however, is only one side of the coin. As David Reimers and others have shown, Americans have throughout their history often been ambivalent about immigration. In all periods, fear of "alien cultures," competition in the labor market, and—more recently—the alleged abuse of welfare benefits, have added fuel to anti-immigrant movements. From the 1980s onward, anti-immigrant groups have targeted immigration from developing countries, and legal and illegal newcomers from Latin America in particular. In contrast to Europe, these lobbies have not been able to change the immigration policy in a fundamental way, although some provisions have been closed to recent immigrants and illegal immigrants. Moreover, it is interesting that both the pro-immigrant and anti-immigrant groups are a combination of the Right and the Left, even of the very far Right and Left, as is illustrated by the environmentalist critique on ongoing immigration.[21]

In European nation-states this is quite different. Many, except those who embrace multiculturalism, largely and increasingly resist the idea of being immigrant nations. They are less confident about the attractiveness of their culture, fear that immigrants with a different background will remain alien bodies in their midst, and therefore have trouble accepting ethnic differences.

## The Welfare State

The fear for "large and problematic" groups of immigrants is strengthened by a second major difference with the United States: the emergence of full-scale *welfare states* in western Europe, especially in the period 1945–70. This has had repercussions in the selection of those who came and in the determination of those who stayed, and it has influenced their structural integration, as has been put forward by scholars like Hollifield and Bommes.[22] The greater and more favorable self-selection of migrants in the United States, both among legals and illegals, and the high demands on self-sufficiency and private initiative may in the end lead to a higher degree of social and economic integration. Although even in this system, the few benefits left (education and food stamps) may interfere with the pure demand-supply mechanism and constitute an extra-economic pull.[23] It seems to be no coincidence, therefore, that the public opinion in the United States is more favorable toward illegal immigrants than it is in Europe—notwithstanding the fact that illegal immigration became a criminal offense in the United States in the 1990s.[24] Whereas in America, illegal immigrants are generally considered to be tough and enterprising workers, in Western Europe they are associated primarily with poverty and criminality.[25] The downside of the American system is that those who fail or get stuck in the second segment of the labor market, like many Mexicans in the United States, face high costs, both physically and emotionally.

## Color and Colonialism

A third obvious difference in the case of the United States is the significance of color, which in America is very much framed by the legacy of an internal slavery tradition and thereby associated with an African ancestry. For a balanced comparison with Europe, I therefore confine myself to colonial migrants with an African background. The chapter on the West Indians in Great Britain shows that they were faced almost immediately with racism and discrimination, as the riots against them at the end of the 1950s testify. However, West Indians, both in Great Britain and in the Netherlands, do better than the almost-white former guest workers and their children and are more accepted in cultural and social respects than colored colonial migrants from a Hindu or Muslim background. In contrast to the Indians and Pakistanis, West Indians are perceived as belonging much more to the "imagined British community." This is very similar to the Surinamese migrants in the Netherlands, both from African and Indian origin. Although most of them are very dark, they are nevertheless considered to be much more Dutch than Turks or Moroccans; they also perform significantly better at school and in the labor market. With the lack of a tradition of internal slavery, color is much less pervasive as an organizing principle. As long as colored colonial migrants share basic cultural norms and values, as is the case with most West Indians, their chances of acceptance are much greater than for white and colored Muslim migrants with different cultural baggage.

## Salad Bowl or Melting Pot?

Notwithstanding contextual differences between the United States and western Europe, there are a number of similarities where the integration process is concerned that allow us to look critically at the claims of those scholars who see primarily change and discontinuity. One of the central issues in the old and new debate in the United States is the question of whether a form of assimilation or integration is likely for today's "large and problematic" immigrants and their descendants. The evidence from the European case supports the assimilation school more than those, like Alejandro Portes,[26] who expect a much more pluralistic development with transnationalism, segmented assimilation, and enclave economies as persisting factors. From the three case studies in the second part of this book, it is clear that integration may be a slow, gendered, and differentiated process, but also that children of migrants gradually become more similar to the established population, both in *structural* and *identificational* respects.

There is little evidence that new developments, such as transnationalism, or a greater cultural distance, especially in the case of Islamic migrants, will block integration. Transnationalism, both with regard to the influence exercised by the states of origin and in the sense of a transnational ethnic bond between people from the same culture, clearly plays a role. States like Turkey, Algeria, and Morocco try to keep "their" migrants under control, but these attempts often stop with the second generation, whose orientation is increasingly geared toward the society where they were born and where they see their future. The most radical break with the nation of origin is found among children of Algerian migrants who demand to be treated as French citizens. Contacts with kin in the country of origin become increasingly artificial as the second generation is regarded as more and more alien by those who stayed behind. Children of former Turkish guest workers are labeled as *Almancik* ("Germans"), which is partly true, because the second generation loses the cultural and linguistic affinity needed to establish or maintain a meaningful contact. A vague pan-ethnic feeling is easier to keep up, but at the same time it is more superficial and symbolic—similar to what Hubert Gans called "symbolic ethnicity."[27] Also among the second generation of some groups there exists a kind of diasporic identity, but it is highly doubtful that this will last, let alone outstrip the day-to-day integration in the society where the offspring of the new migrants live and work. Even pan-ethnic and pan-religious forms of transnationalism are not necessarily incompatible with integration, a notion that was recently expressed by Stephen Howe when he wrote: "Members of minority groups in Britain, as elsewhere in Europe, identify themselves in various ways: sometimes by their or their families' country of origin, sometimes by colour, often (and perhaps increasingly, especially young Muslims) by religion. But survey evidence shows that for the vast majority, such identifications are not necessarily left to be in conflict or competition with a sense of Britishness."[28]

## Monoculture or Multiculture?

Now that we have addressed the three key questions posed in the introduction, I would like to conclude by going back to where it all began: the public debate in western Europe since the Rushdie affair about the assimilability of non-Western migrants. The argument in this book, supported by historical and contemporaneous evidence, is that the predictions of multiculturalists and of those who consider the new migrants to be a Trojan horse are highly unlikely predictions at best. Proponents of the multicultural ideal are right, in the sense that at present, through immigration from other parts of the world, cultural diversity has increased considerably and that these new influences will change the face of western European societies, if only by increasing diversity of religions, of which Islam is the most important. Whether this proliferation of cultures will, in the end, also lead to the persistence of distinct ethnic cultures separate from the established society, whose members over generations will continue to identify as separate, is doubtful. Not only can we learn from past examples (the emancipation process of Jews in Europe; Irish and Polish nationalism; Catholicism among migrants) that such cultures lose their "master status."[29] We can also see that the fast cultural changes, loss of language, and religious conformity among the new migrants points more in the direction of ongoing integration than toward the dawn of a multicultural society where descendants of immigrants remain visible and culturally distinct groups. In this sense, the outcomes of this study are largely compatible with the evaluation of present-day immigration by American sociologists like Richard Alba and Victor Nee, who stress the ongoing assimilation process.[30] Furthermore, the linguistic and cultural assimilation in western Europe, especially among the second generation, bears some striking similarities with Latinos in the United States, as described by (among others) Alejandro Portes and Rubén Rumbaut.[31]

The fear on the part of rabid opponents to the multicultural ideal that fundamentalist Muslim immigrants will act as a sort of fifth column, undermining the secular and liberal values of the West, is thereby equally unfounded and unrealistic, at least as migration history is concerned.[32] Although some of the descendants of the new "large and problematic" migrants may have bleak prospects and will possibly end up in a sort of ethnically tainted underclass, this does not imply that such a process of minority formation is the result of their innate tribal or otherwise backward culture. Much more, it has to do with of the inability of the receiving societies to integrate new migrants in a structural way and to combat discrimination. As the situation of the second generation of Algerians in France (the *beurs*) shows, their worrisome prospects are not so much explained by their Islamic culture, which most of them denounce, but by their exclusion and isolation from mainstream French society. Some members of the second generation of West Indians in Great Britain, Moroccans in Belgium and the Netherlands, and Turks in Germany face a similar situation. It is still too early to know whether this scenario will continue, but in the meantime, other migrants—women more than men—will find their way up through the educational system. In the long run they will blend into western European societies, adding to it new flavors and colors, as so many migrants have done in the remote and recent past. Europe will be—as it has been for ages already—a multicultural continent.

# Notes

## Introduction

1. For criticism on this interpretation, see Kepel, *Les banlieues de l'Islam*, 9–13. See also Roy, *Globalised Islam*, 102–4.

2. In statistics, a distinction is often made between a broad and a narrow definition of *allochtones*, with the narrower definition referring only to those born in the non-Western part of the world. Neither definition equals "immigrants."

3. Finkielkraut, *La défaite*; Finkielkraut, *Au nom de l'autre*.

4. For a recent overview of global migration movements, see Hoerder, *Cultures in Contact*, and McKeown, "Global Migration 1846–1940."

5. Huntington, *Clash of Civilizations*, 254–65.

6. Pryce-Jones, *Closed Circle*, 21–33; Todd, *Le destin des immigrés*, 389–90; Lewis, *Crisis of Islam*; Tibi, *Islamische Zuwanderung*. For a critical assessment, see Lewis, *Islamic Britain*, and Roy, *Globalised Islam*.

7. Taylor, *Multiculturalism*, 38; Kymlicka, *Multicultural Citizenship*.

8. For a critical assessment, see Kivisto, "The Transplanted"; Kazal, "Revisiting Assimilation"; Gans, "Toward a Reconciliation"; and recently, Alba and Nee, *Remaking the American Mainstream*, 17–66.

9. Foner, *From Ellis Island*; Alba and Nee, *Remaking the American Mainstream*. See also "Forum: Old and New Immigrants: On Nancy Foner's Book *From Ellis Island to JFK*," in *Journal of American Ethnic History* 21 (Summer 2002) 4:55–119 (with contributions by Carmel Chiswick, Caroline Brettel, Brian Gratton, Nancy Foner, and Leo Lucassen).

10. Vertovec and Cohen, *Migration*.

11. The most influential proponents of this view in the American context are Alejandro Portes and his associates; see Portes, Guarnizo, and Landolt, "Transnationalism," 224–27. See also Levitt, *Transnational Villagers*.

12. Sterne, "Beyond the Boss," 36; Gerstle and Mollenkopf, "Political Incorporation," 13–14.

13. Zhou, "Segmented Assimilation," 999; Portes, "Immigration Theory," 814; and Joppke, *Immigration,* 182–83.

14. Glazer and Moynihan, *Beyond the Melting Pot.*

15. Such as Foner, *From Ellis Island.*

16. Perlmann and Waldinger, "Second Generation Decline?" 94.

17. Waldinger and Feliciano, "Downward Assimilation?" 395.

18. For a fundamental criticism on their interpretation of the past see Morawska, "Immigrants, Transnationalism, and Ethnicization," 179–93; and Waldinger and Fitzgerald, "Transnationalism in Question," 1188. Foner takes a middle position in *From Ellis Island,* 168–87. For the importance of return migration, see Wyman, *Round-Trip America.*

19. Perlmann and Waldinger, "Second Generation Decline?" 903–4; Foner, *From Ellis Island,* 143–49.

20. Guglielmo, *White on Arrival,* 26–31.

21. Kazal, "Revisiting Assimilation"; Morawska, "Assimilation Model"; Brubaker, "Return of Assimilation?"; Arias, "Change in Nuptiality Patterns." See also Joppke and Morawska, *Toward Assimilation and Citizenship;* Alba and Nee, *Remaking the American Mainstream.*

22. The distinction between assimilation as a process and assimilation as a program was already made by Gordon, *Assimilation in American Life,* 106, where he dismisses the Americanization crusade as "pressure-cooking assimilation."

23. This discussion took place at a so-called "forward look" workshop of the European Science Foundation (ESF) with the title "Immigration and the Construction of Identities in Contemporary Europe: Transnational Ties and Identities; Past and Present," organized by Anita Böcker and Leo Lucassen at the Netherlands Institute of Advanced Study (NIAS), in Wassenaar, Neth., December 6–7, 2002.

24. Green, "Terms and Concepts," 41–42.

25. As argued in Lucassen, "Old and New Migrants," 95–97.

26. Dignan, "Europe's Melting Pot," 137.

27. Roediger, *The Wages of Whiteness;* Roediger, *Abolition of Whiteness;* Ignatief, *Irish Became White.* For a more nuanced interpretation of the whitening process, see Guglielmo, *White on Arrival,* 26–31.

28. See also Alba, *Ethnic Identity,* 140.

29. Lieberson, *Piece of the Pie,* 378.

30. Bade, *Europa in Bewegung,* 82, 422–28; Moch, *Moving Europeans,* 125.

31. Sanua, "Jewish College Fraternities."

32. Foner, *From Ellis Island,* 227.

33. Lucassen, Willems, and Cottaar, *Gypsies;* Willems, *True Gypsy.*

34. Lucassen and Penninx, *Newcomers,* 196–97.

35. Feldman, *Englishmen and Jews,* 329–52; Frankel and Zipperstein, *Assimilation and Community.*

36. Hansen, *Citizenship and Immigration*, 10–34; Lunn, "Immigration and Reaction," 339; and Willems, *Uittocht uit Indië*, 335.

37. Guterl, *Color of Race*, 190–91.

38. For criticism on his interpretation, see Schönwälder, *Einwanderung*, 116–17, 129–30.

39. Willems, "No Sheltering Sky."

40. Van Niekerk, *Premigration Legacies*, 240; Vermeulen and Penninx, *Immigrant Integration*, 219.

41. Lamont, *Dignity of Working Men*, 190.

42. A recent exception is the thematic issue "Immigration et logiques nationales" of *Le Mouvement Social* (July–September 1999), no. 188. Edited by Marie-Claude Blanc-Chaléard; Blanc-Chaléard, "Des logiques," 3–15.

43. Nora, *Les lieux de mémoire*.

44. For example, the virtual European Migration Museum (http://www.emz-berlin.de/emz/emm); and the virtual Swiss Migration Museum (http://www.migrationsmuseum.ch).

45. See http://www.historisches-museum-bremerhaven.de and http://www.museumsnett.no/emigrantmuseum. See also the interesting virtual Malta Emigration Museum (http://www.maltamigration.com).

46. Although there was a short but significant increase in the 1950s in the Netherlands and Germany: Freund, *Aufbrüche*, 391–93.

47. And countries like the Netherlands even much earlier (from the end of the sixteenth century onward): Lucassen and Penninx, *Newcomers*, 19–20. For the early modern period in general, see Moch, *Moving Europeans*, 31–57.

48. Noiriel, *Le creuset français*, 15–21.

49. Lucassen and Lucassen, "Introduction," 33. See also Hoerder and Moch, *European Migrants*, 7.

50. Noiriel, *La tyrannie du national*, 85; Bade, *Europa in Bewegung*, 186; Hoerder, *Cultures in Contact*, 446–47.

51. Noiriel, *Le creuset français*, 50–67.

52. Hoerder, "Historical Dimensions," 121.

53. Vermeulen and Penninx, *Immigrant Integration*, 229.

54. Fetzer, *Public Attitudes*, 95.

55. Borjas, "Welfare Reform."

56. See also Feldman, "L'immigration," 51.

57. For Dutch workers in Germany see Lucassen, "Many-Headed Monster," 249–50; Van Eijl and Lucassen, "Holland Beyond the Borders."

58. Hollifield, *Immigrants, Markets, and States*, 231.

59. Pioneers are Gérard Noiriel and Klaus Bade: Noiriel, *Le creuset français*; Bade, *Deutsche im Ausland*. Good overviews are: Bade, *Europa in Bewegung*; and Moch, *Moving Europeans*.

60. Exceptions are: Moch, *Moving Europeans*; Green, *Ready-to-Wear*; Lucassen and Penninx, *Newcomers*; Bade, *Europa in Bewegung*; Blanc-Chaléard, *Les Italiens*.

61. Oltmer, *Migration und Politik,* 46–48; Gabaccia, *Italy's Many Diasporas,* 136–40.

62. Good examples are: Moch, *Moving Europeans;* Lucassen and Penninx, *Newcomers;* Bade, *Europa in Bewegung;* and Green, "The Comparative Method."

63. Noiriel, *Le creuset français,* 341–56.

64. Blanc-Chaléard, *Les Italiens.*

65. Bade, *Deutsche im Ausland;* Herbert, *Foreign Labor.*

66. Lucassen and Penninx, *Newcomers;* see also Lucassen and Lucassen, "Introduction."

67. Moch, *Moving Europeans;* and Bade, *Europa in Bewegung.*

68. Green, *Ready-to-Wear.*

69. Esser, *Aspekte;* Esser and Friedrichs, *Generation und Identität.*

70. Gordon, *Assimilation,* 68–83.

71. For a good example of domain differentiation see: Morawska, *Insecure Prosperity,* 133–35.

72. A definition proposed by Lucassen and Penninx (*Newcomers,* 15), according to which full assimilation is reached when both the offspring of the migrants as well as the receiving society do not regard the descendants of immigrants primarily as different.

73. Many scholars, especially demographers, use intermarriage rates as a sort of litmus test to measure greater interaction between ethnic groups (Keeley, "Demography and International Migration," 57). See also Alba and Nee, *Remaking the American Mainstream,* 90.

74. Colley, *Britons,* 18–19.

75. Huntington, *Clash of Civilizations,* 200.

76. For a good overview of the current situation of the second generation in western Europe, see Crul and Vermeulen, "Second Generation."

## Chapter 1: The Religious Threat

1. Nugent, *Crossings,* 27–37.

2. Moch, *Moving Europeans;* Bade, *Europa in Bewegung.*

3. Pooley and Turnbull, *Migration and Mobility;* Hochstadt, *Mobility and Modernity;* Rosental, *Les sentiers invisibles.*

4. Suurenbroek, "Friezen in Amsterdam"; Jones and Rees, *Liverpool Welsh;* Moch, "Networks among Bretons?"

5. Bade, *Europa in Bewegung;* Moch, *Moving Europeans;* Noiriel, *Le creuset français;* Holmes, *John Bull's Island.*

6. Lucassen and Lucassen, "Introduction," 33–36.

7. For a good overview see Oltmer, "Deutsche Migrationsverhältnisse," 487–88.

8. Excellent overviews have been written in *A New History of Ireland:* Fitzpatrick, "Peculiar Tramping People"; Fitzpatrick, "Emigration, 1801–70"; see also Feldman, "Migration," 193–97.

9. Lucassen, *Migrant Labour in Europe,* 133–45.

10. Pooley, "The Irish in Liverpool," 72.

11. Akenson, *Irish Diaspora,* 22.

12. Davis, *Irish in Britain,* 11–13. According to Davis (p. 21), the myth of the Great Famine as cause of emigration was successfully propagated by the ultranationalist journalist and historian John Mitchel (1815–75), who was editor of the *United Irishman.* He was supported by the Irish (land-owning) middle classes who thus could put the blame on the English.

13. Miller, *Emigrants and Exiles;* Mokyr, *Why Ireland Starved,* 8–15.

14. Davis, *Irish in Britain,* 14–16.

15. Miller, *Emigrants and Exiles,* 31–35.

16. Neal, *Sectarian Violence,* 52.

17. Jackson, *Irish in Britain,* 12; Busteed, "Little Islands of Erin," 100.

18. Jackson, *Irish in Britain,* 191, table VII.

19. Delaney, *Demography, State and Society,* 45.

20. Even after the foundation of the Irish Republic in 1921, the Irish could migrate freely as subjects of the British crown.

21. Feldman, "Migration," 735–38. For Germany, see Fahrmeir, "Nineteenth-Century German Citizenship," 195.

22. Lowe, *Victorian Lancashire,* 22–25; Feldman, "L'immigration," 56.

23. Neal, *Black '47,* chapter 9.

24. Millward, "Stockport Riots of 1852," 215.

25. Pooley, "The Irish in Liverpool," 83.

26. Finnegan, "The Irish in York," 63.

27. Thompson, *English Working Class,* 480, cited in O'Tuathaigh, "The Irish in Nineteenth-Century Britain," 13.

28. Swift, "Historians and the Irish," 19; see also Busteed, "Little Islands of Erin," 94.

29. Akenson, *Irish Diaspora,* 190; Davis, *Irish in Britain,* 59–63; Fitzpatrick, "Peculiar Tramping People," 634–35.

30. Pooley, "Irish in Liverpool," 75–79; Lowe, *Irish,* 68.

31. Neal, *Sectarian Violence,* 14.

32. Busteed, "Little Islands of Erin," 111.

33. Chinn, "Sturdy Catholic Emigrants," 64.

34. Dennis, *English Industrial Cities,* 38; see also Finnegan, "Irish in York," 74.

35. Lees, *Exiles of Erin,* 63.

36. Belchem, "Liverpool-Irish Enclave," 129.

37. Davis, *Irish in Britain,* 58–61; Dennis, *English Industrial Cities,* 35.

38. Morawska, *Insecure Prosperity,* xviii–xix.

39. Engels, *Working-Class,* 90–92.

40. Feldman, "Class," 181.

41. Jackson, *Irish in Britain,* 84–85.

42. Lees, *Exiles of Erin*, 88–99.

43. Jackson, *Irish in Britain*, 83.

44. To a certain extent, the presence of Irish workers in English textile centers can have been regarded as part of a specific textile migration system and therefore constituted highly selective migration patterns. For an earlier example, see Lucassen and De Vries, "Rise and Fall."

45. Lawton, "Irish Immigration," 48.

46. Davis, *Irish in Britain*, 108–9.

47. Lawton, "Irish Immigration," 49–52.

48. O'Leary, *Immigration and Integration*, 134–38.

49. Lucassen, "Great War," 47–50.

50. O'Leary, *Immigration and Integration*, 135; MacRaild, *Culture*, 17.

51. MacRaild, *Culture*, 71.

52. Lowe, *Irish*, 87.

53. Williamson, "Impact of the Irish," 18–19; Davis, *Irish in Britain*, 90–91.

54. Akenson, *Irish Diaspora*, 199.

55. Swift, "Historians," 19.

56. Miskell, "Irish Migrants," 32.

57. Lobban, "Irish Community," 271–73.

58. Dennis, *English Industrial Cities*, 232; Fielding, *Class and Ethnicity*, 29–30; Lees, *Exiles of Erin*, 58; Lowe, *Irish*, 93.

59. Gallagher, "Two Cities," 109.

60. O'Tuathaigh, "Irish," 19.

61. Hickman, *Religion, Class and Identity*, 24–26; Canny, *Making Ireland British*, 53–54.

62. Hickman, *Religion, Class and Identity*, 25–30.

63. Colley, *Britons*, 25.

64. Cited in Hickman, *Religion, Class and Identity*, 48–49.

65. O'Tuathaigh, "Irish," 22.

66. Since the work of Curtis (*Apes and Angels*), who advanced with force the racist character of the anti-Irish stereotype, a lively discussion developed. Gilley ("English Attitudes") has criticized Curtis for being too one-sided and by pointing at the many contradictions within the racist discourse. Finally, Curtis has been backed up, albeit in a much more nuanced fashion, by Miles and Hickman. See for this discussion Hickman, *Religion, Class and Identity*, 46–56.

67. Fielding, *Class and Ethnicity*, 6–7.

68. Colley, *Britons*, 329.

69. Neal, *Sectarian Violence*, 251.

70. Lowe, *Irish*, 156.

71. Millward, "Stockport Riots," 207.

72. Fielding, *Class and Ethnicity*, 7.

73. Arnstein, "Murphy Riots," 52–53.

74. Ibid., 59.

75. Belchem, "Liverpool-Irish Enclave," 135; Fielding, *Class and Ethnicity*, 12; Lowe, *Irish*, 109–12.

76. Connolly, "Irish and Catholic" 229–30. Tridentine refers to the Council of Trent (1545–63), which shaped the destiny of modern Catholicism (Palmer and Colton, *History*, 84).

77. Lees, *Exiles of Erin*, 165–77.

78. Canny, *Making England British*, 534–37.

79. Lees, *Exiles of Erin*, 214.

80. Anderson, *Imagined Communities*; Gabaccia, *Italy's Many Diasporas*, 26–28.

81. Jacobson, *Special Sorrows*, 19.

82. Lees, *Exiles of Erin*, 133.

83. Fielding, *Class and Ethnicity*, 73.

84. O'Leary, *Immigration and Integration*, 194.

85. Belchem, "Liverpool-Irish Enclave," 136–37.

86. Lowe, *Irish*, 191.

87. Moran, "Nationalists in Exile," 212–35.

88. Fielding, *Class and Ethnicity*, 79.

89. Lees, *Exiles of Erin*, 222.

90. O'Leary, *Immigration and Integration*, 242.

91. O'Day, "Political Behaviour," 84–85.

92. Fielding, *Class and Ethnicity*, 73.

93. MacRaild, *Culture, Conflict and Migration*, 2; Belchem, "Class, Creed and Country," 191–93; Fielding, *Class and Ethnicity*, 2–11; and Pooley, "Irish in Liverpool," 81.

94. Fielding, *Class and Ethnicity*, 2.

95. Lees, *Exiles of Erin*, 18.

96. Belchem, "Class, Creed and Country," 191.

97. O'Tuathaigh, "Irish," 19–20.

98. Lawton, "Irish Immigration," 52.

99. Zhou, "Segmented Assimilation."

100. Lowe, *Irish*, 36.

101. Fielding, *Class and Ethnicity*, 68.

102. Davis, *Irish in Britain*, 71; Finnegan, "Irish in York," 69; O'Leary, *Immigration and Integration*, 184; Lowe, *Irish*, 36–37; Swift, "Stafford Street Row," 182.

103. Finnegan, "Irish in York," 59; Fielding, *Class and Ethnicity*, 70; Large, "Irish in Bristol" 50; O'Leary, *Immigration and Integration*, 238; Lees, *Exiles of Erin*, 149–53; Lowe, *Irish*, 121; Millward, "Stockport Riots," 211.

104. Pooley, "Irish in Liverpool," 80.

105. Fielding, *Class and Ethnicity*, 71.

106. Lees, *Exiles of Erin*, 149.

107. Daniels, *Exile or Opportunity?*

## Chapter 2: A Threat to the Nation

1. Although, as we have seen in the preceding chapter, anti-Catholicism was an integral part of English nationalism (and hence the two cannot be separated), and the Irish migrants developed a distinct nationalism, the emphasis differed in both cases.

2. The Protestant Masurians, although they spoke a Polish dialect, were loyal to the Prussian state and did not join the Polish national movement. They lived in the southeastern part of East Prussia (around Allenstein and Lorzen). See for the linguistic aspects Glück, *Sprachenpolitik*, 106–7.

3. "Poles" in this chapter means German citizens from the eastern parts of the German empire: Upper Silesia, East and West Prussia, and Posen.

4. Poland had been partitioned in 1791 and 1795 by Russia (eastern part), Austria-Hungary (southwest), and Prussia (the western part and Silesia).

5. Klessmann, *Polnische*, 23–27.

6. This term means "the process of becoming Polish," culturally and politically.

7. Wehler, *Krisenherde des Kaiserreich*, 189–93.

8. Bade, "Preussengänger," 111.

9. Ibid., 96–97.

10. Brandt, *Polen und die Kirche*, 40.

11. Reczynska, "Ruhr Basin," 94; Brandt, *Polen*, 40–41.

12. Klessmann, *Polnische Bergarbeiter*, 39.

13. Ibid., 38.

14. Brepohl, *Aufbau des Ruhrvolkes*, 102.

15. Lucassen, *Migrant Labour*; Moch, *Moving Europeans*, 40–43.

16. Murzynowska, *Erwerbsauswanderer*, 25. The numbers in table 4 include also the "Masurians" from East Prussia.

17. Per 100 "Polish" men in 1890 there were 40 women, compared to 61 in 1900, 70 in 1905, and 77 in 1910 (Klessmann, *Polnische Bergarbeiter*, 268). The Masurians probably aimed from the start at definitive emigration and brought their wives much earlier: Murzynowska, *Erwerbsauswanderer*, 35.

18. Murzynowska, *Erwerbsauswanderer*, 88.

19. Ibid., 29.

20. Murphy, *Gastarbeiter*, 34.

21. Murzynowska, *Erwerbsauswanderer*, 48.

22. Barfuss, "*Gastarbeiter*," 184; Hauschildt, *Polnische Arbeitsmigranten*, 207–12; Eder, "Aspekte," 43–60.

23. Ponty, *Polonais méconnus*, 398–402.

24. Klessmann, *Polnische Bergarbeiter*, 161–63.

25. Oenning, "*Mitti polnischen Farben*," 44.

26. Franke, *Ruhrgebiet*, 103.

27. Bernhard, *Polnische Gemeinwesen*, 182.

28. Peters-Schildgen, *"Schmelztiegel" Ruhrgebiet,* 47.

29. Oenning, *"Mitti polnischen Farben,"* 15.

30. Franke, *Ruhrgebiet und Ostpreussen,* 78.

31. Croon and Utermann, *Zeche und Gemeinde,* 151.

32. Klessmann, "Long-Distance Migration," 106. See also Murphy, *Gastarbeiter,* 52. For the sample that Murphy took, he included women but did not analyze men and women separately, so the percentage of the mining industry is significantly lower than that of Klessmann.

33. Henkes, *Heimat in Holland;* Lucassen, "Administrative," 330–31; Franke, *Ruhrgebiet und Ostpreussen,* 67.

34. Klessmann, *Polnische Bergarbeiter,* 265.

35. Ibid., 35.

36. Peters-Schildgen, *"Schmelztiegel" Ruhrgebiet,* 42.

37. Oenning, *"Mitti polnischen Farben",* 13.

38. Klessmann, *Polnische Bergarbeiter,* 71.

39. Stefanski, *Zum Prozess der Emanzipation,* 128–29.

40. Franke asserts that almost all sons followed their fathers, whereas Stefanski argues that in 1900 only 40% of the sons became miners: Franke, *Ruhrgebiet und Ostpreussen,* 66; Stefanski, *Zum Prozess,* 129.

41. Waterkamp, *Bevölkerung von Duisburg,* 38–42. The sample comprised 6,743 questionnaires (14% of the children who had filled it out).

42. Ibid., 79.

43. Brepohl, *Aufbau des Ruhrvolkes,* 142–43. See also Klessman's criticism (*Polnische Bergarbeiter,* 177).

44. Murphy, *Gastarbeiter,* 61.

45. Brandt, *Polen,* 3.

46. Wehler, *Deutsche Kaiserreich,* 96.

47. Many Catholic monastic orders decided to leave Germany and a number of these settled in the bordering Dutch provinces, especially in the Catholic South (Limburg).

48. Wehler, *Krisenherde,* 186.

49. Delbrück, *Polenfrage,* 5.

50. This conviction was widespread and even voiced by distinguished scholars as Max Weber (*Verhältnisse der Landarbeiter,* 803).

51. Glück, *Sprachenpolitik,* 129–30.

52. Kulczycki, *School Strikes,* 15.

53. Canny, *Making England British,* 301–8.

54. Wehler, *Krisenherde,* 189–90; Neubach, *Ausweisungen.*

55. The "colonization commission" (*Ansiedlungskommission*) hardly bought any Polish land, but instead many German *Junkers* profited by selling their land above the market price: Wehler, *Krisenherde,* 190.

56. A combination of the first letters of the family names of the founders of the

*Ostmarkenverein,* Hansemann, Kennemann, and Tiedemann. On the origin of the *Deutschtum* policy, see also Oltmer, *Migration und Politik,* 42–52; and Dann, *Nation und Nationalismus,* 185–98.

57. See, for example, the case of the Italians: Gabaccia, *Italy's Many Diasporas,* 66–67.

58. Brandt, *Polen,* 7.

59. Ibid., 9.

60. Murzynowska, *Erwerbsauswanderer,* 98.

61. Brandt, *Polen,* 10–11.

62. According to Klesmann, Liss was not a real nationalist but primarily a Catholic who tried to further Catholicism by using the Polish language as medium (*Polnische Bergarbeiter,* 58–59).

63. Stefanski, *Zum Prozess,* 26–27.

64. Murphy, *Gastarbeiter,* 141.

65. Stefanski, *Zum Prozess,* 158–62.

66. Klessmann, *Polnische Bergarbeiter,* 105–7.

67. Stefanski asserted that the argument of miscommunication was only used as a cover for a clear-cut, anti-Polish attitude, and he reminds us that only few Polish miners were fired because they did not master German (*Zum Prozess,* 132).

68. Tenfelde, "Krawalle von Herne"; See also Kulczycki, *Foreign Worker,* 117–28.

69. Kulczycki, *Foreign Worker,* 222.

70. Kulczycki, *Polish Coal Miners' Union,* 249–50.

71. Klessmann, *Polnische Bergarbeiter,* 125.

72. Blecking, *Geschichte,* 29–32.

73. Ibid., 113.

74. Ibid., 118.

75. Klessmann, *Polnische Bergarbeiter,* 19, 86. The official name was "Zentralstelle für Überwachung der Polenbewegung im rheinisch-westfälischen Industriegebiet." The specialization of the police with regard to alleged "dangerous groups" was a general tendency in this period, as the *Zigeunerzentrale* of the Munich police in 1905 shows (Lucassen, *Zigeuner,* 175).

76. Blecking, *Geschichte,* 113.

77. Murzynowska, *Erwerbsauswanderer,* 151.

78. Ibid., 149.

79. Cited in Kulczycki, *Foreign Worker,* 127.

80. Peters-Schildgen, *"Schmelztiegel" Ruhrgebiet,* 194–95; Bernhard, *Polnische Gemeinwesen,* 401.

81. Barfuss, "*Gastarbeiter,*" 184–85.

82. Klessmann, *Polnische Bergarbeiter,* 145–46.

83. Oenning, "*Mitti polnischen Farben,*" 52.

84. Ibid., 129.

85. In 1926, 122 children from Wanne Eickel went for several weeks to Poland: Pe-

ters-Schildgen, *"Schmelztiegel" Ruhrgebiet*, 214. See also Oenning, *"Mitti polnischen Farben,"* 129.

86. Klessmann, *Polnische Bergarbeiter*, 174; Oenning, *"Mitti polnischen Farben,"* 75–82.

87. Murphy, *Gastarbeiter*, 144–46.

88. Klessmann, *Polnische Bergarbeiter*, 72; Reif, *Verspätete Stad*, 510.

89. For Polish women, the percentage of mixed marriages was much smaller than for men.

90. Peters-Schildgen, *"Schmelztiegel" Ruhrgebiet*, 365.

91. Barfuss, *"Gastarbeiter,"* 199.

92. 42% compared to 21%, respectively, of all first-generation Polish men at the end of their working careers in 1943.

93. Such as Waterkamp, Franke, and Brepohl.

94. Brepohl, *Aufbau des Ruhrvolkes*, 126; Waterkamp, *Bevölkerung von Duisburg*, 59; Franke, *Ruhrgebiet und Ostpreussen*, 94–95; Murphy, *Gastarbeiter*, 113–15; Hauschildt, *Polnische Arbeitsmigranten*, 270–71.

95. Franke, *Ruhrgebiet und Ostpreussen*, 69.

96. Stefanski, *Zum Prozess*, 27, footnote 23.

97. Croon and Utermann, *Zeche und Gemeinde*, 20; Stefanski, *Zum Prozess*, 13.

98. Hauschildt, *Polnische Arbeitsmigranten*, 268.

99. The bulk of the changes probably took place after 1918, as has been found for Wilhelmsburg (Hauschildt, *Polnische Arbeitsmigranten*, 268–69).

100. Franke, "Einbürgerungen," 25.

101. Brandt, *Polen*, 166–67.

102. See on this organization Hagen, *Germans, Poles and Jews*, 173.

103. Oenning, *"Mitti polnischen Farben,"* 95–96.

104. Klessmann, "Long-Distance Migration," 111.

105. Hughes, "Dilemmas."

## Chapter 3: A Threat to the Native Workers

1. Gabaccia, *Italy's Many Diasporas*, 68. After 1918, European destinations have become dominant (52%, compared with 25% for North America and 19% for South America): (Gabaccia, *Italy's Many Diasporas*, 135). For Germany and Switzerland, see Del Fabbro, *Transalpini*; and Vuilleumier, *Flüchtlinge und Immigranten*.

2. Gabaccia, "Yellow Peril"; Lequin, *Les ouvriers*.

3. Lucassen, *Migrant Labour*, 195–96.

4. Milza, *Voyage en Ritalie*, 59–75.

5. Deduced from Milza, "L'émigration italienne," 65. In 1901, France counted 221,784 naturalized citizens (compared with 34,510 in 1876). As Italians (32% of the total foreign population in 1901) made up 24% of all naturalizations in 1886 (Mauco, *Les étrangers en France*, 60), the estimation of 50,000 is even a conservative one.

6. In 1933, Italians were responsible for 40% of all naturalizations (then 28% of the population): Baroin, *La main-d'oeuvre étrangère*, 188.

7. Gabaccia, *Italy's Many Diasporas;* Lucassen, "Bringing Structure Back In," 507–8.

8. Milza, *Voyage en Ritalie*, 75.

9. Mauco, *Les étrangers*, 521.

10. Mauco, *Les étrangers*, 38; Schor, *Histoire de l'immigration*, 58–60.

11. Milza, *Voyage en Ritalie*, 81. Whereas before 1918 only 8% of all Italian migrants came from Veneto, this increased to 31% thereafter. The importance of Piedmont (28% versus 18%) and Tuscany (22% versus 8%) decreased accordingly.

12. For Italians in Marseille before 1870, see the excellent study of Sewell's (*Structure and Mobility*).

13. Milza, *Français et Italiens*, 216.

14. Bonnet, Santini, and Barthélemy, "Appartenance politique," 65–66.

15. Noiriel, "Les immigrés italiens"; Noiriel, *Longwy*.

16. Seine counted 50,000 Italians in 1901, with almost 22,000 in Paris itself: Milza, *Français et Italiens*, 233.

17. Zucchi, *Little Slaves*, 42–75. For itinerant musicians in general see Lucassen, "A Blind Spot."

18. Paulucci di Calboli, *Larmes et sourires*, 158.

19. Blanc-Chaléard, *Les Italiens*, 79.

20. Perrot, *Les ouvriers en grève*, 170–71.

21. It should be added that these kinds of conflicts were common among migrant and indigenous navvies. See Lucassen, *Migrant Labour*, 70–71; Gabaccia, *Italy's Many Diasporas*, 112.

22. Gabaccia, *Italy's Many Diasporas*, 165.

23. For example, in the *Société d'économie politique* in 1881, and in Leroy-Beaulieu's book *Essai sur la répartition des richesses*, published in 1883 (Ibid., 165).

24. Lequin, *Les ouvriers*, 153. See also Lartigue-Vecchie, "Les grèves," 148.

25. This section is based on Liens, "Les 'Vèpres Marseillaises.'"

26. Vertone, "Antécedents et causes," 111.

27. Ibid.

28. Cubero, *Nationalistes et étrangers*, 53–54.

29. Témime, "Histoire de Marseilles," 174.

30. Bonnet, "Les Italiens," 98–99.

31. Paris, "Les Italiens," 63.

32. Lartigue-Vecchie, "Les grèves," 154–55.

33. Milza, "L'intégration," 189–90.

34. Noiriel, *Longwy*, 80–95.

35. Bertrand, *L'invasion*. For the small impact of legal measures, see also Green, *Repenser*, 43.

36. These arguments are also put forward by Le Conte, *Étude*, 233–36. Le Conte

also voices the fear that Italians in the border area (Alpes Maritimes) will press for joining this part of France to Italy.

37. Blanc, *L'immigration en France.* See also Chandèze, *L'émigration,* 118.

38. As argued in Lucassen, "The Great War," 55.

39. Bertillon, *La problème.*

40. For a discussion of the act, see Brubaker, *Citizenship and Nationhood,* 85–114.

41. He opposes automatic naturalization of the children of foreigners born in France because people should first express a deep-felt will to become French (Blanc, *L'immigration en France,* 133–35). For an interesting discussion of the demographic fear, see Green, *Repenser,* 40–43.

42. Mauco, *Les étrangers en France,* 60; Milza, "L'émigration," 64–65.

43. Milza, *Français et Italiens,* 271.

44. Bonnet, "Note sur les dossiers," 231

45. Mauco, *Les étrangers en France,* 549.

46. Milza, *Français et Italiens,* 208.

47. Ibid., 235–38.

48. For Lyon, see Bonnet, "Les Italiens," 90–96. For Nice, see Milza, *Français et Italiens,* 227.

49. Noiriel, "Les immigrés italiens," 631.

50. For the reaction of Italian consuls around 1900, see *Emigrazione e colonie.*

51. Milza, *Francais et Italiens,* 220.

52. Schnapper, *La communauté des citoyens.*

53. Bonnet, "Les Italiens," 96–97; Couder, "Les italiens de la région parisienne," 514; Témime, "Les journaux italiens," 220.

54. Témime, "Les journaux italiens," 209.

55. Milza, *Français et Italiens,* 229.

56. Gabaccia, *Italy's Many Diasporas,* 143.

57. George, "L'immigration italienne en France," 45.

58. Cross, *Immigrant Workers,* 213–19.

59. Freeman, "Immigrant Labour," 163.

60. Lucassen, "Great War," 55–58; Moch, *Moving Europeans,* 161–71; Bade, *Europa in Bewegung,* 254–58; Lucassen, "Bringing Structure Back In," 503–6.

61. For a comparison between France and the United States see: Noiriel, *Le creuset français,* 19–40; and Green, *Repenser,* 37–76.

62. Ignatief, *Irish Became White;* for more in general see Foner, *From Ellis Island,* 225–28.

63. Schor, *L'opinion française,* 140.

64. Schor, "Les Italiens," 602.

65. Noiriel, *Le creuset français,* 62–63.

66. Cited by Schor, "L'image de l'Italien," 91.

67. Mauco, *Les étrangers en France,* 269.

68. As well as anti-Semitism (Green, "Religion et ethnicité," 140, footnote 40).

69. MacMaster, *Colonial Migrants and Racism*, 223.

70. Schor, *L'opinion française*, 140.

71. Baroin, *La main d'oeuvre*, 101; Blanc, *L'immigration en France*, 61.

72. Schor, "L'image de l'Italien," 98–101; see also Blanc-Chaléard, *Les Italiens*, 97.

73. Milza, *Français et Italiens*, 183, 234; and *Emigrazione*, 204.

74. Milza, *Français et Italiens*, 234.

75. Rainhorn, "Enclaves."

76. Blanc-Chaléard, *Les Italiens*, 119.

77. For the relationship between chain migration and niche formation, see Lesger, Lucassen, and Schrover, "Migrant Network?" 29–32.

78. Blanc-Chaléard, *Les Italiens*, 170–71.

79. Munoz-Perez and Tribalat, "Mariages d'étrangers," 433–35.

80. Girard and Stoetzel, *Français et immigrés*, 70. It has to be remarked that in the data of Munoz-Perez and Tribalat ("Mariages d'étrangers"), the Swiss, who had even higher exogamy rates than the Belgians, were lacking (Mauco, *Les étrangers en France*, 532).

81. Munoz-Perez and Tribalat, "Mariages d'étrangers," 444–45.

82. Greeley, *Be Like Us?*

83. Mauco, *Les étrangers en France*, 227; see also Milza, "Les Italiens," 78, and Videlier, "Les Italiens," 674–75.

84. Ray, *Les Marocains*, 88; in 1937 there were 65,000 North Africans in France, of whom 12,000 to 15,000 were Moroccans.

85. Hamed-Touati, *Immigration maghrébine*, 73–78; MacMaster, *Colonial Migrants*, 75–77.

86. MacMaster, *Colonial Migrants*, 78.

## Chapter 4: Old Threats, New Threats

1. The fear of immigrants as scabs was widespread, not only in Europe, but also in the United States: Montgomery, *House of Labor*, 81–82; Mink, *Old Labor*, 33.

2. See chapter 2.

3. Research requested by the Dutch government, for example, focuses on migrant problems and strengthens the tendency to equate migrants with social and political problems. Those migrants who do not fit the problematic mask are ignored.

4. Feldman, "L'Immigration," 51–52.

5. Tilly, *Coercion*, 107–13.

6. Hutchinson, *Legislative History*; Reimers, *Unwelcome Strangers*, 5–24.

7. Gans, "Filling in Some Holes," 77.

8. Borjas, "Welfare Reform."

9. See also chapter 1 on the Irish.

10. Kok, "Choices and Constraints"; Pooley and Turnbull, *Migration and Mobility*; and Rosental, *Les sentiers invisibles*.

11. See for the Irish: Feldman, "L'Immigration," 53–55.

12. Foner, *From Ellis Island*, 143–46.

13. Weber, *Die Verhältnisse*, 803.

14. Mauco, *Les étrangers en France*, 334: " . . . les Slaves plus moutonniers, plus passifs et habitués, pour une certain nombre, à la discipline allemande."

15. Chevalier, *Classes laborieuses*; and Stedman Jones, *Outcast London*. For an excellent critical discussion on Chevalier, see Sewell, *Structure and Mobility*, 159–61.

16. Gabaccia, *Italy's Many Diasporas*.

17. Foner, *From Ellis Island*, 225–26.

18. Taylor, "Travellers in Britain."

## Chapter 5: The Discomfort of Color

1. Sherwood, *Many Struggles*, 38–61.

2. Hiro, *Black British*, 7.

3. MacMaster, *Colonial Migrants*, 58; Summerskill, *Western Front*.

4. Cottaar, "Onzedelijk of preuts?" Apart from the Surinamese, there were also several hundred Chinese men who worked on steamships but who were laid off in the 1920s. The police also considered them to be unwanted aliens, and many were deported in the 1930s.

5. Foner, *From Ellis Island*, 168.

6. Vertovec, "Indo-Caribbean Experience."

7. Banton, *Coloured Quarter*; Banton, *White and Coloured*; Richmond, "Economic Insecurity and Stereotypes"; Richmond, *Colour Prejudice in Britain*; Richmond, *The Colour Problem*; Patterson, *Dark Strangers*; and Little, *Negroes in Britain*.

8. Collins, "Pride and Prejudice," 392.

9. The most important scholar in the new field of "race relations" was the sociologist John Rex. See Rex and Moore, *Race, Community and Conflict*; and Rex, *Race Relations*.

10. Phizacklea and Miles, *Labour and Racism*; Phizacklea and Miles, *Labour and Racism*; Solomos, *Black Youth*; and Paul, *Whitewashing Britain*. See also Tabili, "The Construction of Racial Difference," 56.

11. Gilroy, *Union Jack*, 22–25. See also Miles for criticizing Stuart Hall for reifying race by regarding it as an "active force which has its own, real effects. . . ." (Miles, *Racism and Migrant Labour*, 176.)

12. Peach, *West Indian Migration*; Peach, "Trends in Levels of Caribbean Segregation"; Foner, *Jamaica Farewell*; Model, "Ethnic Inequality in England"; Model and Fisher, "Unions Between Blacks and Whites," 728–54.

13. Sherwood, *Many Struggles*, 79; Drake, "Colour Problem," 201.

14. Cockcroft, Frank, and Johnson, *Dependence and Underdevelopment*; see also Wallerstein, *Modern World-System*.

15. Grosfoguel, "Colonial Caribbean Migration," 597; Grosfoguel, "Cultural Racism," 410–11.

16. Peach, "Caribbean in Europe," 4–5.

17. Ibid., 7.

18. Mesmer was Prime Minister between 1972 and 1974 and was nominated minister of DOM-TOM (French overseas departments and territories) in 1971 in the cabinet Chaban-Delmas.

19. Freeman, "Caribbean Migration," 186.

20. See also Cross and Johnson's criticism of a too rigidly Marxist segmentation interpretation, which also highlights the great differences between Caribbean experiences in the core zones: "Mobility Denied," 76.

21. Fraser, "Nineteenth-Century," 25.

22. Hennessy, "Workers of the Night," 38–39.

23. Hansen, Citizenship and Immigration, 37–40.

24. Peach, "Afro-Caribbean Migration," 80.

25. Peach, West Indian Migration, 93.

26. Philpott, West Indian Migration, 168–71.

27. Byron, Post-War, 149. See also Chessum, From Immigrants, 52.

28. Foner, Jamaica Farewell, 41–42.

29. Patterson, Dark Strangers, 129; and Byron, Post-War, 115.

30. Pilkington, Beyond the Mother Country, 27.

31. Tabili, "Racial Difference," 97.

32. Drake, "Colour Problem."

33. Little, Negroes in Britain, 57; Richmond, Colour Problem, 235.

34. Rowe, "Sex, 'Race' and Riot," 56–57.

35. Ibid., 58.

36. Tabili, "Racial Difference," 56–57.

37. Drake, "Colour Problem," 197–204.

38. Griffith, Henderson, Usborne, and Wood, Coloured Immigrants, 3.

39. Rex and Tomlinson, Colonial Immigrants, 49–50.

40. See also Rex and Moore, Race, Community and Conflict.

41. Wickenden, Colour in Britain, 31–35.

42. Pilkington, Beyond the Mother Country, 116.

43. Hansen and Lofstrom, "Immigrant Assimilation," 109–10.

44. Peach, "Trends in Levels," 204.

45. The Commonwealth Immigrants Act (1968) and the Immigration Act (1971). See for a thorough discussion of the political discussions around these acts: Hansen, Citizenship and Immigration, 179–206; Layton-Henry, Politics of Immigration, 77–85.

46. See www.theoccidentalquarterly.com/vol1no1/ep-rivers.html.

47. Layton-Henry, Politics of Immigration, 77.

48. Patterson, Immigration and Race, 362.

49. Hall, Critcher, Jefferson, Clarke, and Roberts, Policing the Crisis, 354–58. These movements were not very successful and had only a limited range: Collins, "Pride and Prejudice," 415.

50. Solomos, *Black Youth*, 237.

51. Layton-Henry, *Politics of Immigration*, 147. Layton-Henry explains this by reference to racial profiling by the police who would arrest far more African West Indians than Asians, but this remains speculative and, moreover, could easily be a circular argument.

52. Hiro, *Black British*, 84.

53. Layton-Henry, *Politics of Immigration*, 127.

54. In the same period, the violence against "blacks," especially with an Asian background, often organized by the *National Front*, became almost daily routine, adding to the already tense atmosphere.

55. Solomos, *Black Youth*, 199–209.

56. Model, "Ethnic Inequality," 968–70.

57. Layton-Henry, *Politics of Immigration*, 143; Clancy, Hough, Aust, and Kershaw, *Crime*, 23.

58. Katznelson, *Black Men*, 199.

59. Nickel, "Unemployment in Britain," 45.

60. Cross and Entzinger, *Caribbean Minorities*, 22.

61. Foner shows that the level of schooling among West Indians in London was significantly lower than among this group in New York (Foner, *Jamaica Farewell*, 19; Foner, "Towards a Comparative Perspective," 537).

62. As argued by Peach, and rejected by scholars who focus on racism, such as: Harris, "Post-War Migration," 29.

63. Chessum, *Ethnic Minority*, 154.

64. Wrench, Hassan, and Qureshi, "Labour Market," 55; Heath, McMahon, and Roberts, "Ethnic Differences," 35–36.

65. Byron, *Post-War*, 113–15.

66. Model, "Ethnic Inequality," 985.

67. Nickel, "Unemployment in Britain," 15.

68. The negative effects of ethnic clustering have recently been shown by research on the effect of enclaves on employment and earnings: Clark and Drinkwater, "Enclaves," 24.

69. Lewis, *Five Families*, 1–3.

70. Steinberg, "Cultural Fallacy," 64–66.

71. Heath, McMahon, and Roberts, "Ethnic Differences," 20.

72. See, for example, Bonds, "School Response," 82–86; Troyna, "British Schooling," 183; Richmond and Mendoza, "Education and Qualifications."

73. Cross and Johnson, "Mobility Denied," 94.

74. Heath, McMahon, and Roberts, "Ethnic Differences," 27–28. Their research concerned the period 1992–97 and people economically active (ages 21–49), born in Britain.

75. See http://www.statistics.gov.uk/cci/.

76. Pathak, *Race Research*, 5.

77. Peach, "Trends in Levels," 207.

78. Ibid., 214.

79. Carter, Harris, and Joshi, "The 1951–55 Conservative Government," 340.

80. Alba, "Assimilation's Quiet Tide," 13.

81. Collins, "Pride and Prejudice," 406.

82. Banton, *Coloured Quarter*, 182; Banton, *White and Coloured*, 178–84.

83. Banton, *White and Coloured*, 184.

84. See for example Griffith, Henderson, Usborne, and Wood, *Coloured Immigrants*, 17, 69; Benson, *Ambiguous Ethnicity*.

85. Benson, *Ambiguous Ethnicity*, 13.

86. See for example Hiro, *Black British*, 310.

87. Analyzed by Dale and Holdsworth, "Analysis of Ethnicity," 163–73; Model and Fisher, "Unions," 734–35.

88. Brown, *Black and White Britain*, 33; Dale and Holdsworth, "Analysis of Ethnicity," 173. I have computed the 1991 percentages because Dale and Holdsworth only give differentiated percentages.

89. Model and Fisher, "Unions," 741.

90. Tizard and Phoenix, *Mixed Race?* 36–37.

91. Banton, *Coloured Quarter*, 279.

92. Foner, *From Ellis Island*, chapter 6; Waters, *Black Identities*, 172–81; see also Kalmijn, "Intermarriage," 143, note 10.

93. Waters, *Black Identities*, 172–81.

94. Model, "West Indian Prosperity," 541.

95. Lucassen, "Old and New Migrants," 89–90.

96. Boris and Janssens, "Complicating Categories."

97. Foner, *Jamaica Farewell*, 70–71; Van Niekerk, *Premigration Legacies*, 101–3.

98. Van Niekerk, *Premigration Legacies;* Byron and Condon, "Comparative Study." For France, the trends seem less positive (Giraud, "Les migrations," 437–42).

99. Byron and Condon, "Comparative Study," 94.

100. In France, the unemployment rate among Caribbean migrants is about the same as for the white, native French.

101. Van Niekerk, *Premigration Legacies*, 139–40.

## Chapter 6: Foreigners Within?

1. See, for example, Wimmer, "Explaining Xenophobia," 30–32.

2. Brubaker, *Citizenship and Nationhood*, 10.

3. Esser, "Ausländerproblem," 171; Voelker, "More Foreign Workers," 333.

4. Mandel, "Fortress Europe," 114–15.

5. Bade, *Europa in Bewegung*, 409–17.

6. For the inclusion of colonial migrants from Indonesia in the Netherlands, see Willems, "No Sheltering Sky."

7. Schönwälder, "Zukunftsblindheit," 123–44.

8. Abadan-Unat, *Turkish Workers*, 387. The numbers given here are lower than in

more recent studies, but because of the differentiation between origins they give a good idea of the growth of the Turkish share. See also Schönwälder, *Einwanderung,* 159.

9. Apart from naturalizations in 1998, more and more children born in Germany automatically became citizens with an option to choose at age 18. In 2000 alone, this amounted to 40,000 of the total immigrant population (probably at least 10,000 of Turkish parenthood): Dornis, "Zwei Jahre," 167–70.

10. Mandel, "Shifting Centres," 154.

11. For a critique on the push-pull model, see: Hoerder, "Segmented Macrosystems," 74.

12. Sezer, "Zur Geschichte," 235; Abadan-Unat, "Turkish Migration," 5–6.

13. Abadan-Unat, *Turkish Workers,* 9.

14. Kürsat-Ahlers, "Turkish Minority," 118.

15. Cepni, *Türkische Arbeitnehmer,* 7–9.

16. Ibid., 42.

17. Ibid., 222.

18. For the Italians, see Von Oswald, "Stippvisiten"; Rieker, *"Ein Stück Heimat,"* 47–48.

19. See Manfrass, *Türken,* 58: "Gesetz zur Föderung der Rückkehrbereitschaft von Ausländern" (November 29, 1983).

20. Motte, "Vom 'Wirtschaftswunder,'" 253; Sezer, "Zur Geschichte," 245–46.

21. Von Oswald, Schönwälder, and Sonnenberg, "Einwanderungsland," 26.

22. Penninx and Roosblad, *Trade Unions,* 187.

23. Hollifield, *Immigrants,* 231.

24. In 1971, the new work-permit regulation (*Arbeitserlaubnisverordnung*) stated that foreign workers who had worked for more than five years would automatically receive a work permit for five more years, irrespective of the situation in the labor market: Herbert, *Geschichte der Ausläderpolitik,* 226.

25. Manfrass, *Türken,* 2.

26. Leggewie, "How Turks," 104.

27. Von Oswald, "Stippvisiten," 245–46.

28. Rieker, "Südländer," 248–51.

29. Von Oswald, Schönwälder, and Sonnenberg, "Einwanderfungsland," 25.

30. Herbert, *Geschichte,* 218.

31. Esser, "Ist das Ausländerproblem?" 171; Mandel, "Fortress Europe," 120.

32. Herbert, *Geschichte,* 240.

33. Ibid., 253.

34. Stolcke, "Talking Culture," 3.

35. Manfrass, *Türken,* 72–75.

36. Herbert, *Geschichte,* 320.

37. Bade, "Immigration and Social Peace," 86.

38. Hagedorn, "Bilanz," 37–41. See also Joppke, *Immigration,* 631–38.

39. Thränhardt, "Prophecies."

40. Good examples are Bielefeld, *Inländische Ausländer;* and Wilpert, "Foundations of Racism," 67–70.

41. Bade, *Europa in Bewegung,* 166–67.

42. Koopmans, "Zachte heelmeesters," 87–92; Böcker and Thränhardt, "Is het Duitse," 33–44.

43. Hinken, "Die betriebliche Integration."

44. Bade, *Legal and Illegal,* 15–25.

45. Amiraux, "Turkish Islam," 37.

46. This resembles the anti-Catholic discourse in the nineteenth century in France, Germany, and Great Britain, where similar accusations were voiced. For criticism on the term *Leitkultur,* see Esser, "What Substance," 48.

47. Stolcke, "Talking Culture," 1–3.

48. For a critical discussion of this concept, see Hafez, "Zwischen Parallelgesellschaft," 728–36.

49. Schiffauer, *Migranten aus Subay,* 341–43.

50. Karakasoglu, "Turkish Cultural," 166–67.

51. Ibid., 169. See also Heitmeyer, Müller, and Schröder, *Verlockender,* 183–96; and Schiffauer, *Die Gottesmänner,* 315–20.

52. Amiraux, "Turkish Islam," 49.

53. See Doomernik, "Institutionalization"; Rath, Penninx, and Groenendijk, *Western Europe;* and Schiffauer, "Islamische Gemeinschaft," 92–94.

54. Leggewie, "How Turks," 79–80.

55. Leggewie, "Turcs, Kurdes et Allemands," 116.

56. Glebe, "Housing," 130.

57. Ibid., 140–50.

58. The segregation index expresses the percentage of people from a certain social or ethnic group who would have to move to different neighborhoods to make their current neighborhood non-segregated.

59. Musterd and Deurloo, "Unstable Immigrant Concentrations in Amsterdam," 494.

60. Friedrichs, "Ethnic Segregation in Cologne," 1754–56.

61. Hanhörster and Mölder, "Konflikt."

62. Alpleis, "Erschwert, " 181.

63. Nauck, "Sozial-ökologischer Kontext," 325–26.

64. Von Oswald, Schönwälder, and Sonnenberg, "Einwanderungsland," 23.

65. Cepni, *Türkische Arbeitnehmer,* 118–22; Bender, Rürup, Seifert, and Sesselmeier, "Migration und Arbeitsmarkt," 59–84; Herbert, *Geschichte,* 213.

66. Cepni, *Türkische Arbeitnehmer,* 118.

67. It should be noted that unemployment rates in the Netherlands, both for natives and Turks, were considerably lower during the 1990s than in Germany.

68. Böcker and Thränhardt, "Erfolge und Misserfolge der Integration," 10–15.

69. Thränhardt, "Einwanderungsland," 58–59.

70. Schultze, *Berufliche Integration,* 51–53.

71. Leggewie, "Integration and Segregation," 86–95.

72. Faist, "From School to Work," 321–22.

73. Seifert, "Die zweite," 688–91; Seifert, "Berufliche" 254–57.

74. Herwartz-Emden, "Einwandererkinder im." For similar developments in the Netherlands, see Crul, "Breaking the Circle."

75. Herbert, *Geschichte,* 295.

76. *Statistisches Bundesamt,* Arbeitstabelle zur Fachserie 11, Reihe 1 (2000/2001).

77. Alba, *Ethnic Identity,* 220.

78. Venema and Grimm, *Arbeitnehmer,* 194, table 14.2.

79. Hunger and Thränhardt, "Bildungserfolg," table 7.

80. Mehrländer, Ascheberg, and Ueltzhöffer, *Repräsentativuntersuchung '95.*

81. Source: *Zuwanderung gestalten,* 215 (table IV.4.); Solga, "Jugendliche ohne Schulabschluss," 723–24.

82. Salentin and Wilkening, "Ausländer," 294.

83. In the beginning of the 1990s, some 20% of all foreign students in Bavaria were still placed in bilingual classes (Hunger and Thränhardt, "Der Bildungserfolg").

84. Ibid.

85. Alba, Handle, and Müller, "Ethnische Ungleichheit," 228–33.

86. Abali, "Kulturelle," 328–29.

87. White, "Turks," 755; Mandel, "Shifting Centres," 154–58.

88. Diehl and Bohm, "Rights or Identity?"; Salentin and Wilkening, "Ausländer," 278.

89. White, "Turks," 756; Hafez, "Zwischen Parallelgesellschaft," 729.

90. Böcker, "Paving," 174–75.

91. White, "Turks," 760. See also Mandel, "Shifting Centers," 163.

92. Esser, "Interethnische Freundschaften," 187.

93. Esser, "Interethnische Freundschaften," 201–6.

94. Thränhardt, "Einwanderungsland," 55.

95. Seifert, "Berufliche," 258: Münz, Seifert, and Ulrich, *Zuwanderung,* 101.

96. Seifert, "Berufliche," 258.

97. Venema and Grimm, *Arbeitnehmer,* 47.

98. For the Netherlands see: Hooghiemstra, *Trouwen over de grens,* 26.

99. See also Thränhardt, "Prophecies," 28.

100. Venema and Grimm, *Arbeitnehmer,* table 5.24.

## Chapter 7: Islam and the Colonial Legacy

1. Hargreaves, *Immigration,* 125–27. See also Silverman, *Deconstructing the Nation,* 111–18.

2. "Loi encadrant, en application du principe de laïcité, le port de signes ou de

tenues manifestant une appartenance religieuse dans les écoles, collèges et lycées publics" (Act no. 2004-228, March 15, 2004): http://www.senat.fr.

3. Jazouli, *L'Action collective;* and Aïssou, *Les beurs.*

4. Roy, "Islam in France," 56.

5. Todd, *Le destin des immigrés,* 383–90.

6. Such as Dominique Schnapper, Gérard Noiriel, and Hervé Le Bras.

7. Todd, *Le destin des immigrés,* 293.

8. Stora, *Ils venaient d'Algérie,* 14–15.

9. An excellent overview of the colonial roots of Algerian migration to France is offered by MacMaster, *Colonial Migrants.* See also Gilllette and Sayad, *L'immigration,* chapter 2, and a number of chapters in Costa-Lascoux and Temime, *Les Algériens en France.*

10. Laid down in the so-called *Senatus* Law of 1865.

11. MacMaster, *Colonial Migrants,* 7.

12. Lucassen, *Migrant Labour;* Moch, *Moving Europeans,* 40–42; Bade, *Europa in Bewegung,* 31–42.

13. Also within Kabylia there were huge differences in emigration rates, explained by the coexistence of "closed" and "open" (depending on seasonal labor) villages: MacMaster, *Colonial Migrants,* 45.

14. Mauco, *Les étrangers en France,* 269. As remarks throughout his (otherwise fairly balanced) pioneering study show, Mauco himself was also clearly influenced by anti-"Arab" as well as anti-Jewish stereotypes. For the anti-Semitic tendencies, see Green, "Religion et ethnicité," 140, footnote 40.

15. Ibid., 296.

16. Cross, *Immigrant Workers,* 213–15.

17. Possibly because during the summer Kabyle migrants returned home to do their own harvesting.

18. Mauco, *Les étrangers,* 170, 197. See also Hamed-Touati, *Immigration maghrébine,* 63.

19. MacMaster, *Colonial Migrants,* 67.

20. Ibid., 110–12.

21. Girard, *Francais et immigrés,* 96. See also Stora, who mentions 5,000 families in 1953 (*Ils venaient d'Algérie,* 95–97).

22. Stora, *Ils venaient d'Algérie,* 94, 144–45.

23. Hargreaves, *Immigration,* 16.

24. MacMaster, *Colonial Migrants,* 203–5.

25. Stora, *Ils venaient d'Algérie,* 402.

26. Hargreaves, *Immigration,* 11.

27. On the Harkis, see Manfrass, *Türken in der Bundesrepublik,* 31; Jordi and Hamoumou, *Les harkis;* Hamoumou, *Et ils sont;* and Kepel, *Les banlieues de l'Islam,* 322–25.

28. Lucassen and Penninx, *Newcomers,* 41–42.

29. The term *pieds noirs* became common at the beginning of the war of independence in 1954: Cohen, "Pied-Noir Memory," 129.

30. Jazouli, *L'Action collective*, 113–14.

31. Hargreaves, *Immigration*, 182.

32. The main proponent is Rogers Brubaker (*Citizenship and Nationhood*), who is on this point rightly criticized by Ezra, *The Colonial Unconscious*, 149–51.

33. Although also under Ottoman rule, the best land may have been in the hands of the (then-) ruling class.

34. MacMaster, *Colonial Migrants*, 2–8. See also Belbahri, *Immigration et situations postcoloniales*.

35. MacMaster, *Colonial Migrants*, 126.

36. Cited by MacMaster in *Colonial Migrants*, 127.

37. Ibid., 135.

38. Mauco, *Les étrangers en France*, 269, 485, and 532. See also Baroin, *La main d'oeuvre*, 101.

39. Girard, *Francais et immigrés*, 21.

40. Fetzer, *Public Attitudes*, 111.

41. See chapter 5.

42. Stora, *Ils venaient d'Algérie*, 206.

43. MacMaster, *Colonial Migrants*, 200.

44. Gastaut, *L'immigration*, 262–68.

45. Ibid., 268–88.

46. Schwab, *Integration von Moslems*, 155.

47. Silverman, *Deconstructing the Nation*, 95–106; Hargreaves, *Immigration*, xiv–xvi.

48. Reid, "Immigrant Workers," 269.

49. Schnapper, *L'Europe des immigré*, 168, 180–81; Le Bras, *Le démon des origines*.

50. Alba and Silberman, "Decolonization Immigrations," 1175.

51. Tribalat, *Faire France*, 8–17.

52. For a useful discussion of the remaining statistical possibilities, see Spire and Merllié, "La question des origines."

53. See for example Manfrass, *Türken*, 37–48.

54. Ogden, "Foreigners in Paris," 32.

55. White, "Immigrants," 198. See also Manfrass, *Türken*, 38; and MacMaster, *Colonial Migrants*, 193.

56. *Société Nationale de Construction de Logements pour les Travailleurs Algériens*.

57. Gourévitch, *La France africaine*, 109.

58. Wieviorka, Bataille, Jacquin, Martucelli, Peralva, and Zawadzki, *La France raciste*, 156–58.

59. Manfrass, *Türken*, 39; see also Lamont, Morning, and Mooney, "Particular Universalisms," 394.

60. De Rudder, "Les conditions de logement," 328–29.

61. Silverman, *Deconstructing the Nation*, 95–106.

62. Manfrass, *Türken*, 47.

63. Not only for immigrants, but for French from all parts of the country. See in this respect the classic study by Weber, *Peasants into Frenchmen.*

64. See also Alba and Silberman, "Decolonization Immigrations," 1184.

65. Aïssou, *Les beurs.*

66. It involves a sample of 13,000 migrants (except for Italians and Tunisians) and a control group of native French. These people (both first and second generation under age 30) were approached at the end of 1992 with questionnaires focusing on employment, schooling, religion, marriage, and intermarriage.

67. Tribalat, *Faire France*, 24.

68. Ibid., 47.

69. Khellil, *L'intégration*, 102.

70. Some authors argue that girls have fewer chances to drop out and are less influenced by the norms and values reigning in the public space in the *banlieues* (Hassini, *L'école*, 227–31).

71. Tribalat, *Faire France*, 177. In contrast to the Portuguese, Algerian men (53%) have an even more difficult time than Algerian women (47%).

72. Ibid., 175.

73. Tunisians tend to do somewhat better.

74. This therefore excludes youngsters who left school and never found jobs.

75. Tribalat, *Faire France*, 161.

76. Ibid., 124.

77. See also Neyrand and M'Sili, "Les couples mixtes," 589.

78. Tribalat, *Faire France*, 69–77; See also Kaltenbach and Tribalat, *La République et l'islam*, 18.

79. Tribalat, *Faire France*, 85.

80. Hargreaves, *Immigration*, 134.

81. Lebon, *Immigration*, 95.

82. Kepel, *Les banlieues de l'Islam*, 3–6.

83. Ibid., 367.

84. Hargreaves, *Immigration*, 125.

85. Ibid., 97. Eighteen percent of the girls pray regularly and another 24 percent only now and then. Children of mixed marriages are even less religious, especially the girls.

86. Roy, "Islam in France," 65.

87. See also Témime, "La politique française," 84.

88. Tribalat, *Faire France*, 150.

## Conclusion

1. Morawska, "Sociology and Historiography," 1878; Lucassen and Lucassen, "Introduction," 25; Brettell and Hollifield, "Migration Theory," 15–16.

2. Perlmann and Waldinger, "Second Generation Decline?" 917.

3. Our knowledge about the Dutch situation suggests that it is even possible to extend this conclusion to the early modern period (Lucassen and Penninx, *Newcomers*).

4. Noiriel, *Le creuset français;* Moch, *Moving Europeans;* Hoerder and Moch, *European Migrants;* Hoerder, *Cultures in Contact.* See also Lucassen and Penninx, *Newcomers.*

5. Paz, *Popular Anti-Catholicism.*

6. Colley, *Britons,* 25.

7. Dann, *Nation und Nationalismus,* 185–98. See also Oltmer, *Migration und Politik.*

8. Green, "Terms and Concepts."

9. Penninx and Roosblad, "Conclusion," 187.

10. Schönwälder, *Einwanderung,* 163–66; Cottaar, *in Den Haag,* 141–46.

11. Here, a parliamentary committee researched the results of thirty years of integration policies with the implicit assumption that this policy had largely failed.

12. On self-selection, see Chiswick, "Self-Selected?" 71.

13. Bade, *Vom Auswanderungsland?;* Bade, *Europa in Bewegung,* 319–20.

14. Hollifield, *Immigrants,* 92.

15. With the exception of Spain (already in the 1970s) and Italy and Greece (from the 1980s onward).

16. Van Niekerk, *Premigration Legacies,* 209; Van Niekerk, "Afro-Caribbeans."

17. Hooghiemstra, *Trouwen over de grens,* 141.

18. Doomernik, *Institutionalization,* 59.

19. Crul and Vermeulen, "The Second Generation," 969.

20. Huntington, *Who Are We?*

21. Reimers, *Unwelcome Strangers.* See also Zolberg, "Reforming the Back Door," 316.

22. Hollifield, *Immigrants,* 204–10; Bommes and Geddes, *Immigration and Welfare,* 250–52.

23. Borjas, "Welfare Reform," 1121.

24. Schuck, "Law," 197–99. See also Fetzer, *Public Attitudes,* 95.

25. Bade, *Legal and Illegal,* 15.

26. Portes, "Immigration Theory," 812–16.

27. Gans, "Symbolic Ethnicity."

28. Howe, "Britishness," 36. See also Modood, Beishon, and Virdee, *Changing Ethnic Identities;* Modood et al., *Ethnic Minorities,* 329.

29. As defined by Hughes, "Dilemmas."

30. Alba and Nee, *Remaking the American Mainstream,* 274.

31. Portes and Schauffler, "Language," 28; Portes and Rumbaut, *Immigrant America,* 299–300.

32. This may be complicated, of course, by major (geo)political changes in the future.

# Bibliography

Abadan-Unat, Nermin. "Turkish Migration to Europe, 1960–1975: A Balance Sheet of Achievement and Failures." In *Turkish Workers in Europe: 1960–1975: A Socio-Economic Reappraisal,* edited by Nermin Abadan-Unat, 1–46. Leiden, Neth.: E. J. Brill, 1976.

——— ed., *Turkish Workers in Europe, 1960–1975: A Socio-Economic Reappraisal.* Leiden, Neth.: E. J. Brill, 1976.

Abali, Ünal. "Kulturelle Identität und Sprache: Türkische Schülerinnen und Schüler in Deutschland; Eine empirische Untersuchung." *Deutsch Lernen* 4 (2000): 310–31.

Aïssou, Abdel. *Les beurs, l'école et la France.* Paris: L'Harmattan/CIEMI, 1987.

Akenson, Donald Harman. *The Irish Diaspora: A Primer.* Toronto: P. D. Meany Co., 1996.

Alba, Richard D. *Ethnic Identity: The Transformation of White America.* New Haven, Conn.: Yale University Press, 1990.

———. "Assimilation's Quiet Tide." *The Public Interest* 119 (1995): 1–18.

Alba, Richard D., Johann Handl, and Walter Müller. "Ethnische Ungleichheit im deutschen Bildungssystem." *Kölner Zeitschrift für Soziologie und Sozialpsychologie* 46 (1994) 2:209–37.

Alba, Richard D., and Victor Nee. *Remaking the American Mainstream: Assimilation and Contemporary Immigration.* Cambridge, Mass.: Harvard University Press, 2003.

Alba, Richard D., and Roxane Silberman. "Decolonization Immigrations and the Social Origins of the Second Generation: The Case of North Africans in France." *International Migration Review* 36 (2002) 4:1169–93.

Alpleis, Hannes. "Erschwert die etnische Konzentration die Eingliederung?" In *Generation und Identität: Theoretische und empirische Beiträge zur Migrationssozi-*

*ologie*, edited by Hartmut Esser and Jürgen Friedrichs, 209–37. Opladen, Ger.: Westdeutscher Verlag, 1990.

Amiraux, Valérie. "Turkish Islam in Germany: Between Political Overdetermination and Cultural Affirmation." In *Political Participation and Identities of Muslims in Non-Muslim States*, edited by W. A. R. Shadid and P. S. van Koningsveld, 36–52. Kampen, Neth.: Kok-Pharos Publishing House, 1996.

Anderson, Benedict. *Imagined Communities: Reflections on the Origin and Spread of Nationalism*. London: Verso Editions, 1983.

Arias, Elizabeth. "Change in Nuptiality Patterns among Cuban Americans: Evidence of Cultural and Structural Assimilation." *International Migration Review* 35 (2001) 2:525–56.

Arnstein, Walter L. "The Murphy Riots: A Victorian Dilemma." *Victorian Studies* 19 (1975) 1:51–71.

Bade, Klaus J. *Vom Auswanderungsland zum Einwanderungsland? Deutschland 1880 bis 1980*. Berlin: Colloquium, 1983.

———. "'Preussengänger' und 'Abwehrpolitik': Ausländerbeschäftigung, Ausländerpolitik und Ausländerkontrolle auf dem Arbeitsmarkt in Preussen vor dem Ersten Weltkrieg." *Archiv für Sozialgeschichte* 24 (1984): 91–162.

———, ed. *Deutsche im Ausland, Fremde in Deutschland: Migration in Geschichte und Gegenwart*. Munich: Beck, 1992.

———. "Immigration and Social Peace." *Daedalus* Winter (1994): 85–106.

———. *Europa in Bewegung: Migration vom späten 18. Jahrhundert bis zur Gegenwart*. Munich: C. H. Beck, 2000.

———. *Legal and Illegal Immigration into Europe: Experiences and Challenges, Ortelius Lectures*. Wassenaar, Neth.: NIAS, 2003.

———. *Migration in European History*. Oxford: Blackwell Publishing, 2003.

Banton, Michael. *The Coloured Quarter: Negro Immigrants in an English City*. London: Jonathan Cape, 1955.

———. *White and Coloured: The Behaviour of British People towards Coloured Immigrants*. London: Jonathan Cape, 1959.

Barfuss, Karl Marten. *"Gastarbeiter" in Nordwestdeutschland 1884–1918*. Vol. 52. Bremen, Ger.: Selbstverlag des Staatsarchivs der freien Stadt Bremen, 1986.

Baroin, Henri. *La main-d'oeuvre étrangère dans la région lyonnaise*. Lyon: Bosc Frères & Riou, M. L., 1935.

Belbahri, Aldelkader. *Immigration et situations postcoloniales*. Paris: L'Harmattan/CIEMI, 1987.

Belchem, John. "Class, Creed and Country: The Irish Middle Class in Victorian Liverpool." In *The Irish in Victorian Britain: The Local Dimension*, edited by Roger Swift and Sheridan Gilley, 190–211. Dublin: Four Courts Press, 1999.

———. "The Liverpool-Irish Enclave." *Immigrants and Minorities* 18 (1999) 2–3:128–46.

Bender, Stefan, Bert Rürup, Wolfgang Seifert, and Werner Sesselmeier. "Migration und Arbeitsmarkt." In *Migrationsreport 2000*, edited by Klaus J. Bade and Rainer Münz, 59–84. Frankfurt am Main, Ger.: Campus, 2000.

Benson, Susan. *Ambiguous Ethnicity: Interracial Families in London*. Cambridge: Cambridge University Press, 1981.

*Bericht der Beauftragten der Bundesregierung für Ausländerfragen über die Lage der Ausländer in der Bundesrepublik Deutschland*. Berlin: Beauftragte der Bundesregierung für Ausländerfragen, 2000.

Bernhard, Ludwig. *Das Polnische Gemeinwesen im preussischen Staat: Die Polenfrage*. Leipzig, Ger.: Duncker & Humblot, 1907.

Bertillon, Jacques. *La problème de la dépopulation*. Paris: Armand Colin, 1897.

Bertrand, Louis. *L'invasion: Roman contemporaine*. Paris: Bibliothèque Charpentier, 1907.

Bielefeld, Uli. *Inländische Ausländer: Zum gesellschaftlichen Bewusstsein türkischer Jugendlicher in der Bundesrepublik*. Frankfurt am Main, Ger.: Campus Verlag, 1988.

Blanc, Albert. *L'immigration en France: Le travail national*. Lyon: A. Rey, 1901.

Blanc-Chaléard, Marie-Claude, "Des logiques nationales aux logiques ethniques?" *Mouvement Social* (1999) 188:3–15.

———. *Les Italiens dans l'est Parisien: Une histoire d'intégration (1880–1960)*. Rome: École Française de Rome, 2000.

Blecking, Diethelm. *Die Geschichte der Nationalpolnischen Turnorganisation "Sokol" im Deutschen Reich 1884–1939*. Münster, Ger.: LIT Verlag, 1986.

Böcker, Anita. "Paving the Way to a Better Future: Turks in the Netherlands." In *Immigrant Integration: The Dutch Case*, edited by Hans Vermeulen and Rinus Penninx, 153–77. Amsterdam: Spinhuis, 2000.

Böcker, Anita, and Dietrich Thränhardt. "Erfolge und Misserfolge der Integration: Deutschland und die Niederlande im Vergleich." *Das Parlament* (23-6-2003): 3–11.

———. "Is het Duitse integratiebeleid succesvoller, en zo ja, waarom? Reactie op Ruud Koopmans." *Migrantenstudies* 19 (2003): 33–44.

Bommes, Michael, and Andrew Geddes, eds. *Immigration and Welfare: Challenging the Borders of the Welfare State*. London: Routledge, 2000.

Bonds, Thomas William. "School Response to West Indian Youth Immigrating to England, 1960–1970." *Pylon: The Atlanta University Review of Race and Culture* 41 (1980): 72–88.

Bonnet, Jean-Charles. "Les Italiens dans l'agglomération lyonnaise à l'aube de la 'Belle Époque.'" In *L'emigrazione italiana in Francia prima del 1914*, edited by Jean Baptiste Duroselle and Enrico Serra, 87–106. Milan: Franco Angeli, 1978.

———. "Note sur les dossiers de naturalisation des italiens du Rhône de 1880 à 1915." In *L'emigrazione italiana in Francia prima del 1914*, edited by Jean Baptiste Duroselle and Enrico Serra, 225–38. Milan: Franco Agneli, 1978.

Bonnet, Serge, Charles Santini, and Hubert Barthélemy. "Appartenance politique et attitude religieuse dans l'émigration Italienne en Lorraine sidérurgique." *Archives de Sociologie des Religions* 13 (1962): 45–72.

Boris, Eileen, and Angélique Janssens. "Complicating Categories: An Introduction." *International Review of Social History* 44 (1999) 7:1–14.

Borjas, George J. "Welfare Reform and Immigrant Participation in Welfare Programs." *International Migration Review* 36 (2002) 4:1093–1123.

Brandt, Hans Jürgen. *Die Polen und die Kirche im Ruhrgebiet 1871–1919.* Münster, Ger.: Aschendorf, 1987.

Brepohl, Wilhelm. *Die Aufbau des Ruhrvolkes im Zuge der Ost-West-Wanderung: Beiträge zur deutschen Sozialgeschichte des 19. und 20. Jahrhunderts.* Dortmund, Ger.: Sozialforschungsstelle, 1948.

Brettell, Caroline B., and James F. Hollifield. "Migration Theory: Talking Across Disciplines." In *Migration Theory: Talking Across Disciplines,* edited by Caroline B. Brettell and James F. Hollifield, 1–26. New York: Routledge, 2000.

Brown, Colin. *Black and White Britain: The Third PSI Survey.* Aldershot, Eng.: Gower, 1984.

Brubaker, Rogers. *Citizenship and Nationhood in France and Germany.* Cambridge, Mass.: Harvard University Press, 1992.

———. "The Return of Assimilation? Changing Perspectives on Immigration and Its Sequels in France, Germany, and the United States." *Ethnic and Racial Studies* 24 (2001) 4:531–48.

Busteed, Mervyn. "Little Islands of Erin: Irish Settlement and Identity in Mid–Nineteenth-Century Manchester." *Immigrants and Minorities* 18 (1999) 2–3:94–127.

Byron, Margaret. *Post-war Caribbean Migration to Britain: The Unfinished Cycle.* Aldershot, Eng.: Avebury, 1994.

Byron, Margaret, and Stéphanie Condon. "A Comparative Study of Caribbean Return Migration from Britain and France: Towards a Context-Dependent Explanation." *Transactions* 21 (1996) 1:91–104.

Canny, Nicholas. *Making Ireland British, 1580–1650.* Oxford: Oxford University Press, 2001.

Carter, Bob, Clive Harris, and Shirley Joshi. "The 1951–55 Conservative Government and the Racialization of Black Immigration." *Immigrants and Minorities* 6 (1987): 335–47.

Cepni, Musa Koral. *Türkische Arbeitnehmer in der Bundesrepublik Deutschland: Ihr Einsatz im Gastgeberland und ihr Beitrag zur wirtschaftliche Entwicklung ihres Heimatlandes.* Freiburg: Hochschulverlag, 1980.

Chessum, Lorna. *From Immigrants to Ethnic Minority: Making Black Community in Britain.* Aldershot, Eng.: Ashgate, 2000.

Chevalier, Louis. *Classes laborieuses et classes dangereuses à Paris, pendant la première moitié du XIX siècle.* Paris: Librairie Genéral Française, 1978.

Chinn, Carl. "'Sturdy Catholic Emigrants': The Irish in Early Victorian Birmingham." In *The Irish in Victorian Britain: The Local Dimension,* edited by Roger Swift and Sheridan Gilley, 52–74. Dublin: Four Courts Press, 1999.

Chiswick, Barry R. "Are Immigrants Favorably Self-Selected? An Economic Analysis." In *Migration Theory: Talking Across Disciplines*, edited by Caroline Brettell and James F. Hollifield, 61–76. New York: Routledge, 2000.

Clancy, Anna, M. Hough, R. Aust, and C. Kershaw. *Crime, Policing and Justice: The Experience of Ethnic Minorities; Findings from the 2000 British Crime Survey.* London: Home Office, 2001.

Clark, Kenneth, and Stephen Drinkwater. "Enclaves, Neighbourhood Effects and Employment Outcomes: Ethnic Minorities in England and Wales." *Journal of Population Economics* 15 (2002) 1:5–30.

Cockcroft, James D., André Gunder Frank, and Dale L. Johnson. *Dependence and Underdevelopment: Latin America's Political Economy.* Garden City, N. Y.: Anchor Books, 1972.

Cohen, William B. "Pied-Noir Memory, History, and the Algerian War." In *Europe's Invisible Migrants*, edited by Andrea L. Smith, 129–46. Amsterdam: Amsterdam University Press, 2003.

Colley, Linda. *Britons: Forging the Nation, 1707–1837.* London: Yale University Press, 1992.

Collins, Marcus. "Pride and Prejudice: West Indian Men in Mid–Twentieth-Century Britain." *Journal of British Studies* 40 (2001): 391–418.

Connolly, Gerard. "Irish and Catholic: Myth or Reality? Another Sort of Irish and the Renewal of the Clerical Profession Among Catholics in England, 1791–1918." In *The Irish in the Victorian City*, edited by Roger Swift and Sheridan Gilley, 225–54. London: Croom Helm, 1985.

Costa-Lascoux, Jacqueline, and Émile Temime, eds. *Les Algériens en France (Genèse et devenir d'une migration).* Paris: Publisud, 1985.

Cottaar, Annemarie. *Ik had een neef in Den Haag: Nieuwkomers in de twintigste eeuw.* Zwolle, Neth.: Waanders, 1998.

———. "Onzedelijk of preuts? Surinaamse modellen in de hoofdstad." *Optima* (2003) 4:125–35.

Couder, Laurent. "Les italiens de la région parisienne dans les années 1920." In *Les Italiens en France de 1914 à 1940*, edited by Pierre Milza, 501–46. Rome: École française de Rome, 1986.

Croon, Helmuth, and Kurt Utermann. *Zeche und Gemeinde: Untersuchungen über Strukturwandel einer Zechengemeinde im nördlichen Ruhrgebiet.* Tübingen, Ger.: J. C. B. Mohr, 1958.

Cross, Gary S. *Immigrant Workers in Industrial France: The Making of a New Laboring Class.* Philadelphia: Temple University Press, 1983.

Cross, Malcolm, and Han Entzinger, "Caribbean Minorities in Britain and the Netherlands: Comparative Questions." In *Lost Illusions: Caribbean Minorities in Britain and the Netherlands*, edited by Malcolm Cross and Hans Entzinger, 1–33. London: Routledge 1988.

———, eds. *Lost Illusions: Caribbean Minorities in Britain and the Netherlands.* London: Routledge, 1988.

Cross, Malcolm, and Mark Johnson. "Mobility Denied: Afro-Caribbean Labour and the British Economy." In *Lost Illusions: Caribbean Minorities in Britain and the Netherlands,* edited by Malcolm Cross and Han Entzinger, 73–105. London: Routledge, 1988.

Crul, Maurice. "Breaking the Circle of Disadvantage: Social Mobility of Second-Generation Moroccans and Turks in the Netherlands." In *Immigrants, Schooling and Social Mobility: Does Culture Make a Difference?* edited by Hans Vermeulen and Joel Perlmann, 225–44. Houndmills, Eng.: Macmillan, 2000.

Crul, Maurice, and Hans Vermeulen. "The Second Generation in Europe: Introduction." *International Migration Review* 37 (2003) 4:965–86.

Cubero, José. *Nationalistes et étrangers: Le massacre d'Aigues-Mortes.* Paris: Éditions Imago, 1996.

Curtis, L. P. *Apes and Angels: The Irishman in Victorian Caricature.* Newton Abbot, Eng.: David and Charles, 1971.

Dale, Angela, and Clare Holdsworth. "Issues in the Analysis of Ethnicity in the 1991 British Census: Evidence from Microdata." *Ethnic and Racial Studies* 20 (1997) 1:160–81.

Daniels, Mary. *Exile or Opportunity? Irish Nurses and Midwives in Britain.* Liverpool: The Institute of Irish Studies, Occasional Papers in Irish Studies, no. 5, 1993.

Dann, Otto. *Nation und Nationalismus in Deutschland, 1770–1990.* Munich: Beck, 1996.

*Daten und Fakten zur Ausländersituation.* Berlin: Beauftragte der Bundesregierung für Ausländerfragen, 2002.

Davis, Graham. *The Irish in Britain, 1815–1914.* Dublin: Gill and Macmillan, 1991.

Delaney, Enda. *Demography, State and Society: Irish Migration to Britain, 1921–1971.* Liverpool: Liverpool University Press, 2000.

Delbrück, Hans. *Die Polenfrage.* Berlin: Verlag von Hermann Walther, 1984.

Dennis, Richard. *English Industrial Cities of the Nineteenth Century: A Social Geography.* Cambridge: Cambridge University Press, 1984.

De Rudder, Véronique. "Les conditions de logement des Algériens en France: Un problème racial?" In *Les Algériens en France (Genèse et devenir d'une migration),* edited by Jacqueline Costa-Lascoux and Émile Temime, 320–35. Paris: Publisud, 1985.

Diehl, Claudia, and Michael Bohm. "Rights or Identity? Naturalization Processes Among 'Labor Migrants' in Germany." *International Migration Review* 37 (2003) 1:133–62.

Dignan, Don. "Europe's Melting Pot: A Century of Large-Scale Immigration Into France." *Ethnic and Racial Studies* 4 (1981) 2:137–52.

Doomernik, Jeroen. "The Institutionalization of Turkish Islam in Germany and The Netherlands: A Comparison." *Ethnic and Racial Studies* 18 (1995) 1:46–63.

Dornis, Christian. "Zwei Jahre nach der Reform des Staatsangehörigkeitsrechts: Bilanz und Ausblick." In *Migrationsreport 2002,* edited by Klaus J. Bade and Rainer Münz, 163–78. Frankfurt am Main, Ger.: Campus, 2002.

Drake, St. Clair. "The Colour Problem in Britain: A Study in Social Definitions." *The Sociological Review* 3 (1955) 5:197–217.

Eder, Angelika. "Aspekte polnischen Lebens in Hamburg." In *Die Migration von Polen nach Deutschland: Zu Geschichte und Gegenwart eines europäischen Migrationssystems*, edited by Christian Pallaske, 43–60. Baden-Baden, Ger.: Nomos Verlagsgesellschaft, 2001.

*Emigrazione e colonie: Raccolta di rapporti dei RR; Agenti diplomatici e consolari.* Rome: Ministerio degli affari esteri, 1903.

Engels, Frederick. *The Condition of the Working-Class in England in 1844.* London: Swan Sonnenschein & Co., 1892.

Esser, Hartmut. *Aspekte der Wanderungssoziologie: Assimilation und Integration von Wanderern, ethnischen Gruppen und Minderheiten.* Darmstadt, Ger.: Luchterhand, 1980.

———. "Ist das Ausländerproblem in der Bundesrepublik ein 'Türkenproblem'?" In *Fremde raus? Fremdenangst und Ausländerfeindlichkeit*, edited by Rolf Italiaander, 169–79. Frankfurt am Main, Ger.: Fischer Taschenbuchverlag, 1983.

———. "Interethnische Freundschaften." In *Generation und Identität, Theoretische und empirische Beiträge zur Migrationssoziologie*, edited by Hartmut Esser and Jürgen Friedrichs, 185–206. Opladen, Ger.: Westdeutscher Verlag, 1990.

———."What Substance Is There to the Term 'Leitkultur'?" In *The Challenge of Diversity: European Social Democracy Facing Migration, Integration, and Multiculturalism*, edited by René Cuperus, Karl A. Duffek, and Johannes Kandel, 47–58. Innsbruck: Studienverlag, 2003.

Esser, Hartmut, and Jürgen Friedrichs, eds. *Generation und Identität: Theoretische und empirische Beiträge zur Migrationssoziologie.* Opladen, Ger.: Westdeutscher Verlag, 1990.

Ezra, Elisabeth. *The Colonial Unconscious: Race and Culture in Interwar France.* Ithaca, N.Y.: Cornell University Press, 2000.

Fahrmeir, Andreas. "Nineteenth-Century German Citizenship: A Reconsideration." *The Historical Journal* 40 (1997) 3:721–52.

———. *Citizens and Aliens: Foreigners and the Law in Britain and the German States, 1789–1870.* New York: Berghahn, 2000.

Faist, Thomas. "From School to Work: Public Policy and Underclass Formation among Young Turks in Germany during the 1980s." *International Migration Review* 27 (1993) 2:306–31.

Feldman, David. *Englishmen and Jews: Social Relations and Political Culture, 1840–1914.* New Haven, Conn.: Yale University Press, 1994.

———. "L'immigration, les immigrés et 'État en Grande-Bretagne aux XIXe et XXe siècles." *Le Mouvement Social* (1999) 188:43–60.

———. "Migration." In *Cambridge Urban History of Britain*, edited by Martin Daunton, 185–206. Cambridge: Cambridge University Press, 2000.

———. "Class." In *History and Historians in the Twentieth Century*, edited by Peter Burke, 181–206. Oxford: Oxford University Press, 2002.

Fetzer, Joel S. *Public Attitudes toward Immigration in the United States, France, and Germany*. Cambridge: Cambridge University Press, 2000.

Fielding, Steven. *Class and Ethnicity: Irish Catholics in England, 1880–1939*. Buckingham/Philadelphia: Open University Press, 1993.

Finkielkraut, Alain. *La défaite de la pensée: Essai*. Paris: Gallimard, 1987.

———. *Au nom de l'autre: Réflexions sur l'antisémitisme qui vient*. Paris: Gallimard, 2003.

Finnegan, Frances. "The Irish in York." In *The Irish in the Victorian City*, edited by Roger Swift and Sheridan Gilley, 59–84. London: Croom Helm, 1985.

Fitzpatrick, David. "Emigration, 1801–70." In *A New History of Ireland: Ireland Under the Union, I, 1801–70*, edited by W. E. Vaughan, 562–622. Oxford: Oxford University Press, 1989.

———. "A Peculiar Tramping People: The Irish in Britain, 1801–70." In *A New History of Ireland: Ireland under the Union, I, 1801–70*, edited by W. E. Vaughan, 623–60. Oxford: Oxford University Press, 1989.

Foner, Nancy. *Jamaica Farewell: Jamaican Migrants in London*. Berkeley: University of California Press, 1978.

———. "Towards a Comparative Perspective on Caribbean Migration." In *Caribbean Migration: Globalised Identities*, edited by Mary Chamberlain, 47–60. London: Routledge, 1998.

———. *From Ellis Island to JFK: New York's Two Great Waves of Immigration*. New Haven, Conn.: Yale University Press, 2000.

Franke, Eberhard. *Das Ruhrgebiet und Ostpreussen: Geschichte, Umfang und Bedeutung der Ostpreusseneinwanderung*. Essen, Ger.: Walter Bacmeisters Nationalverlag, 1936.

———. "Einbürgerungen und Namensänderungen im Ruhrgebiet." *Westfälische Forschungen* 2 (1939) 1:19–28.

Frankel, Jonathan, and Steve J. Zipperstein, eds. *Assimilation and Community: The Jews in Nineteenth-Century Europe*. Cambridge: Cambridge University Press, 1992.

Fraser, Peter D. "Nineteenth-Century West Indian Migration to Britain." In *In Search For a Better Life: Perspectives on Migration From the Caribbean*, edited by Ransford W. Palmer, 19–38. New York: Praeger, 1990.

Freeman, Gary P. "Caribbean Migration to Britain and France: From Assimilation to Selection." In *The Caribbean Exodus*, edited by Barry B. Levine, 185–203. New York: Praeger, 1987.

———. "Immigrant Labour and Racial Conflict: the Rôle of the State." In *Migrants in Modern France: Population Mobility in the Later 19th and 20th Centuries*, edited by Philip E. Ogden and Paul E. White, 160–76. London: Unwin Hyman, 1989.

Freund, Alexander. *Aufbrüche nach dem Zusammenbruch: Die deutsche Nordameri-*

*ka-Auswanderung nach dem zweiten Weltkrieg.* Göttingen, Ger.: V&R unipress, 2004.

Friedrichs, Jürgen. "Ethnic Segregation in Cologne, Germany, 1984–94." *Urban Studies* 35 (1998) 10:1745–64.

Gabaccia, Donna R. "The 'Yellow Peril' and the 'Chinese of Europe': Global Perspectives on Race and Labor, 1815–1930." In *Migration, Migration History, History: Old Paradigms and New Perspectives,* edited by Jan Lucassen and Leo Lucassen, 177–96. Bern: Peter Lang, 1997.

———. *Italy's Many Diasporas.* London: UCL Press, 2000.

Gallagher, Tom. "A Tale of Two Cities: Communal Strife in Glasgow and Liverpool Before 1914." In *The Irish in the Victorian City,* edited by Roger Swift and Sheridan Gilley, 106–29. London: Croom Helm, 1985.

Gans, Herbert J. "Symbolic Ethnicity and Symbolic Religiosity: Towards a Comparison of Ethnic and Religious Acculturation." *Ethnic and Racial Studies* 17 (1994) 4:577–92.

———. "Towards a Reconciliation of 'Assimilation' and 'Pluralism': The Interplay of Acculturation and Ethnic Retention." *International Migration Review* 31 (1997) 4:875–92.

———. "Filling in Some Holes: Six Areas of Needed Immigration Research." In *Immigration Research for a New Century: Multidisciplinary Perspectives,* edited by Nancy Foner, Rubén G. Rumbaut, and Steven J. Gold, 76–92. New York: Russell Sage Foundation, 2002.

Gastaut, Yvan. *L'immigration et l'opinion en France sous la Ve République.* Paris: Éditions du Seuil, 2000.

George, Pierre. "L'immigration italienne en France de 1920 à 1939: Aspects démographiques et sociaux." In *Les Italiens en France de 1914 à 1940,* edited by Pierre Milza, 45–67. Rome: École française de Rome, 1986.

Gerstle, Gary, and John Mollenkopf. "The Political Incorporation of Immigrants, Then and Now." In *E Pluribus Unum? Contemporary and Historical Perspectives on Immigrant Political Incorporation,* edited by Gary Gerstle and John Mollenkopf, 1–32. New York: Russell Sage Foundation, 2001.

Gilley, Sheridan. "English Attitudes to the Irish in England, 1780–1900." In *Immigrants and Minorities in British Society,* edited by Colin Holmes. London: Allen & Unwin, 1978.

Gillette, Alain, and Abdelmalek Sayad. *L'Immigration algérienne en France.* Paris: Éditions Entente, 1984.

Gilroy, Paul. *There Ain't No Black in the Union Jack: The Cultural Politics of Race and Nation.* London: Hutchinson, 1987.

Girard, Alain, ed. *Francais et immigrés: Nouveaux documents sur l'adaption.* Paris: Presses Universitaires de France, 1954.

Girard, Alain, and Jean Stoetzel. *Francais et immigrés: L'attitude francaise; L'adaption des Italiens et des Polonais.* Paris: Presses Universitaires de France, 1953.

Giraud, Michel. "Les migrations guadeloupéenne et martiniquaise en France métropolitaine." *Review* 22 (1999) 4:435–48.

Glazer, Nathan, and Patrick Moynihan. *Beyond the Melting Pot: The Negroes, Puerto Ricans, Jews, Italians, and Irish of New York City.* Cambridge, Mass.: MIT Press, 1970.

Glebe, Günther. "Housing and Segregation of Turks in Germany." In *Turks in European Cities: Housing and Urban Segregation,* edited by Sule Özüekren and Ronald van Kempen, 122–57. Utrecht, Neth.: Ercomer, 1997.

Glück, Helmut. *Die preussisch-polnische Sprachenpolitik, Eine Studie zur Theorie und Methodologie der Forschung über Sprachenpolitik, Sprachenbewustsein and Sozialgeschichte am Beispiel der preussisch-deutschen Politik gegenüber der polnischen Minderheit vor 1914.* Hamburg: Helmut Buske Verlag, 1979.

Gordon, Milton. *Assimilation in American Life: The Role of Race, Religion, and National Origins.* New York: Oxford University Press, 1964.

Gourévitch, Jean-Paul. *La France africaine: Islam, intégration, insécurité; Infos et intox.* Paris: Le Pré aux Clercs, 2000.

Greeley, Andrew M. *Why Can't They Be Like Us? America's White Ethnic Groups.* New York: A. P. Dutton, 1971.

Green, Nancy L. "The Comparative Method and Poststructural Structuralism: New Perspectives For Migration Studies." In *Migration, Migration History, History: Old Paradigms and New Perspectives,* edited by Jan Lucassen and Leo Lucassen, 57–72. Bern: Peter Lang, 1997.

———. *Ready-to-Wear, Ready-to-Work: A Century of Industry and Immigrants in Paris and New York.* Durham, N.C.: Duke University Press, 1997.

———. "Religion et ethnicité: De la comparaison spatiale et temporelle." *Annales HSS* (2002) 1:127–44.

———. *Repenser les migrations.* Paris: PUF, 2002.

———. "Terms and Concepts, Then and Now." In *Immigration and the Construction of Identities in Contemporary Europe: Transnational Ties and Identities,* edited by Anita Böcker and Leo Lucassen, 40–44. Wassenaar, Neth.: NIAS, 2002.

Griffith, J. A. G., Judith Henderson, Margaret Usborne, and Donald Wood. *Coloured Immigrants in Britain.* London: Oxford University Press, 1960.

Grosfoguel, Ramón. "Colonial Caribbean Migration to France, the Netherlands, Great Britain and the United States." *Ethnic and Racial Studies* 20 (1997) 3:594–612.

———. "'Cultural Racism' and Colonial Caribbean Migrants in Core Zones of the Capitalist World Economy." *Review* 22 (1999) 4:409–34.

Guglielmo, Thomas A. *White on Arrival: Italians, Race, Color, and Power in Chicago, 1890–1945.* Oxford: Oxford University Press, 2003.

Guterl, Matthew Pratt. *The Color of Race in America, 1900–1940.* Cambridge, Mass.: Harvard University Press, 2001.

Hafez, Kai. "Zwischen Parallelgesellschaft, strategischer Ethnisierung und Transkultur: Die türkische Medienkultur in Deutschland." *Blätter für deutsche und internationale Politik* 45 (2000) 6:728–36.

Hagedorn, Heike. "Bilanz der Einbürgerungspolitik in Deutschland und Frankreich." In *Migration in erklärten und 'unerklärten' Einwanderungsländern: Analyse und Vergleich*, edited by Uwe Hunger, Karin Meendermann, Bernhard Santel, and Wichard Woyke, 37–64. Münster, Ger.: LIT, 2001.

Hagen, William W. *Germans, Poles and Jews: The Nationality Conflict in the Prussian East, 1772–1914.* Chicago: University of Chicago Press, 1980.

Hall, Stuart, Chas Critcher, Tony Jefferson, John Clarke, and Brian Roberts. *Policing the Crisis: Mugging, the State, and Law and Order.* New York: Holmes & Meier, 1978.

Hamed-Touati, M'Barka. *Immigration maghrébine et activités politiques en France: De la première guerre mondiale à la veille du front populaire.* Tunis: Université de Tunis I, 1994.

Hamoumou, Mohand. *Et ils sont devenus harkis.* Paris: Fayard, 1993.

Hanhörster, Heike, and Margit Mölder. "Konflikt- und Integrationsräume im Wohnbereich." In *Bedrohte Stadtgesellschaft: Soziale Desintegrationsprozesse und ethnisch-kulturelle Konfliktkonstellationen*, edited by Wilhelm Heitmeyer and Reimund Anhut, 347–400. Weinheim, Ger.: Juventa, 2000.

Hansen, Jörgen, and Magnus Lofstrom. "Immigrant Assimilation and Welfare Participation: Do Immigrants Assimilate Into or Out of Welfare?" Working paper 2430. London: Centre for Economic Policy Research, 2000.

Hansen, Randall. *Citizenship and Immigration in Post-war Britain: The Institutional Origins of a Multicultural Nation.* Oxford: Oxford University Press, 2000.

Hargreaves, Alec G. *Immigration, 'Race' and Ethnicity in Contemporary France.* London: Routledge, 1995.

Harris, Clive. "Post-war Migration and the Industrial Reserve Army." In *Inside Babylon: The Caribbean Diaspora in Britain*, edited by Winston James and Clive Harris, 9–54. London: Verso, 1993.

Hassini, Mohamed. *L'école: Une chance pour les filles de parents maghrébins.* Paris: CIEMI/L'Harmattan, 1997.

Hauschildt, Elke. *Polnische Arbeitsmigranten in Wilhelmsburg bei Hamburg während des Kaiserreichs und der Weimarer Republik.* Dortmund, Ger.: Forschungsstelle Ostmitteleuropa, 1986.

Heath, Anthony, Dorren McMahon, and Jane Roberts. "Ethnic Differences in the Labour Market: A Comparison of the SARS and LFS." Working paper 71. Oxford: CREST, 1999.

Heitmeyer, Wilhelm, Joachim Müller, and Helmut Schröder. *Verlockender Fundamentalismus: Türkische Jugendlichen in Deutschland.* Frankfurt am Main, Ger.: Suhrkamp, 1997.

Hennessy, Alistair. "Workers of the Night: West Indians in Britain." In *Lost Illusions: Caribbean Minorities in Britain and the Netherlands*, edited by Malcolm Cross and Han Entzinger, 36–53. London: Routledge, 1988.

Herbert, Ulrich. *A History of Foreign Labor in Germany, 1880–1980: Seasonal Workers, Forced Laborers, Guest Workers.* Ann Arbor: University of Michigan Press, 1990.

———. *Geschichte der Ausländerpolitik in Deutschland: Saisonarbeiter, Zwangsarbeiter, Gastarbeiter, Flüchtlinge*. Munich: C. H. Beck, 2001.

Herwartz-Emden, Leonie. "Einwandererkinder im deutschen Bildungswesen." In *Das Bildungswesen in der Bundesrepublik Deutschland: Strukturen und Entwicklungen im Überblick*, edited by Kai S. Cortina et al., 661–709. Berlin: Rowohlt Taschenbuch Verlag, 2003.

Hickman, Mary J. *Religion, Class, and Identity: The State, the Catholic Church, and the Education of the Irish in Britain*. Aldershot, Eng.: Avebury, 1995.

Hinken, Günter. "Die betriebliche Integration von Arbeitsmigranten in Deutschland: Institutionelle und programmatische Inklusionsofferten innerhalb des 'deutschen Modells.'" In *Migration in erklärten und unerklärten Einwanderungsländern: Analyse und Vergleich*, edited by Uwe Hunger, Karin Meendermann, Bernhard Santel, and Wichard Woyke, 167–94. Münster, Ger.: LIT, 2001.

Hiro, Dilip. *Black British, White British: A History of Race Relations in Britain*. London: Grafton Books, 1991.

Hochstadt, Steven. *Mobility and Modernity: Migration in Germany, 1820–1989*. Ann Arbor: University of Michigan Press, 1999.

Hoerder, Dirk. "Segmented Macrosystems and Networking Individuals: The Balancing Functions of Migration Processes." In *Migration, Migration History, History: Old Paradigms and New Perspectives*, edited by Jan Lucassen and Leo Lucassen, 73–84. Bern: Peter Lang, 1997.

———. "Historical Dimensions of Many-Cultured Societies in Europe: The Case of Hamburg, Germany." In *Socio-Cultural Problems in the Metropolis: Comparative Analyses*, edited by Dirk Hoerder and Rainer-Olaf Schultze, 121–140. Hagen, Ger.: ISL-Verlag, 2000.

———.*Cultures in Contact: World Migrations in the Second Millennium*. Durham, N. C.: Duke University Press, 2002.

Hoerder, Dirk, and Leslie Page Moch, eds. *European Migrants: Global and Local Perspectives*. Boston: Northeastern University Press, 1996.

Hollifield, James F. *Immigrants, Markets, and States: the Political Economy of Postwar Europe*. Cambridge, Mass.: Harvard University Press, 1992.

Holmes, Colin. *John Bull's Island: Immigration and British Society, 1871–1971*. Basingstoke, Eng.: Macmillan, 1988.

Hooghiemstra, Erna. *Trouwen over de grens: Achtergronden van partnerkeuze van Turken en Marokkanen in Nederland*. The Hague: Sociaal Cultureel Planbureau, 2003.

Howe, Stephen. "Britishness and Multiculturalism." In *The Challenge of Diversity: European Social Democracy Facing Migration, Integration, and Multiculturalism*, edited by René Cuperus, Karl A. Duffek, and Johannes Kandel, 31–46. Innsbruck: Studienverlag, 2003.

Hughes, Everett C. "Dilemmas and Contradictions of Status." *American Journal of Sociology* 50 (March 1945): 353–59.

Hunger, Uwe, and Dietrich Thränhardt. "Der Bildungserfolg von Einwandererkindern in den Bundesländern: Diskrepanzen zwischen der PISA-Studie und den offiziellen Schulstatistiken." In *Schieflagen im Bildungssystem: Die Benachteiligung der Migrantenkinder,* edited by Georg Auernheimer, 51–77. Opladen, Ger.: Leske und Budrich, 2003.

Huntington, Samuel P. *The Clash of Civilizations and the Remaking of World Order.* New York: Simon & Schuster, 1996.

———. *Who Are We? The Cultural Core of American National Identity.* New York: Simon & Schuster, 2004.

Hutchinson, Edward Prince. *Legislative History of American Immigration Policy, 1798–1965.* Philadelphia: University of Pennsylvania Press, 1981.

Ignatief, Noel. *How the Irish Became White.* New York: Routledge, 1995.

Jackson, John Archer. *The Irish in Britain.* London: Routledge and Kegan Paul, 1963.

Jacobson, Matthew Fry. *Special Sorrows: The Diasporic Imagination of Irish, Polish and Jewish Immigrants in the United States.* Cambridge, Mass.: Harvard University Press, 1995.

Jazouli, Adil. *L'Action collective des jeunes Maghrébins de France.* Paris: CIEMI/L'Harmattan, 1986.

Jones, Trevor. *Britain's Ethnic Minorities: An Analysis of the Labour Force Survey.* London: Policy Studies Institute, 1993.

Jones, R. Merfyn, and D. Ben Rees. *The Liverpool Welsh and Their Religion: Two Centuries of Welsh Calvinist Methodism.* Liverpool: Modern Welsh Publications, 1984.

Joppke, Christian. *Immigration and the Nation-State: The United States, Germany, and Great Britain.* Oxford: Oxford University Press, 1999.

Joppke, Christian, and Ewa Morawska, eds. *Toward Assimilation and Citizenship: Immigrants in Liberal Nation-States.* Houndmills, Eng.: Palgrave Macmillan, 2003.

Jordi, Jean-Jacques, and Mohand Hamoumou. *Les Harkis, une mémoire enfouie.* Paris: Éditions Autrement, 1999.

Kalmijn, Matthijs. "Trends in Black/White Intermarriage." *Social Forces* 7 (1993) 1:119–46.

Kaltenbach, Jeanne-Hélène, and Michèle Tribalat. *La République et l'islam: Entre crainte et aveuglement.* Paris: Gallimard, 2002.

Karakasoglu, Yasemin. "Turkish Cultural Orientations in Germany and the Role of Islam." In *Turkish Culture in German Society Today,* edited by David Horrocks and Eva Kolinsky, 157–80. Providence, R.I.: Berghahn, 1996.

Katznelson, Ira. *Black Men, White Cities: Race, Politics, and Migration in the United States, 1900–30, and Britain, 1948–68.* London: Oxford University Press, 1973.

Kazal, Russell A. "Revisiting Assimilation: The Rise, Fall, and Reappraisal of a Concept in American Ethnic History." *American Historical Review* 100 (1995) 2:437–71.

Keeley, Charles B. "Demography and International Migration." In *Migration Theory: Talking Across Disciplines*, edited by Caroline Brettell and James F. Hollifield, 43–60. New York: Routledge, 2000.

Kepel, Gilles. *Les banlieues de l'Islam: Naissance d'une religion en France.* Paris: Seuil, 1991.

Khellil, Mohand. *L'intégration des Magrébins en France.* Paris: Presses Universitaires de France, 1991.

Kivisto, Peter. "The Transplanted Then and Now: The Reorientation of Immigration Studies from the Chicago School to the New Social History." *Ethnic and Racial Studies* 13 (1990) 4:455–81.

Klessmann, Christoph. *Polnische Bergarbeiter im Ruhrgebiet 1870–1945: Soziale Integration und nationale Subkultur einer Minderheit in der deutschen Industriegesellschaft.* Göttingen, Ger.: Vandenhoeck & Ruprecht, 1978.

———. "Long-Distance Migration, Integration, and Segregation of an Ethnic Minority in Industrial Germany: The Case of the Ruhr-Poles." In *Population, Labour and Migration in 19th- and 20th-Century Germany*, edited by Klaus J. Bade, 101–14. Leamington Spa, Eng.: Berg, 1987.

Kok, Jan. "Choices and Constraints in the Migration of Families: The Central Netherlands, 1850–1940." *The History of the Family* 9 (2004) 2:137–58.

Koopmans, Ruud. "Zachte heelmeesters . . . Een vergelijking van de resultaten van het Nederlandse en Duitse integratiebeleid en wat de WRR daaruit niet concludeert." *Migrantenstudies* 18 (2002) 2:87–92.

Kulczycki, John J. *School Strikes in Prussian Poland, 1901–1907: The Struggle over Bilingual Education.* New York: Columbia University Press, 1981.

———. *The Foreign Worker and the German Labour Movement: Xenophobia and Solidarity in the Coal Fields of the Ruhr, 1871–1914.* Oxford: Berg, 1994.

———. *The Polish Coal Miners' Union and the German Labor Movement in the Ruhr, 1902–1934.* Oxford/New York: Berg, 1997.

Kürsat-Ahlers, Elcin. "The Turkish Minority in German Society." In *Turkish Culture in German Society Today*, edited by David Horrocks and Eva Kolinsky, 113–36. Providence, R. I.: Berghahn, 1996.

Kymlicka, Will. *Multicultural Citizenship: A Liberal Theory of Minority Rights.* Oxford: Clarendon Press, 1995.

Lamont, Michelle. *The Dignity of Working Men: Morality and the Boundaries of Race, Class, and Immigration.* Cambridge, Mass.: Harvard University Press, 2000.

Lamont, Michelle, Ann Morning, and Margarita Mooney. "Particular Universalisms: North African Immigrants Respond to French Racism." *Ethnic and Racial Studies* 25 (2002) 3:390–414.

Large, David. "The Irish in Bristol in 1851: A Census Enumeration." In *The Irish in the Victorian City*, edited by Roger Swift and Sheridan Gilley, 37–58. London: Croom Helm, 1985.

Lartigue-Vecchie, M. "Les grèves des dockers à Marseille de 1890 à 1903." *Provence Historique* 10 (1960): 146–79.

Lawton, R. "Irish Immigration to England and Wales in the Mid-Nineteenth Century." *Irish Geography* 4 (1959) 1:35–54.

Layton-Henry, Zig. *The Politics of Immigration.* Oxford: Blackwell, 1992.

Lebon, André. *Immigration et présence étrangère en France 1997/1998.* Paris: Ministère de l'Emploi et de la Solidarité: Direction de la Population et des Migrations, 1998.

Le Bras, Hervé. *Le démon des origines: Démographie et extrême droite.* Latour d'Aigues, Fr.: Éditions de l'Aube, 1998.

Le Conte, René. *Étude sur l'émigration italienne.* Paris: Librairie des facultés A. Michalon, 1908.

Lees, Lynn Hollen. *Exiles of Erin: Irish Migrants in Victorian London.* Manchester, Eng.: Manchester University Press, 1979.

Leggewie, Claus. "How Turks Became Kurds, Not Germans." *Dissent* 43 (1996) 3:79–83.

———. "Turcs, Kurdes et Allemands: Histoire d'une migration; de la stratification sociale à la différenciation culturelle, 1961–1990." *Le Mouvement Social* 188 (1999): 103–18.

———. "Integration and Segregation." In *Migrationsreport 2000,* edited by Klaus J. Bade and Rainer Münz, 85–108. Frankfurt am Main, Ger.: Campus, 2000.

Lequin, Yves. *Les ouvriers de la région lyonnaise (1848–1914): La formation de la classe ouvrière régionale.* 2 vols. Lyon: Presses Universitaires de Lyon, 1977.

Lesger, Clé, Leo Lucassen, and Marlou Schrover. "Is There Life Outside the Migrant Network? German Immigrants in XIXth Century Netherlands and the Need for a More Balanced Migration Typology." *Annales de Démographie Historique* (2002) 2:29–50.

Levitt, Peggy. *The Transnational Villagers.* Berkeley: University of California Press, 2001.

Lewis, Bernard. *The Crisis of Islam: Holy War and Unholy Terror.* London: Weidenfeld & Nicolson, 2002.

Lewis, Oscar. *Five Families: Mexican Case Studies in the Culture of Poverty.* New York: Basic Books, 1959.

Lewis, Philip. *Islamic Britain: Religion, Politics and Identity among British Muslims.* London: I. B. Tauris, 2002.

Lieberson, Stanley. *A Piece of the Pie: Blacks and White Immigrants since 1880.* Berkeley: University of California Press, 1980.

Liens, Georges. "Les 'Vèpres Marseillaises' (Juin 1881) ou la crise franco-italienne au lendemain du traité du Bardo." *Revue d'Histoire Moderne et Contemporaine* 14 (1967): 1–30.

Little, K. L. *Negroes in Britain: A Study of Racial Relations in English Society.* London: Kegan Paul, 1947.

Lobban, R. D. "The Irish Community in Greenock in the Nineteenth Century." *Irish Geography* VI (1971): 270–81.

Lowe, W. J. *The Irish in Mid-Victorian Lancashire: The Shaping of a Working Class Community.* New York: Peter Lang, 1989.

Lucassen, Jan. *Migrant Labour in Europe: The Drift to the North Sea.* London: Croom Helm, 1987.

Lucassen, Jan, and Leo Lucassen. "Introduction." In *Migration, Migration History, History: Old Paradigms and New Perspectives,* edited by Jan Lucassen and Leo Lucassen, 1–38. Bern: Peter Lang, 1997.

———, eds. *Migration, Migration History, History: Old Paradigms and New Perspectives.* Bern: Peter Lang, 1997.

Lucassen, Jan, and Rinus Penninx. *Newcomers: Immigrants and Their Descendants in the Netherlands.* Amsterdam: Spinhuis, 1997.

Lucassen, Leo. "A Blind Spot: Migratory and Travelling Groups in Western European Historiography." *International Review of Social History* 38 (1993): 209–35.

———. *Zigeuner: Die Geschichte eines polizeilichen Ordnungsbegriffes in Deutschland, 1700–1945.* Cologne: Böhlau, 1996.

———. "Eternal Vagrants? State Formation, Migration, and Travelling Groups in Western Europe, 1350–1914." In *Migration, Migration History, History: Old Paradigms and New Perspectives,* edited by Jan Lucassen and Leo Lucassen, 225–52. Bern: Peter Lang, 1997.

———. "The Great War and the Origins of Migration Control in Western Europe and the United States (1880–1920)." In *Regulation of Migration: International Experiences,* edited by Anita Böcker, Kees Groenendijk, Tetty Havinga, and Paul Minderhoud, 45–72. Amsterdam: Spinhuis, 1998.

———. "A Many-Headed Monster: The Evolution of the Passport System in the Netherlands and Germany in the Long Nineteenth Century." In *Documenting Individual Identity: The Development of State Practices in the Modern World,* edited by Jane Caplan and John Torpey, 235–55. Princeton, N.J.: Princeton University Press, 2001.

———. "Old and New Migrants in the Twentieth Century: A European Perspective." *Journal of American Ethnic History* 21 (2002) 4:85–101.

———. "Administrative Into Social Control: The Aliens Police and Foreign Female Servants in the Netherlands, 1918–1940." *Social History* 27 (2002) 3:327–42.

———. "Bringing Structure Back In: Economic and Political Determinants of Immigration in Dutch Cities, 1920–1940." *Social Science History* 26 (2002) 3:503–29.

Lucassen, Leo, and Boudien de Vries. "The Rise and Fall of a Western European Textile-Worker Migration System: Leiden, 1586–1700." *Revue du Nord* 15 (Hors serie) (2001): 23–42.

Lucassen, Leo, Wim Willems, and Annemarie Cottaar. *Gypsies and Other Itinerant Groups: A Socio-Historical Approach.* New York: St. Martin's Press, 1998.

Lunn, Kenneth. "Immigration and Reaction in Britain, 1880–1950: Rethinking the 'Legacy of Empire.'" In *Migration, Migration History, History: Old Paradigms and New Perspectives*, edited by Jan Lucassen and Leo Lucassen, 335–49. Bern: Peter Lang, 1997.

MacMaster, Neil. *Colonial Migrants and Racism: Algerians in France, 1900–62*. Houndmills, Eng.: Macmillan, 1997.

MacRaild, Donald M. *Culture, Conflict and Migration: The Irish in Victorian Cumbria*. Liverpool: Liverpool University Press, 1998.

Mandel, Ruth. "Shifting Centres and Emergent Identities: Turkey and Germany in the Lives of Turkish Gastarbeiter." In *Muslim Travellers: Pilgrimage, Migration, and the Religious Imagination*, edited by Dale F. Eickelman and James Piscatori, 153–74. London: Routledge, 1990.

———. "'Fortress Europe' and the Foreigners Within: Germany's Turks." In *The Anthropology of Europe: Identities and Boundaries in Conflict*, edited by Victoria A. Goddard, Joseph R. Llobera, and Chris Shore, 113–24. Oxford: Berg, 1994.

Manfrass, Klaus. *Türken in der Bundesrepublik: Nordafrikaner in Frankreich; Ausländerproblematik im deutsch-französischen Vergleich*. Bonn: Bouvier Verlag, 1991.

Mauco, Georges. *Les étrangers en France: Leur rôle dans l'activité économique*. Paris: Librairie Armand Colin, 1932.

McKeown, Adam. "Global Migration, 1846–1940." *Journal of World History* 15 (2004) 2:155–89.

Mehrländer, Ursula, Carsten Ascheberg, and Jörg Ueltzhöffer. *Repräsentativuntersuchung '95: Situation der ausländischen Arbeitnehmer und ihrer Familienangehörigen in der Bundesrepublik Deutschland*. Bonn: Bundesministerium für Arbeit und Sozialordnung, 1996.

Miles, Robert. *Racism and Migrant Labour*. London: Routledge and Kegan Paul, 1982.

Miller, Kerby A. *Emigrants and Exiles: Ireland and the Irish Exodus to North America*. Oxford: Oxford University Press, 1985.

Millward, Pauline. "The Stockport Riots of 1852: A Study of Anti-Catholic and Anti-Irish Sentiment." In *The Irish in the Victorian City*, edited by Roger Swift and Sheridan Gilley, 207–24. London: Croom Helm, 1985.

Milza, Olivier. "Les Italiens dans l'économie française (1919–1939)." In *Les Italiens en France de 1914 à 1940*, edited by Pierre Milza, 69–88. Rome: École française de Rome, 1986.

Milza, Pierre. "L'émigration italienne en France de 1870 à 1914." In *L'emigrazione italiana in Francia prima del 1914*, edited by Jean Baptiste Duroselle and Enrico Serra, 63–86. Milan: Franco Angeli, 1978.

———. "L'intégration des Italiens dans le mouvement ouvrier français à la fin du XIX et au début du XX siècle; le cas de la région Marseillaise."In *L'emigrazione italiana in Francia prima del 1914*, edited by Jean Baptiste Duroselle and Enrico Serra, 171–208. Milan: Franco Agneli, 1978.

————. *Français et Italiens à la fin du XIXe siècle: Aux origines du rapprochement franco-italien de 1900–1902.* 2 vols. Rome: École française de Rome, 1981.

————. *Voyage en Ritalie.* Paris: Éditions Payot & Rivages, 1995.

Mink, Gwendolyn. *Old Labor and New Immigrants in American Political Development: Union, Party, and State, 1875–1920.* Ithaca, N. Y.: Cornell University Press, 1986.

Miskell, Louise. "Irish Migrants in Cornwall: The Camborne Experience, 1861–82." In *The Irish in Victorian Britain: The Local Dimension,* edited by Roger Swift and Sheridan Gilley, 31–51. Dublin: Four Courts Press, 1999.

Moch, Leslie Page. *Moving Europeans: Migration in Western Europe since 1650.* Bloomington: Indiana University Press, 2003.

————. "Networks Among Bretons? The Evidence for Paris, 1875–1925." *Continuity and Change* 18 (2003) 3:431–56.

Model, Suzanne. "West Indian Prosperity: Fact or Fiction?" *Social Problems* 42 (1995) 4:535–53.

————. "Ethnic Inequality in England: An Analysis Based on the 1991 Census." *Ethnic and Racial Studies* 22 (1999) 6:966–90.

Model, Suzanne, and Gene Fisher. "Unions Between Blacks and Whites: England and the U.S. Compared." *Ethnic and Racial Studies* 25 (2002) 5:728–54.

Modood, Tariq, et al. *Ethnic minorities in Britain: Diversity and Disadvantage.* London: Policies Studies Institute, 1997.

Modood, Tariq, Sharon Beishon, and Satnam Virdee. *Changing Ethnic Identities.* London: Policy Studies Institute, 1994.

Mokyr, Joel. *Why Ireland Starved: A Quantitative and Analytical History of the Irish Economy, 1800–1850.* London: Allen & Unwin, 1983.

Montgomery, David. *The Fall of the House of Labor: The Workplace, the State, and American Labor Activism, 1865–1925.* Cambridge: Cambridge University Press, 1987.

Moran, Gerard. "Nationalists in Exile: The National Brotherhood of St. Patrick in Lancashire, 1861–5." In *The Irish in Victorian Britain: The Local Dimension,* edited by Roger Swift and Sheridan Gilley, 212–35. Dublin: Four Courts Press, 1999.

Morawska, Ewa. "The Sociology and Historiography of Immigration." In *Immigration Reconsidered: History, Sociology and Politics,* edited by Virginia Yans-McLaughlin, 187–240. Oxford: Oxford University Press, 1990.

————. "In Defence of the Assimilation Model." *Journal of American Ethnic History* 13 (1994) 2:76–87.

————. *Insecure Prosperity: Small-Town Jews in Industrial America, 1890–1940.* Princeton, N.J.: Princeton University Press, 1996.

————. "Immigrants, Transnationalism, and Ethnicization: A Comparison of This Great Wave and the Last." In *E Pluribus Unum? Contemporary and Historical Perspectives on Immigrant Political Incorporation,* edited by Gary Gerstle and John Mollenkopf, 175–212. New York: Russell Sage Foundation, 2001.

Motte, Jan. "Vom 'Wirtschaftswunder' bis zur Stahlkrise: Die Beschäftigung von Arbeitern aus der Türkei im Hüttenwerk Salzgitter, 1963–1984." In *Zuwanderung und Integration in Niedersachsen seit dem Zweiten Weltkrieg*, edited by Klaus J. Bade and Jochen Oltmer, 253–72. Osnabrück, Ger.: Rasch, 2002.

Munoz-Perez, Francisco, and Michèle Tribalat. "Mariages d'étrangers et mariages mixtes en France: Évolution depuis la Première Guerre." *Population* (1984) 3:427–462.

Münz, Rainer, Wolfgang Seifert, and Ralf Ulrich. *Zuwanderung nach Deutschland: Strukturen, Wirkungen, Perspektiven.* Frankfurt am Main, Ger.: Campus Verlag, 1997.

Murphy, Richard C. *Gastarbeiter im Deutschen Reich: Polen in Bottrop, 1891–1933.* Wuppertal, Ger.: Peter Hammer Verlag, 1982.

Murzynowska, Krystyna. *Die polnischen Erwerbsauswanderer im Ruhrgebiet während der Jahre 1880–1914.* Dortmund, Ger.: Forschungsstelle Ostmitteleuropa, 1979.

Musterd, Sako, and Rinus Deurloo. "Unstable Immigrant Concentrations in Amsterdam: Spatial Segregation and Integration of Newcomers." *Housing Studies* 17 (2002) 3:487–503.

Nauck, Bernhard. "Sozial-ökologischer Kontext und ausserfamiliäre Beziehungen: Ein interkultureller und interkontextueller Vergleich am Beispiel von deutschen und türkischen Familien." *Kölner Zeitschrift für Soziologie und Sozialpsychologie* 29 (1988): 310–27.

Neal, Frank. *Sectarian Violence: The Liverpool Experience 1819–1914; An Aspect of Anglo-Irish History.* Manchester: Manchester University Press, 1988.

———. *Black '47: Britain and the Famine Irish.* New York: St. Martins Press, 1998.

———. "The Foundations of the Irish Settlement in Newcastle Upon Tyne: The Evidence in the 1851 Census." *Immigrants and Minorities* 18 (1999) 2&3:71–93.

Neubach, Helmut. *Die Ausweisungen von Polen und Juden aus Preussen, 1885/86: Ein Beitrag zu Bismarcks Polenpolitik und zur Geschichte des deutsch-polnischen Verhältnisses.* Wiesbaden, Ger.: Harrassowitz, 1967.

Neyrand, Gérard, and Marine M'Sili. "Les couples mixtes dans la France contemporaine: Mariage, acquisition de la nationalité française et divorce." *Population* 52 (1997) 3:571–606.

Nickel, Stephen. "Unemployment in Britain." In *The State of Working Britain*, edited by Paul Gregg and Jonathan Wadsworth, 7–28. Manchester: Manchester University Press, 1999.

Noiriel, Gérard. *Longwy: immigrés et prolétaires, 1880–1980.* Paris: Presses Universitaires de France, 1984.

———. "Les immigrés italiens en Lorraine pendant l'entre-deux-guerres: Du rejet xénophobe aux stratégies d'intégration." In *Les Italiens en France de 1914 à 1940*, edited by Pierre Milza. Rome: École française de Rome, 1986.

———. *Le creuset français: Histoire de l'immigration, XIXe-XXe siècles.* Paris: Éd. du Seuil, 1988.

———. *La tyrannie du national: Le droit d'asile en Europe (1793–1993)*. Paris: Calmann-Lévy, 1991.

Nora, Pierre. *Les lieux de mémoire*. Paris: Gallimard, 1997.

Nugent, Walter. *Crossings: The Great Transatlantic Migrations, 1870–1914*. Bloomington: Indiana University Press, 1992.

O'Day, Alan. "The Political Behaviour of the Irish in Great Britain in the Late 19th and Early 20th Century." In *Irish and Polish Migration in Comparative Perspective*, edited by John Belchem and Klaus Tenfelde, 75–92. Essen, Ger.: Klartext, 2003.

Oenning, Ralf Karl. *"Du da mitti polnischen Farben . . .": Sozialisationserfahrungen von Polen im Ruhrgebiet, 1918 bis 1939*. Münster, Ger.: Waxmann, 1991.

Ogden, Philip E. "Foreigners in Paris: Residential Segregation in the Nineteenth and Twentieth Centuries." London: Department of Geography, Occasional Papers, 1979.

O'Leary, Paul. *Immigration and Integration: The Irish in Wales, 1789–1922*. Cardiff: University of Wales Press, 2000.

Oltmer, Jochen. "Deutsche Migrationsverhältnisse: Neuere Forschungsergebnisse zur Wanderungsgeschichte im Kaiserreich und in der Weimarer Republik." *Historisches Jahrbuch* 122 (2002): 483–520.

O'Tuathaigh, M. A. G. "The Irish in Nineteenth-Century Britain: Problems of Integration." In *The Irish in the Victorian City*, edited by Roger Swift and Sheridan Gilley, 13–36. London: Croom Helm, 1985.

Palmer, R. R., and Joel Colton. *A History of the Modern World*. 5th ed. New York: Alfred A. Knopf, 1978.

Paris, Robert. "Les Italiens et le mouvement ouvrier français de 1870 à 1915." In *L'intégration italienne en France*, edited by Antonio Bechelloni, Michel Dreyfus, and Pierre Milza, 59–70. Paris: Éditions complexe, 1995.

Pathak, Shalini. *Race Research for the Future: Ethnicity in Education, Training and the Labour Market*. London: Department for Education and Employment, 2000.

Patterson, Sheila. *Dark Strangers: A Sociological Study of the Absorption of a Recent West Indian Migrant Group in Britain, South London*. London: Tavistock Publications, 1963.

———. *Immigration and Race Relations in Britain, 1960–1967*. London: Oxford University Press, 1969.

Paul, Kathleen. *Whitewashing Britain: Race and Citizenship in the Postwar Era*. Ithaca, N. Y.: Cornell University Press, 1997.

Paulucci di Calboli, Raniero. *Larmes et sourires de l'émigration italienne*. Paris: Librairie Félix Juven, 1909.

Paz, Denis G. *Popular Anti-Catholicism in Mid-Victorian England*. Stanford, Calif.: Stanford University Press, 1992.

Peach, Ceri. *West Indian Migration to Britain*. London: Oxford University Press, 1968.

———. "Patterns of Afro-Caribbean Migration and Settlement in Great Britain." In *The Caribbean in Europe: Aspects of the West Indian Experience in Britain, France, and the Netherlands*, edited by Colin Brock, 62–64. London: Frank Cass, 1986.

———.*The Caribbean in Europe: Contrasting Patterns of Migration and Settlement in Britain, France, and the Netherlands*. Coventry, Eng.: Centre for Research in Ethnic Relations, 1991.

———. "Trends in Levels of Caribbean Segregation, Great Britain, 1961–91." In *Caribbean Migration: Globalised Identities*, edited by Mary Chamberlain, 203–16. London: Routledge, 1998.

Penninx, Rinus, and Judith Roosblad, eds. *Trade Unions, Immigration, and Immigrants in Europe, 1960–1993: A Comparative Study of Trade Unions in Seven West European Countries*. New York: Berghahn, 2000.

Perlmann, Joel, and Roger Waldinger. "Second Generation Decline? Children of Immigrants, Past and Present: A Reconsideration." *International Migration Review* 31 (1997) 4:893–922.

Perrot, Michelle. *Les ouvriers en grève: France, 1871–1890*. 2 vols. Lille, Fr: Université de Lille III, 1975.

Peters-Schildgen, Susanne. *"Schmelztiegel" Ruhrgebiet: Die Geschichte der Zuwanderung am Beispiel Herne bis 1945*. Essen, Ger.: Klartext Verlag, 1997.

Philpott, Stuart B. *West Indian Migration: The Montserrat Case*. London: The Athlone Press, 1973.

Phizacklea, Annie, and Robert Miles. *Labour and Racism*. London: Routledge and Kegan Paul, 1980.

Pilkington, Edward. *Beyond the Mother Country: West Indians and the Notting Hill White Riots*. London: I. B. Tauris, 1988.

Ponty, Janine. *Polonais méconnus: Histoire des travailleurs immigrés en France dans l'entre-deux-guerres*. Paris: Publications de la Sorbonne, 1990.

Pooley, Colin G. "The Irish in Liverpool circa 1850–1940." In *Ethnic Identity in Urban Europe*, edited by Max Engman, 71–98. New York: New York University Press, 1992.

Pooley, Colin G., and Jean Turnbull. *Migration and Mobility in Britain Since the Eighteenth Century*. London: UCL Press, 1998.

Portes, Alejandro, ed. *The New Second Generation*. New York: Russell Sage Foundation, 1996.

———. "Immigration Theory for a New Century: Some Problems and Opportunities." *International Migration Review* 31 (1997) 4:799–826.

Portes, Alejandro, Luis E. Guarnizo, and Patricia Landolt. "The Study of Transnationalism: Pitfalls and Promise of an Emergent Research Field." *Ethnic and Racial Studies* 22 (1999) 2:217–37.

Portes, Alejandro, and Rubén G. Rumbaut. *Immigrant America: A Portrait*. 2nd ed. Berkeley: University of California Press, 1996.

Portes, Alejandro, and Richard Schauffler. "Language and the Second Generation: Biligualism Yesterday and Today." In *The New Second Generation,* edited by Alejandro Portes, 8–29. New York: Russell Sage Foundation, 1996.

Pryce-Jones, David. *The Closed Circle: An Interpretation of the Arabs.* Chicago: I. Dee, 2002.

Rainhorn, Judith. "Enclaves et creusets matrimoniaux à Paris et à New York: Perspective compareé de deux expériences de mixité matrimoniale au sein de l'émigration italienne." *Annales de Démographie Historique,* (2002) 2:79–100

Rath, Jan, Rinus Penninx, and Kees Groenendijk. *Western Europe and Its Islam.* Leiden, Ger.: Brill, 2001.

Ray, Joanny. *Les Marocains en France.* Paris: Maurice Lavergne, 1937.

Reczynska, Anna. "America and the Ruhr Basin in the Expectations of Polish Peasant Migrants." In *Distant Magnets: Expectations and Realities in the Immigrant Experience, 1840–1930,* edited by Dirk Hoerder and Horst Rössler, 84–104. New York: Holmes & Meier, 1993.

Reid, Donald. "The Politics of Immigrant Workers in Twentieth-Century France." In *The Politics of Immigrant Workers: Labor Activism and Migration in the World Economy since 1830,* edited by Camille Guerin-Gonzales and Carl Strikwerda, 245–78. New York: Holmes & Meier, 1993.

Reif, Heinz. *Die verspätete Stadt: Industrialisierung, städtischer Raum und Politik in Oberhausen 1846–1929.* Oberhausen, Ger.: Landschaftsverband Rheinland, 1993.

Reimers, David M. *Unwelcome Strangers: American Identity and the Turn Against Immigration.* New York: Columbia University Press, 1998.

Rex, John. *Race Relations in Sociological Theory.* New York: Schocken Books, 1970.

Rex, John, and Robert Moore. *Race, Community and Conflict: A Study of Sparkbrook.* London: Oxford University Press, 1967.

Rex, John, and Sally Tomlinson. *Colonial Immigrants in a British City: A Class Analysis.* London: Routledge and Kegan Paul, 1979.

Richmond, Anthony. "Economic Insecurity and Stereotypes as Factors in Colour Prejudice." *The Sociological Review* 42 (1950): 147–70.

———. *Colour Prejudice in Britain: A Study of West Indian Workers in Liverpool, 1941–1951.* London: Routledge and Kegan Paul, 1954.

———. *The Colour Problem: A Study of Racial Relations.* Harmondsworth, Eng.: Penguin, 1955.

Richmond, Anthony, and Aloma Mendoza. "Education and Qualifications of Caribbean Immigrants and Their Children in Britain and Canada." In *In Search of a Better Life: Perspectives on Migration from the Caribbean,* edited by Ransford W. Palmer, 141–70. New York: Praeger, 1990.

Rieker, Yvonne. "Südländer, Ostagenten oder Westeuropäer? Die Politik der Bundesregierung und das Bild der italienischen Gastarbeiter, 1955–1970." *Archiv für Sozialgeschichte* 40 (2000): 231–58.

———. *"Ein Stück Heimat findet man ja immer."* Die italienische Einwanderung in die Bundesrepublik. Essen, Ger.: Klartext Verlag, 2003.

Roediger, David. *The Wages of Whiteness: Race and the Making of the American Working Class.* London: Verso, 1991.

———. *Towards the Abolition of Whiteness: Essays on Race, Politics, and Working Class History.* London: Verso, 1994.

Rosental, Paul André. *Les sentiers invisibles: Espace, familles, et migrations dans la France du 19e siècle.* Paris: Éditions de l'École des Hautes Études en Sciences Sociales, 1999.

Rowe, Michael. "Sex, 'Race' and Riot in Liverpool, 1919." *Immigrants and Minorities* 19 (2000) 2:53–70.

Roy, Olivier. "Islam in France: Religion, Ethnic Community or Social Ghetto?" In *Muslims in Europe,* edited by Bernard Lewis and Dominique Schnapper, 54–66. London and New York: Pinter Publishers, 1994.

———. *Globalised Islam: The Search for a New Ummah.* London: Hurst and Company, 2004.

Salentin, Kurt, and Frank Wilkening. "Ausländer, Eingebürgerte, und das Problem einer realistischen Zuwanderer-Integrationsbilanz." *Kölner Zeitschrift für Soziologie und Sozialpsychologie* 55 (2003) 2:278–98.

Sanua, Marianne R. "Jewish College Fraternities in the United States, 1895–1968: An Overview." *Journal of American Ethnic History* 19 (2001) 2:3–42.

Schiffauer, Werner. *Die Migranten aus Subay: Türken in Deutschland; eine Ethnographie.* Stuttgart: Klett-Cotta, 1991.

———. *Die Gottesmänner: Türkische Islamisten in Deutschland; Eine Studie zur Herstellung religiöser Evidenz.* Frankfurt am Main, Ger.: Suhrkamp, 2000.

———. "Die Islamische Gemeinschaft Milli Görüs: Ein Lehrstück zum verwickelten Zusammenhang von Migration, Religion, und sozialer Integration." In *Migrationsreport 2004: Fakten, Analysen, Perspektiven,* edited by Klaus J. Bade, Michael Bommes, and Rainer Münz, 67–96. Frankfurt am Main, Ger.: Campus, 2004.

Schnapper, Dominique. *L'Europe des immigrés: Essai sur les politiques d'immigration.* Paris: Éditions François Bourin, 1992.

———. *La communauté des citoyens: Sur l'idée moderne de nation.* Paris: Gallimard, 1994.

Schönwälder, Karen. *Einwanderung und ethnische Pluralität: Politische Entscheidungen und öffentliche Debatten in Großbritannien und der Bundesrepublik von den 1950er bis zu den 1970er Jahren.* Esssen, Ger.: Klartext Verlag, 2001.

———. "Zukunftsblindheit oder Steuerungsversagen? Zur Ausländerpolitik der Bundesregierung der 1960er und frühen 1970er Jahre." In *Migration Steuern und Verwalten,* edited by Jochen Oltmer, 123–44. Göttingen: V&R unipress, 2003.

Schor, Ralph. *L'opinion française et les étrangers en France, 1919–1939.* Paris: Publications de la Sorbonne, 1985.

———. "Les Italiens dans les Alpes-Maritimes 1919–1939." In *Les Italiens en France de 1914 à 1940*, edited by Pierre Milza, 577–607. Rome: École française de Rome, 1986.

———. "L'image de l'Italien dans la France de l'entre-deux-guerres." In *Les Italiens en France de 1914 à 1940*, edited by Pierre Milza, 89–109. Rome: École française de Rome, 1986.

Schuck, Peter H. "Law and the Study of Migration." In *Migration Theory: Talking Across Disciplines*, edited by Caroline Brettell and James F. Hollifield, 187–204. New York: Routledge, 2000.

Schultze, Günther. *Berufliche Integration türkischer Arbeitnehmer: Vergleich der ersten und zweiten Generation.* Bonn: Dietz, 1991.

Schwab, Christa. *Integration von Moslems in Grossbritannien und Frankreich.* Vienna: WUV-Universitätsverlag, 1997.

Seifert, Wolfgang. "Die zweite Ausländergeneration in der Bundesrepublik: Längschnittbeobachtungen in der Berufseinstiegsphase." *Kölner Zeitschrift für Soziologie und Sozialpsychologie* 44 (1992) 4:677–96.

———. "Berufliche, ökonomische und soziale Mobilität von Arbeitsmigranten zwischen 1984 und 1993." In *Lebenslagen im Wandel: Sozialberichterstattung im Längsschnitt*, edited by Wolfgang Zapf, Jürgen Schupp, and Roland Habich, 240–63. Frankfurt am Main, Ger.: Campus Verlag, 1996.

Sewell, William H. *Structure and Mobility: The Men and Women of Marseille, 1820–1970.* Cambridge: Cambridge University Press, 1985.

Sezer, Ahmet Necati. "Zur Geschichte der türkischen Migration nach Deutschland." In *Migration in erklärten und 'unerklärten' Einwanderungsländern*, edited by Uwe Hunger, Karin Meendermann, Bernhard Santel, and Wichard Woyke, 233–56. Münster, Ger.: LIT, 2001.

Sherwood, Marika. *Many Struggles: West Indian Workers and Service Personnel in Britain (1939–45).* London: Karia Press, 1985.

Silverman, Maxim. *Deconstructing the Nation: Immigration, Racism, and Citizenship in Modern France.* London: Routledge, 1992.

Solga, Heike. "Jugendliche ohne Schulabschluss und ihre Wege in den Arbeitsmarkt." In *Das Bildungswesen in der Bundesrepublik Deutschland: Strukturen und Entwicklungen im Überblick*, edited by Kai S. Cortina, et al., 710–54. Berlin: Rowohlt Taschenbuch Verlag, 2003.

Solomos, John. *Black Youth, Racism, and the State: The Politics of Ideology and Policy.* Cambridge: Cambridge University Press, 1988.

Spire, Alexis, and Dominique Merllié. "La question des origines dans les statistiques en France: Les enjeux d'une controverse." *Le Mouvement Social* 188 (1999): 119–30.

Stedman Jones, Gareth. *Outcast London: A Study in the Relationship Between Classes in Victorian Society.* Oxford: Clarendon Press, 1971.

Stefanski, Valentina-Maria. *Zum Prozess der Emanzipation und Integration von Aus-senseitern: Polnische Arbeitsmigranten im Ruhrgebiet.* Dortmund, Ger.: For-schungsstelle Ostmitteleuropa, 1984.

Steinberg, Stephen. "The Cultural Fallacy in Studies of Racial and Ethnic Mobility." In *Immigrants, Schooling and Social Mobility: Does Culture Make a Difference?* Edited by Hans Vermeulen and Joel Perlmann, 61–71. Houndmills, Eng: Mac-millan, 2000.

Sterne, Evelyn Savidge. "Beyond the Boss: Immigration and American Political Cul-ture from 1880 to 1940." In *E Pluribus Unum? Contemporary and Historical Per-spectives on Immigrant Political Incorporation*, edited by Gary Gerstle and John Mollenkopf, 33–66. New York: Russell Sage Foundation, 2001.

Stolcke, Verena. "Talking Culture: New Boundaries, New Rhetorics of Exclusion in Europe." *Current Anthropology* 36 (1995) 1:1–24.

Stora, Benjamin. *Ils venaient d'Algérie: l'immigration algérienne en France (1912–1992).* Paris: Fayard, 1992.

Summerskill, Michael. *China on the Western Front: Britain's Chinese Work Force in the First World War.* London: M. Summerskill, 1982.

Suurenbroek, Frank. "Friezen in Amsterdam: Groepsvorming onder binnenlandse migranten aan het einde van de negentiende eeuw." *Tijdschrift voor Sociale Ge-schiedenis* 26 (2000) 4:325–42.

Swift, Roger. "'Another Stafford Street Row': Law, Order, and the Irish Presence in Mid-Victorian Wolverhampton." In *The Irish in the Victorian City*, edited by Roger Swift and Sheridan Gilley, 179–206. London: Croom Helm, 1985.

———. "Historians and the Irish: Recent Writings on the Irish in Nineteenth-Cen-tury Britain." *Immigrants and Minorities* 18 (1999) 2&3:14–39.

Tabili, Laura. "The Construction of Racial Difference in Twentieth-Century Britain: The Special Restriction (Coloured Alien Seamen) Order, 1925." *Journal of Brit-ish Studies* 33 (1994): 54–98.

Taylor, Charles. *Multiculturalism and the 'Politics of Recognition.'* Princeton, N.J.: Princeton University Press, 1992.

Taylor, Rebecca. "Travellers in Britain, 1900–1960: A Minority and the State." PhD diss., University of London, Birkbeck College, 2003.

Témime, Émile. "La politique française à l'égard de la migration algérienne: Le poids de la colonisation." *Le Mouvement Social* 188 (1999): 77–87.

Tenfelde, Klaus. "Die 'Krawalle von Herne' im Jahre 1899." *Internationale Wissen-schaftliche Korrespondenz zur Geschichte der deutschen Arbeiterbewegung* 15 (1979): 71–104.

Thompson, E. P. *The Making of the English Working Class.* London: Gollancz, 1963.

Thränhardt, Dietrich. "Einwanderungsland Deutschland: Von der Tabuisierung zur Realität." In *Einwanderungsland Deutschland: Neue Wege nachhaltiger Integration*, edited by Ursula Mehrländer and Günther Schultze, 41–63. Bonn: Dietz, 2001.

————. "Prophecies, *Ius Soli* and Dual Citizenship: Interpreting the Changes in the German Citizenship System." Unpublished paper, Wassenaar, Ger.: NIAS, 2002.

Tibi, Bassam. *Islamische Zuwanderung: Die gescheiterte Integration.* Stuttgart: Deutsche Verlags-Anstalt, 2002.

Tilly, Charles. *Coercion, Capital, and European States, A.D. 990–1992.* Cambridge: Cambridge University Press, 1990.

Tizard, Barbara, and Ann Phoenix. *Black, White, or Mixed Race? Race and Racism in the Lives of Young People of Mixed Parentage.* Revised edition. London: Routledge, 2002.

Todd, Emmanuel. *Le destin des immigrés: Assimilation et ségrégation dans les démocraties occidentales.* Paris: Seuil, 1994.

Tribalat, Michèle. *Faire France: Une grande enquête sur les immigrés et leurs enfants.* Paris: Découverte, 1995.

Troyna, Barry. "British Schooling and the Reproduction of Racial Inequality." In *Lost Illusions: Caribbean Minorities in Britain and the Netherlands,* edited by Malcolm Cross and Han Entzinger, 166–84. London: Routledge, 1988.

Van Eijl, Corrie, and Leo Lucassen, "Les Pays-Bas au-delà de leurs frontières. L'émigration et l'Etat néerlandais, 1850–1940." In *Citoyenneté et ceux qui partent: la politique de l'émigration et de l'expatriation,* edited by Nancy L. Green and Patrick Weil. Paris: École des Hautes Études en Sciences Sociales, forthcoming 2005.

Van Niekerk, Mies. *Premigration Legacies and Immigrant Social Mobility: The Afro-Surinamese and Indo-Surinamese in the Netherlands.* Lanham, Md.: Lexington Books, 2002.

————. "Afro-Caribbeans and Indo-Caribbeans in the Netherlands: Premigration Legacies and Social Mobility." *International Migration Review* 38 (2004) 7:158–83.

Venema, Mathias, and Claus Grimm. *Situation der ausländischen Arbeitnehmer und ihre Familienangehörigen in der Bundesrepublik Deutschland: Tabellenband.* Bonn: Bundesministerium für Arbeit und Sozialordnung, 2002.

Vermeulen, Hans, and Rinus Penninx, eds. *Immigrant Integration: The Dutch Case.* Amsterdam: Spinhuis, 2000.

Vertone, Teodosio. "Antécedents et causes des événements d'Aigues-Mortes." In *L'émigration italienne en France de 1870 à 1914,* edited by Jean Baptiste Duroselle and Enrico Serra, 107–38. Milan: Franco Agneli, 1978.

Vertovec, Steven. "Indo-Caribbean Experience in Britain: Overlooked, Miscategorized, Misunderstood." In *Inside Babylon: The Caribbean Diaspora in Britain,* edited by Winston James and Clive Harris, 165–78. London: Verso, 1993.

Vertovec, Steven, and Robin Cohen, eds. *Migration, Diasporas, and Transnationalism.* Cheltenham, Eng.: Edward Elgar, 1999.

Videlier, Philippe. "Les Italiens de la région lyonnaise." In *Les Italiens en France de 1914 à 1940,* edited by Pierre Milza, 661–91. Rome: École française de Rome, 1986.

Voelker, Gottfried E. "More Foreign Workers: Germany's Labour Problem No. 1." In *Turkish Workers in Europe, 1960–1975: A Socio-Economic Reappraisal,* edited by Nermin Abadan-Unat, 331–45. Leiden, Ger.: E. J. Brill, 1976.

Von Oswald, Anne. "'Stippvisiten' in der 'Autostadt' Volkswagen: Wolfsburg und die italienischen 'Gastarbeiter,' 1962–1975." In *Zuwanderung und Integration in Niedersachsen seit dem zweiten Weltkrieg,* edited by Klaus J. Bade and Jochen Oltmer, 225–52. Osnabrück, Ger.: Rasch, 2002.

Von Oswald, Anne, Karen Schönwälder, and Barbara Sonnenberg. "Einwanderungsland Deutschland: A New Look at Its Post-War History." In *European Encounters: Migrants, Migration, and European Societies since 1945,* edited by Rainer Ohliger, Karen Schönwälder, and Triadafilos Triadafilopoulos, 19–37. Aldershot, Eng.: Ashgate, 2003.

Vuilleumier, Marc. *Flüchtlinge und Immigranten in der Schweiz: Ein historischer Überblick.* 2nd ed. Zürich: Pro Helvetia, 1992.

Waldinger, Roger, and Cynthia Feliciano. "Will the New Second Generation Experience 'Downward Assimilation'? Segmented Assimilation Re-assessed." *Ethnic and Racial Studies* 27 (2004) 3:376–402.

Waldinger, Roger, and David Fitzgerald. "Transnationalism in Question." *American Journal of Sociology* 109 (2004) 5:1177–95.

Wallerstein, Immanuel. *The Modern World-System.* New York: Academic Press, 1974.

Waterkamp, Hermann. *Die Bevölkerung von Duisburg.* Essen, Ger.: Walter Bacmeisters Nationalverlag, 1941.

Waters, Mary C. *Black Identities: West Indian Immigrant Dreams and American Realities.* New York: Russell Sage, 1999.

Weber, Eugen. *Peasants into Frenchmen: The Modernization of Rural France, 1870–1914.* Stanford, Calif.: Stanford University Press, 1976.

Weber, Max. *Die Verhältnisse der Landarbeiter im ostelbischen Deutschland.* Leipzig: Duncker & Humblot, 1892.

Wehler, Hans-Ulrich. *Krisenherde des Kaiserreichs, 1871–1918: Studien zur deutschen Sozial- und Verfassungsgeschichte.* Göttingen, Ger.: Vandenhoeck & Ruprecht, 1979.

———. *Das Deutsche Kaiserreich, 1871–1918.* Göttingen: Vandenhoeck & Ruprecht, 1980.

White, Jenny B. "Turks in the New Germany." *American Anthropologist* 99 (1997) 1: 754–69.

White, Paul E. "Immigrants, Immigrant Areas and Immigrant Communities in Postwar Paris." In *Migrants in Modern France: Population Mobility in the Later Nineteenth and Twentieth Centuries,* editd by Philip E. Ogden and Paul E. White, 195–211. London: Unwin Hyman, 1989.

Wickenden, James. *Colour in Britain.* Oxford: Oxford University Press, 1958.

Wieviorka, Michel, Philippe Bataille, Daniel Jacquin, Danilo Martucelli, Angelina Peralva, and Paul Zawadzki. *La France raciste.* Paris: Éditions du Seuil, 1992.

Willems, Wim. *In Search of the True Gypsy: From Enlightenment to Final Solution.* London: Frank Cass, 1997.

———. *De uittocht uit Indië, 1945–1995.* Amsterdam: Bert Bakker, 2001.

———. "No Sheltering Sky: Migrant Identities of Dutch Nationals from Indonesia." In *Europe's Invisible Migrants,* edited by Andrea L. Smith, 33–59. Amsterdam: Amsterdam University Press, 2003.

Williamson, Jeffrey G. "The Impact of the Irish on British Labor Markets During the Industrial Revolution." *Journal of Economic History* 46 (1986) 3:693–720.

Wilpert, Czarina. "The Ideological and Institutional Foundations of Racism in the Federal Republic of Germany." In *Racism and Migration in Western Europe,* edited by John Wrench and John Solomos, 67–82. Oxford: Berg, 1993.

Wimmer, Andreas. "Explaining Xenophobia and Racism: A Critical Review of Current Research Approaches." *Ethnic and Racial Studies* 20 (1997) 1:17–41.

Wrench, John, Edgar Hassan, and Tarek Qureshi. "From School to the Labour Market in Britain: The Qualitative Exposure of Structures of Exclusion." In *Migrants, Ethnic Minorities, and the Labour Market: Integration and Exclusion in Europe,* edited by John Wrench, Andrea Rea, and Nouria Ouali, 54–71. Houndmills, Eng.: Palgrave, 1999.

Wyman, Mark. *Round-Trip America: The Immigrants Return to Europe, 1880–1930.* Ithaca, N. Y.: Cornell University Press, 1993.

Zhou, Min. "Segmented Assimilation: Issues, Controversies, and Recent Research on the New Second Generation." *International Migration Review* 31 (1997) 4:975–1008.

Zolberg, Aristide. "Reforming the Back Door: The Immigration Reform and Control Act of 1986 in Historical Perspective." In *Immigration Reconsidered: History, Sociology, and Politics,* edited by Virginia Yans-McLaughlin, 315–39. New York: Oxford University Press, 1990.

Zucchi, John E. *The Little Slaves of the Harp: Italian Child Street Musicians in Nineteenth-Century Paris, London and New York.* Liverpool: Liverpool University Press, 1999.

*Zur Integration der Türken in Deutschland: Allgemeine Behauptungen und Ergebnisse von Studien.* Berlin: Botschaft der Republik Türkei in Berlin, 2002.

*Zuwanderung gestalten: Integration fördern.* Berlin: Bundesministerium des Inneren, 2001.

# Index

**LEO LUCASSEN** is an associate professor in the Department of History at the University of Amsterdam. He has published extensively on Gypsies and itinerant groups, and in 1996 he was granted the Dirk Jacob Veegens Award by the Koninklijke Hollandse Maatschappij voor Wetenschappen (Royal Holland Society of Sciences) for his scholarly work on these groups. In 1998 he received a pioneer research grant from the Netherlands Organization for Scientific Research (NWO) for a large-scale research project on immigrants in the Netherlands. Previous books are *Zigeuner: Die Geschichte eines polizeilichen Ordnungbegriffes* (1996) [The labeling of Gypsies by the German police]; *Migration, Migration History, History* (1997, edited with Jan Lucassen); and *Gypsies and Other Itinerant Groups* (1998, with Wim Willems and Annemarie Cottaar). He is coeditor of the forthcoming *European Encyclopedia on the History of Migration and Integration*.

**STUDIES OF WORLD MIGRATIONS**

The Immigrant Threat: The Integration of Old and New Migrants
   in Western Europe since 1850   *Leo Lucassen*

The University of Illinois Press
is a founding member of the
Association of American University Presses.

---

Composed in 10.5/13 Adobe Minion
with Meta display
by Jim Proefrock
at the University of Illinois Press
Manufactured by Sheridan Books, Inc.

University of Illinois Press
1325 South Oak Street
Champaign, IL 61820-6903
www.press.uillinois.edu

5788